TRADE, TRADERS AND
THE ANCIENT CITY

TRADE, TRADERS AND THE ANCIENT CITY

Edited by

HELEN PARKINS and
CHRISTOPHER SMITH

ROUTLEDGE

London and New York

First published 1998
by Routledge
11 New Fetter Lane, London EC4P 4EE

Simultaneously published in the USA and Canada
by Routledge
29 West 35th Street, New York, NY 10001

Typeset in Times by
Florencetype Ltd, Stoodleigh, Devon

Printed and bound in Great Britain by
Creative Print and Design (Wales), Ebbw Vale

British Library Cataloguing in Publication Data
A catalogue record for this book is available
from the British Library

Library of Congress Cataloging in Publication Data
A catalogue record for this book has been requested

ISBN 0–415–16517–2

T 100137960X

Contents

List of figures and tables   vii
Notes on contributors   ix
Preface   xi
List of abbreviations   xii

1 Time for change? Shaping the future of the
  ancient economy   1
  HELEN PARKINS

2 The Old Assyrian merchants   16
  AMÉLIE KUHRT

3 Traders and artisans in archaic central Italy   31
  CHRISTOPHER SMITH

4 Trade on the Black Sea in the archaic and
  classical periods: some observations   52
  GOCHA R. TSETSKHLADZE

5 Ceramics and positivism revisited: Greek
  transport amphoras and history   75
  MARK LAWALL

6 The grain trade of Athens in the fourth
  century BC   102
  MICHAEL WHITBY

7 Land transport in Roman Italy: costs, practice
  and the economy   129
  RAY LAURENCE

vi *Contents*

8 Trade and traders in the Roman world: scale,
   structure, and organisation   149
   JEREMY PATERSON

9 Trade and the city in Roman Egypt   168
   RICHARD ALSTON

10 Trading gods in northern Italy   203
   MARK HUMPHRIES

11 Ancient economies: models and muddles   225
   JOHN K. DAVIES

   Index   257

Figures and tables

Figures

5.1 Chian imports to Athens represented as a
     percentage of total imports in each period   87
5.2 Numbers of Chian imports to Gordion compared
     to total datable imports and the Chian imports
     expressed as a percentage of the total datable
     imports per period   88

9.1 Communications from Oxyrhynchus (excluding
     Oxyrhynchite), first to sixth century AD   188
9.2 Communications from Oxyrhynchus (including
     Oxyrhynchite), second century AD   190
9.3 Communications from Oxyrhynchus (including
     Oxyrhynchite), third century AD   191
9.4 Zones of contact   193

10.1 Map of north-eastern Italy and the north-western
     Balkans, showing the location of bureaux of the
     publicum portorii Illyrici, centres of commercial
     activity by the Barbii family of Aquileia, and
     centres of Isiac and Mithraic worship   209
10.2 Map of northern Italy showing the location of
     Jewish and Christian communities by the early
     fourth century   211
10.3 Plan of the southern part of Aquileia, indicating
     the location of Theodore's church complex, the
     imperial *horreum* and the extent of the tetrarchic
     expansion of the city   219

11.1 Flow diagram of resource movement,
     stage 1: modified household autarky   245

11.2 Flow diagram of resource movement,
stage 2: complex flows 247
11.3 Flow diagram of resource movement,
stage 3: interactions with the public economy 249

Tables

9.1 Roman Egypt: traffic registered in the
customs accounts 179
9.2 Roman Egypt: communities in contact
with Karanis 181

Contributors

Richard Alston is Lecturer in Classics, Royal Holloway, University of London.

John K. Davies is Professor of Ancient History and Classical Archaeology, University of Liverpool.

Mark Humphries is Research Associate, *Gesta Martyrum Romanorum* Project, Department of Religions and Theology, University of Manchester.

Amélie Kuhrt is Professor of Ancient Near Eastern History, University College, University of London.

Ray Laurence is Lecturer in Classics, University of Reading.

Mark Lawall is Adjunct Professor, Classics Department, University of Manitoba.

Helen Parkins is British Academy Postdoctoral Fellow, and Research Fellow, Fitzwilliam College, Cambridge.

Jeremy Paterson is Senior Lecturer in Classics, University of Newcastle.

Christopher Smith is Lecturer in Ancient History, University of St Andrews.

Gocha Tsetskhladze is Research Fellow in Classics, Royal Holloway, University of London.

Michael Whitby is Professor of Classics and Ancient History, University of Warwick.

Preface

In any understanding of the ancient world, the trader must play a role. So much of our archaeological record is represented by goods which have moved from their point of origin to a different point of deposition; how they got there, and who carried them, is the focus of this volume. By focusing on trade and the trader however, it should not be thought that we intend this to be a wholly commercial study; all the contributors show that the exchange of goods is inseparable from social and political factors. Hence, the city; one part of the economic structure of the ancient world.

Several of the chapters here were originally delivered as papers at a conference held at the University of St Andrews on 11 and 12 July 1995. We are grateful to the participants at that conference for the stimulus and excitement they provided, and to the various other scholars who have subsequently offered us papers for publication. We are also grateful to the School of Greek, Latin and Ancient History, the Society for the Promotion of Hellenic Studies, the Classical Association for Scotland, the Foundation for Hellenic Culture, and the Carnegie Trust for financial support. Finally, we would like to acknowledge the encouragement which Professor Geoffrey Rickman has given to the editors individually, and the generous hospitality which he offered at the conference.

Helen Parkins
Christopher Smith

Abbreviations

AA	*Archäologischer Anzeiger*
AE	*L'Année Épigraphique*
Aeg	*Aegyptus*
AEMTh	*To Arkheologiko ergo sti Makedonia kai Thraki*
AHB	*Ancient History Bulletin*
AJN	*American Journal of Numismatics*
AJP	*American Journal of Philology*
ANRW	*Aufstieg und Niedergang der römischen Welt*
ASNP	*Annali della Scuola Normale Superiore di Pisa*
ASP	*American Studies in Papyrology*
BASP	*Bulletin of the American Society of Papyrologists*
BCH	*Bulletin de Correspondance Hellénique*
BIFAO	*Bulletin de l'Institut Français d'Archéologie Orientale*
BS	*Bosporskii Sbornik* (Bosporan Collection) (Moscow)
BSA	*Annual of the British School at Athens*
CAH	*The Cambridge Ancient History*
CE	*Chronique d'Égypte*
CIG	*Corpus Inscriptionum Graecarum*
CIL	*Corpus Inscriptionum Latinarum*
CQ	*Classical Quarterly*
CR	*Classical Review*
DdA	*Dialoghi di Archeologia*
DHA	*Dialogues d'histoire ancienne*
DP	*Drevnee Prichernomor'e* (Ancient Black Sea Littoral: Short Bulletins of the Odessa Archaeological Society) (Odessa)
EAD	*Exploration archéologique de Délos faite par l'Ecole Française d'Athènes*
FGH	F. Jacoby (1923–58). *Die Fragmente der griechischen Historiker* (Berlin)
G&R	*Greece and Rome*

HOPE	*History of Political Economy*
IG	*Inscriptiones Graecae*
IGAIMK	*Izvestiya gosudarstvennoe akademii istorii material'noe kultury*
ILCV	*Inscriptiones Latinae Christianae Veteres*, ed. E. Diehl (Berlin, 1925–31)
ILS	*Inscriptiones Latinae Selectae*, ed. H. Dessau (Berlin, 1892–1916)
IOSPE	*Inscriptiones Antiquae Orae Septentrionalis Ponti Euxini Graecae et Latinae*
IstMitt	*Mitteilungen des Deutschen Archäologischen Instituts* (Istanbuler Abt.)
JEA	*Journal of Egyptian Archaeology*
JEL	*Journal of Economic Literature*
JHS	*Journal of Hellenic Studies*
JJP	*Journal of Juristic Papyrology*
JRA	*Journal of Roman Archaeology*
JRS	*Journal of Roman Studies*
KSIA	*Kratkie soobsheniya instituta arkheologii Akademia Nauk SSSR*
MBAH	*Münsterische Beiträge zur antiken Handelsgeschichte*
MIA	*Materialy i issledovaniya po arkheologii SSSR*
ML	R. Meiggs and D. Lewis. *A Selection of Greek Historical Inscriptions to the End of the Fifth Century* BC (Oxford 1969)
OJA	*Oxford Journal of Archaeology*
PAS	*Peterburgskii Arkheologicheskii Vestnik* (Petersburg Archaeological Herald) (St Petersburg)
PBSR	*Papers of the British School at Rome*
PCPS	*Proceedings of the Cambridge Philological Society*
PdP	*La parola del passato*
PZ	*Prähistorische Zeitschrift*
RAL	*Rendiconti della classe di scienze morali, storiche e filologiche dell'Accademia dei Lincei*
RCRF Acta	*Rei Cretariae Romanae Fautorum Acta*
REA	*Revue des études anciennes*
REconAnth	*Research in Economic Anthropology*
RLA	*Reallexikon der Assyriologie* (Berlin, 1928)
SA	*Sovetskaya Arkheologiya* (Soviet Archaeology) (Moscow)

SEG	*Supplementum Epigraphicum Graecum*
St. Etr.	*Studi Etruschi*
TAPA	*Transactions of the American Philological Association*
TCL	*Textes cunéiformes du Louvre*
TC I	*Tablettes cappadociennes, publiées avec inventaire et tables. TCL 4* (Paris, 1920)
TTAED	*Türk Tarih Arkeoloji ve Etnografya Dergisi*
VDI	*Vestnik Drevnei Istorii* (Journal of Ancient History) (Moscow)
ZA	*Zeitschrift für Assyriologie und verwandte Gebiete*
ZPE	*Zeitschrift für Papyrologie und Epigraphik*

1

Time for change?
Shaping the future of the
ancient economy

Helen Parkins

Crisis, what crisis?

This collection of papers, taken from a 1995 conference with the
same working title, brings together work on two of the currently
most popular, but also most provocative subjects in ancient history
– namely, the ancient economy and the ancient city. To bring these
two subjects together for the specific purpose of joint consideration might be thought overdue for, in the past few years in
particular, much research on the ancient economy has converged
on economic structures engendered by the city, while, at the same
time, discussion of the ancient city has frequently been diverted
towards economic issues.[1] This volume includes chapters on these
subjects in Greek, Roman, and Near Eastern history. The broad
aim, then, is to explore more closely, and to offer new perspectives on, the types of relationships between trade, traders and the
city in antiquity and the ways in which they impacted on one
another.

There are those who might question the value of such an exercise, for the markedly polarised and ideological debate over the

---

[1] The examples are far too numerous to list here, but more recent
instances may be found in papers in *Opus* 6–8 (1987–9); and in Rich and
Wallace-Hadrill (eds) 1991; Cornell and Lomas (eds) 1995; Parkins (ed.)
1997. See also Harris 1993b.

ancient economy has suffered from considerable critical press in more recent years. Keith Hopkins (1983, 1) memorably described the situation as it stood in 1983; the ancient economy, he claimed, is 'an academic battleground ... The contestants campaign under various colours – apologists, marxists, modernizers, primitivists ... the war continues.' The relationship between trade and the city has been a specific focus for this kind of polemic, especially since the Weberian 'consumer city' model was resurrected for ancient historians some twenty-five years ago.[2] But while the various schools of thought have continued to engage in lively combat on the one hand, on the other, to the many innocent by-standers 'there is a danger that familiarity with the debate leads to boredom, as though it did not matter any longer' (Whittaker 1995, 22).[3]

It is partly for these reasons, then, that the study of the ancient economy appears to some, at least, to have taken itself down a cul-de-sac (Kuhrt, this volume), and hence, a tangible sense of crisis has emerged. Now, however, a combination of fresh approaches and new information (most notably, in the case of the latter, from archaeology), offers a way out. The papers brought together here, then, collectively testify to the renewed vitality of research in this field. They also bear witness to something of a sea-change; gone, for the most part, is the apparent confidence of the 1970s and early 1980s in applying all-encompassing models, and in its place is greater caution. The continuing addition of archaeological data to our other sources is without doubt primarily responsible. Since archaeology allows us to study society from the bottom up, as it were, it can reveal detail otherwise obscured by other types of sources, or by generalising models, and puts us in an increasingly strong position to be able to challenge established ideas.

While several chapters in this volume make use of archaeological material in their arguments, those by Smith and Lawall offer pertinent examples of novel perspectives made possible only by archaeology. Smith shows how the role of artisans (as distinct from

[2]   Finley 1973, ch. 2. For a thorough and up-to-date summary and discussion of the consumer, producer, and service city models, see Whittaker 1995. On the origin of the consumer city model, and for a critique there, see now Morley 1996, ch. 1.
[3]   See, similarly, e.g. Mattingly 1997, who speaks of the 'ossification' and 'impasse' of the consumer city debate.

traders) and, more specifically, the goods that they produced (pottery, and terracotta decoration), can shed light on the society and economy of archaic central Italy, and even on the origin of the city. Pottery is also Lawall's chosen diagnostic tool for illuminating Chian history. Through investigation of the shapes and markings primarily of sixth- and fifth-century BC amphoras he uncovers two periods of significant internal economic change on Chios during the fifth century, the extent of which is undocumented by any other source. Both Smith and Lawall demonstrate above all the unique contribution that archaeology continues to make to our understanding of the ancient economy, for it potentially gives much greater geographical and chronological accuracy to our picture of trade than the textual sources by themselves permit. And, as Lawall himself suggests, with more and more archaeological work being undertaken all the time, we can hopefully look forward to increased precision in the years to come.

At the same time, Alston and Kuhrt prove that other sources long since known to historians (papyri, and Near Eastern cuneiform tablets respectively) still have a great deal of potential yet to be tapped, and can extend our knowledge both geographically and temporally.

Alston's chapter, for example, adds to the growing body of impressive work on Roman Egypt, much of which has been directed at exploring systems of landholding and of agricultural management (e.g. Kehoe 1988 and 1992; Rathbone 1991; Rowlandson 1996). Combining detailed papyrological analysis with a broad historical perspective, Alston shows how this particular body of Egyptian source material can be used to construct a wider picture of inter-regional trade, even 'international' trade. Furthermore, with new archaeological survey and excavation happening apace in this most important of Roman provinces,[4] we can expect further dimensions to be added to the picture in the years to come.

At the other end of the chronological spectrum, Kuhrt demonstrates what can be learnt about Assyrian trade mechanisms from Akkadian cuneiform tablets. Indeed, Kuhrt suggests that the debate over the ancient economy may have become sterile because

---

[4] See e.g. papers collected in Bailey (ed.) 1996, on archaeological work currently being conducted in Roman Egypt, and its provisional findings.

of extensive reliance on, and over-working of, Graeco-Roman evidence from the classical period. Fresh life could be injected into the discussion, she proposes, if we were to look more frequently at different historical periods. Her chapter, on trade and traders in Old Assyria, lends considerable weight to her argument, revealing as it does a level of economic sophistication that few might have anticipated.

Old models, new perspectives?

Ever since the 1960s and early 1970s, when Moses Finley and A. H. M. Jones separately set out a 'primitivist' model for understanding the ancient economy, their hugely influential work has set the tone for much of the debate as to the roles and functions of trade, traders, and the ancient city. The crux of their model is that agriculture was the dominant mode of production in antiquity and that, for this reason, there was little or no interest in developing 'industrial'-type production. Towns and cities were thus net consumers, industry remained minimal and local, and commercial activity 'was always a side-issue compared to landowning'.[5]

This model, at the time of its inception, stood in sharp contrast to its 'modernising' predecessor, associated primarily with Rostovtzeff. Much of the debate that has taken place over the last twenty or thirty years has revolved around the question of which of these two pictures, together with similar and related conceptualisations, is the more accurate.[6] Now, however, particularly in the face of a great deal of additional evidence, it has become apparent that, in some respects at least, neither of these models is entirely adequate nor necessarily helpful.[7] As a result, historians are tending away from both ends of the ideological spectrum

[5] Hopkins 1983, xii.
[6] Hence Hopkins's description (quoted above, p. 2), concerning not just the primitivist:modernist oppositions, but also that of closely related dichotomies, such as formalist:substantivist, Marxist:capitalist, and so forth.
[7] This is probably especially true for attempts at understanding the Roman economy. See e.g. Purcell 1990 (on Jongman); Frier 1991, 247, echoed by Harris 1993b, and Mattingly 1994, 235 (in his review of Harris).

and finding novel and different ways of addressing problems in ancient economic history.

A handful of specific themes that recur throughout all the chapters in this book – economic integration, interdependence and the role of traders – illustrate the point particularly emphatically, and underline also the various ways in which new data are serving as a driving force behind current approaches.

Economic interdependence and integration

The primitivist scheme holds that inter-regional trade was minimal, largely because of limited specialised production (due to lack of 'industrial' development) and poor and expensive transport. Especially for the archaic period, but also in later periods, trade is regarded as having been essentially opportunistic, independent, and inherently local, built as it was around a subsistence economy. For these reasons, interdependent markets are believed to have been all but non-existent. In the past few years, however, archaeology has been making an ever more important contribution to this aspect of Greek economic history.[8]

Tsetskhladze tacitly addresses the validity of this picture in his chapter on Greek colonisation during the archaic and early classical periods. The colonising drive of many Greek cities in these periods is conventionally explained by the Greeks' need to secure vital supplies that they lacked, chiefly grain, metals, and slaves. Needing to pay for these imports, the Greek craftsmen were spurred into production; a degree of interdependence is thus envisaged. Using archaeological and other evidence, Tsetskhladze challenges the traditional interpretation of Greek colonisation of the Black Sea region, arguing that the same evidence can in fact be used to reach very different conclusions. Both the Greeks' requirements and the ability of the colonised areas to supply them, it is claimed, have been seriously misjudged.

Robin Osborne (1996) is one of the latest in a line of scholars who have used ceramics to argue that the archaic Greek economy

---

[8] Pottery studies have also, of course, made a significant contribution to the understanding of Roman economic history. See, more recently, e.g. Rodriguez-Almeida 1984; Tchernia 1986 and 1989.

was in fact based on interdependent markets, in which supply and demand can be qualitatively proven.[9] It should be noted, however, that Osborne benefits from the wealth of pottery studies that have materialised only in the last few years. Osborne studied sixth- and fifth-century Attic pottery, concentrating on two main features: the shape and the painter of the pottery. He found that the pottery indicates significant geographical variation in supply and demand according to these two attributes, even in the smaller number of sixth-century samples; put simply, 'different places generated different demand, characteristically met by different workshops' (Osborne 1996, 38). Further, if we accept, as Osborne does, that pots were not 'intrinsically valuable',[10] then the patterns of exchange that they reveal cannot have been created solely by the demand for pottery, which suggests that the pottery trade started on the back of some other kind of trade – maybe that of grain. In sum, Osborne's study points not just perhaps to a greater volume of trade, but to a much greater degree of organisation and integration than previously thought. That the production and consumption of the cities involved seems clearly to be interdependent cannot be explained satisfactorily by trading opportunism.

A similar position is taken in this volume by Mark Lawall, who in effect extends Osborne's argument into the classical period through a study of fifth-century BC Chian amphoras. Using data relating to imports of amphoras at Athens and elsewhere, along with evidence of Chian marking practices and changes in amphora shapes, Lawall's study serves as powerful testimony to the high visibility of trade from the archaic into the classical period and, as mentioned earlier, also brings greater geographical and chronological clarity to our picture of trade during this time. In addition, and more importantly for present purposes, the Chian marking systems demonstrate a striking degree of sensitivity to both internal and external markets. Once again, trading opportunism hardly seems an adequate explanation.

[9] For more caution with regard to what can be proved or otherwise about interdependent markets from Italian amphorae, see Tomber 1993.
[10] Osborne 1996, 39. The question of whether pots were intrinsically valuable or not has provoked a heated debate in recent years. For an introduction to the main arguments, see e.g. Gill 1991.

As we move into the classical period the quality and quantity of evidence improves markedly – as is manifest in Lawall's chapter – especially with regard to those two most atypical of cities, the imperial capitals of Athens and Rome. Indeed, one of the major attractions of studying the ancient economy from the perspective of the big cities is that we have so much information with which to play; if we are to try to prove or disprove economic interdependency, then Athens or Rome would therefore seem good places from which to start. But the greater volume of evidence for this period generates its own potential hazards. The vast array of data (particularly archaeological and epigraphic), once assembled and rendered accessible,[11] can shed important light on a number of areas of economic history. But it can just as easily prove tantalising, deceptive, or simply unreliable. Facts and figures hold out the key to understanding the ancient economy, but in themselves do not necessarily take us further, as Whitby's chapter emphasises. In addressing the long-running debate over Athens' grain supply – once regarded as a key test for the assertion that interdependent markets in antiquity were non-existent[12] – Whitby suggests that the underlying difficulty is the overly quantificatory and technical nature of the debate, which has led to the grain trade being abstracted from its actual context. Whitby argues that more telling than sets of figures and calculations are the many ways in which the Athenians can be shown to have kept tabs on their grain supply.[13] These underline the importance of the grain trade to Athens, and the practical irrelevance to the Athenians of precise information-gathering; much more effective in practice were 'impressions, rumours and hunches'. While as yet these conclusions do not ultimately resolve the question of interdependence, they may at least point in the direction of where more appropriate answers may be found.

[11] The efforts of Duncan-Jones (1982 and 1990) remain unsurpassed in this respect.
[12] Finley 1985a, ch. 7, esp. pp. 178–9.
[13] In this respect, Whitby's observations both confirm and realise Finley's (1985a, 178) earlier claim, that: 'Unfortunately, the problem of interdependence will never be resolved statistically ... the only alternative is to analyse the factors involved in the trade and to draw whatever inferences seem legitimate.'

For the Roman period, a picture of limited integration and interdependence becomes still harder to sustain, since our evidence
indicates extensive trading activity across the Mediterranean.
Hopkins (1980)[14] explained this situation by making Finley's model
more dynamic. While still retaining its basic tenet – namely, that
agriculture was the predominant mode of production – he
suggested a number of refinements. Envisaging more integration
and monetisation of the economy than the original model
admitted, he suggested that taxation of core provinces allowed
expenditure in frontier regions and in Rome, thereby stimulating
long-distance trade and more specialised production, and
increasing the importance of towns.[15]

In support of the argument against economic integration
appears to be the prevalent view that transport costs were generally high, thus deterring large-volume, long-distance trade. In
making his adjustments to the model, Hopkins pointed out that
archaeological evidence testifies to trade of this nature taking place
and, moreover, to its having been conducted on a large scale.[16]
But if we need any additional convincing that the expense of transport should be dismissed as an argument against integrated
markets in the Roman empire, then Laurence's chapter provides
compelling reason to do so. Laurence takes as his starting-point
the data that lie at the heart of this argument: figures calculated
fifty years ago on the cost of haulage by land in Roman times,
showing how their main implication – that land transport was
prohibitively expensive, particularly in comparison to that by sea
– has been accepted and widely used as 'fact' ever since. Disputing
the accuracy of the original data, Laurence redoes the sums,
and arrives at alternative figures for land haulage costs which
suggest that sea and land transport were in fact complementary,
rather than competing systems. Moreover, he demonstrates that

[14]   See also Hopkins 1983. While Hopkins's model allows for genuine
economic growth, it, too, still leaves some areas unresolved; see e.g. Lo
Cascio 1982; Duncan-Jones 1990; Whittaker 1990; and, more recently,
Howgego 1992 and 1994.
[15]   As 'centres in which local craftsmen converted the locally produced
surplus into higher value, lower volume goods for transport and sale to
distant markets' (Hopkins 1983, xx).
[16]   Not only was that trade large scale, but it was also in an astonishingly wide variety of commodities: Harris 1993a.

roads – often paid for and made possible by villa owners – made possible the integration (and survival, or even profitability) of villas into local village or *vicus* economies,[17] which were, in turn, integrated into the larger Italian economy. His findings undoubtedly have important ramifications not only for the interpretation of Roman road use but, more significantly, for our understanding of economic development and integration in Italy and perhaps the Roman empire more generally.

A different study, but one that in passing confirms that trade (particularly long-distance, high-volume trade) was not discouraged by consideration of transport costs, is offered by Alston, who not only substantiates the existence of integrated markets, but also uncovers distinct *hierarchies* of integration. He shows that trade and trade networks centred on urban communities, and that the ways in which they did so were subject to considerable regional variation. Here, too, local economies are found to be at the heart of a broader picture. Some of these urban centres were part of an 'international' trade network, and benefited almost solely from that type of trading contact, whereas others, like the majority of those in Middle Egypt, were linked in production and exchange to local villages. Joined together in this way, city-and-village units were bound up with others in a regional or district system in which trade was facilitated indirectly – by the linking of village and metropolis – through a guild and licensing scheme. As Alston himself suggests, a regional study such as this serves to highlight the difficulties of explaining the ancient city with a single economic model, such as the 'consumer city' ideal-type.[18]

An altogether different kind of inter-regional integration (from that of Roman Egypt) is demonstrated by Old Assyrian trade, specifically by a significant trading colony in north-western Iraq, Kanesh, belonging to a small city, Ashur, hundreds of miles to the south. Ashur's ability to be so influential in trade at such a distance is explained partly in terms of its own strategic position, but more so in its intricate political and administrative structures.

[17] On the villa and *vicus* unit, and the challenge it issues to the consumer city model see also Whittaker 1990.
[18] Cf. now Morley 1996 and esp. 1997, 54–5 on urban 'systems' in Roman Italy, and the need to consider cities in their wider economic context, rather than as to whether or not they conform to the consumer city ideal-type.

Trade itself was carried by representatives of Ashur families, and was essentially oriented around family business. The colony's position at the heart of several important trading networks, together with its high degree of organisation, allowed Ashur to command valuable imports, and to profit from the internal carrying trade.

The role of traders

Kuhrt's study, along with those by Smith and Paterson, presents a forceful case for understanding ancient economies from the perspective of traders and associated groups. For if there is one single overriding problem with previous models of the ancient economy, then it is arguably their tendency to abstract economic activity from its context,[19] thus inherently downplaying the role of the traders themselves. For Finley and Jones, craftsmen and traders were of little significance, reflecting both their low output and the low volume of trade respectively. For Hopkins, taxation was the vital driving force in the economy, and craftsmen are seen as little more than converters of high-bulk goods into transportable commodities.

Neither of these models, however, can adequately explain the existence or success of Kanesh. In a structure more reminiscent of a medieval than an ancient city, Ashur's central governing body, the city assembly, was headed by merchant families – who sent their family members to trading colonies, such as Kanesh. Furthermore, an additional arrangement looks to have helped safeguard the interests and dominance of Ashur's ruling group; families sometimes shared what amounted to the sponsorship of an 'outsider' trader – a non-family member – over a long-term period in a deal that guaranteed the investing parties equal division of the profits.

Nor does a picture in which traders and artisans are marginalised sit easily with the findings of Smith's chapter. He suggests

---

[19] Lin Foxhall (1990, 22–3) recently noted that one problem with Finley's work, particularly given his insistence that the economy was embedded in the socio-political system, is that 'The remainder of *The Ancient Economy* is a treatise on what the ancient economy was not: i.e. commoditised and organised labour, capital investment, corporations, integrated markets, etc.'

that, far from being a sideshow, traders and craftsmen were serious players in economic development, and that their movements and, more specifically, the types of production in which they were engaged, provide the key to understanding the emergence of the Italian economy and even urbanisation during this period. While Smith focuses on the seventh and sixth centuries BC, it may not be unreasonable to suggest that if we are properly to understand the relationship between trade, traders, and the ancient city in later periods, study of the archaic period could offer vital clues.

Paterson focuses on the imperial period, and offers a more direct challenge to Hopkins's long-established model of economic growth, in which traders are central. Rather than regarding taxation as the major stimulus to trade, Paterson argues that the main impetus came instead from the extended trading opportunities that arose from empire. Traders, he points out, often went ahead of the Roman armies, and always had their eyes on the main chance; with the sense of stability and security that empire brought with it, that chance more readily presented itself.

At the same time, that same stability may have contributed to cultural integration, a subject that is taken up by Humphries, who regards trade as the vehicle for the spread of Christianity. While the traditional view holds that individual merchants themselves were responsible for the dissemination of Christianity, Humphries instead highlights a link between trade networks *per se* and the spread of the early church, showing how Christianity's first centres in northern Italy coincided with market or production centres. These networks and their convergence on urban centres, he argues, served to encourage cultural plurality, which in turn facilitated the church's expansion.

A new model?

Each of the chapters in this volume finds a different question to ask of the original working theme, trade, traders and the ancient city. Each answer reveals a different facet to the ancient economy. Given the timespan (roughly two thousand years) and geographical extent (from Assyria to northern Italy) considered in the case studies presented here, such diversity of focus is to be expected. But small wonder, then, that ancient economy has so far largely confounded attempts to accommodate and explain its many aspects with a single coherent model. It is hardly surprising, either, that many scholars choose to stay within their own specialism, be it one of specific subject, such as the ancient city, or of geographical area or historical period – each, as John Davies notes, having its own separate bibliography, and employing its own vocabulary and ideological suppositions. But so long as that remains the case, and no other overall model is ventured, then it is inevitable that much of the research currently carried out into the ancient economy finds itself operating within the terms of previous models, even if those models are generally acknowledged to have outlived their useful purpose. For the most recently dominant, primitivist model, the effort of having to cope with a wide variety of new material is causing it to be stretched to its very limits. The totality of additions, refinements and local variations and exceptions that have been suggested in recent years now make its overhaul a matter of some urgency.[20]

We are left, then, with the problem of finding a replacement framework for understanding the ancient economy which can cope with contemporary developments. And, if we are properly to get to grips with the ancient economy, we surely need first to agree our terms before beginning to fit all the different elements and levels together, from tiny workshops and rural smallholdings through shipping to taxation, and from exchange both within and between individual households through to inter-state trade. To achieve this requires unpicking all previous theories, models, and ideologies – which means those not just of the last couple of decades or so, but those of the more distant past as well – in order to trace the origins of the present impasse, and to overcome perhaps the biggest obstacle of all to progress: scholarly obfuscation. Thus, the 'first task is to make explicit what remained implicit' (Davies, this volume, p. 226).

In a comprehensive survey of the last century of ancient economic history, John Davies not only identifies the several points at which, arguably, we have gone wrong in the past – and have therefore led ourselves down blind alleys – but ultimately

---

[20]   A situation that, broadly speaking, Finley himself anticipated as part of the natural and desirable progress of history; see e.g. Finley 1985b, esp. ch. 1.

gives a tantalising and promising glimpse of where we can go from here. He ventures to construct a new model for the ancient economy that incorporates all levels and types of activity, and which also manages to explain their interrelationship(s); it therefore succeeds, too, in making sense of the range of perspectives put forward by the other contributors to this volume.

Final thoughts

The quest to understand the ancient economy goes on. It is hoped that the chapters in this volume show that research into ancient economic history looks to have a healthy and exciting future, aided by innovative techniques, new evidence, and fresh recruits. Whether Davies's model becomes common currency or not, only time – as always – will tell; in any event, its author makes no claim to a final version. But irrespective of the model's adoption, his chapter delivers a serious message: that we must find a way of communicating with each other, and agreeing the terms and terminology through which we do so, in order that we can more profitably work towards what is, after all, our common goal – to elucidate the ancient economy. To this end, these chapters, taken together, stress the need for extending the dialogue not only between ancient historians and archaeologists – between whom the boundaries are already rapidly blurring – but also between these and other specialists – papyrologists, epigraphists, numismatists, and so forth. Only through continued collaboration can we hope to do justice to the entire spectrum of source material, and subject our interpretations of the ancient economy to proper scrutiny.

Bibliography

Bailey, D. M. (ed. 1996), *Archaeological Research in Egypt: The Proceedings of the 17th Classical Colloquium of the Department of Greek and Roman Antiquities, British Museum, held on 1–4 December 1993 (JRA* suppl. 19; Ann Arbor, Mich.).

Cornell, T., and Lomas, K. (eds 1995), *Urban Society in Roman Italy* (London).

Duncan-Jones, R. (1982), *The Economy of the Roman Empire* (2nd edn, Cambridge).

—— (1990), *Structure and Scale in the Roman Economy* (Cambridge).

Finley, M. I. (1973), *The Ancient Economy* (London).

—— (1984), 'The study of the ancient economy: further thoughts', *Opus* 3: 5–11.

—— (1985a), *The Ancient Economy* (2nd edn, London).

—— (1985b), *Ancient History: Evidence and Models* (London).

Foxhall, L. (1990), 'Olive cultivation within Greek and Roman agriculture: the ancient economy revisited' (Ph.D. thesis, University of Liverpool).

Frier, B. W. (1991), 'Pompeii's society and economy' (review of W. Jongman (1988), *The Society and Economy of Pompeii*), *JRA* 4: 243–7.

Gill, D. W. J. (1991), 'Pots and trade: spacefillers or objets d'art?', *JHS* 111: 29–47.

Harris, W. V. (1993a), 'Between archaic and modern: some current problems in the history of the Roman economy', in W. V. Harris (ed. 1993b), pp. 11–29.

—— (ed. 1993b), *The Inscribed Economy: Production and Distribution in the Roman Empire in the Light of Instrumentum Domesticum* (*JRA* suppl. 6; Ann Arbor, Mich.).

Hopkins, K. (1980), 'Taxes and trade in the Roman Empire (200 BC–AD 400)', *JRS* 70: 101–25.

—— (1983), 'Introduction', in P. Garnsey, K. Hopkins, and C. R. Whittaker (eds), *Trade in the Ancient Economy* (Cambridge).

Howgego, C. (1992), 'The supply and use of money in the Roman world, 200 BC–AD 300', *JRS* 82: 1–31.

—— (1994), 'Coin circulation and the integration of the Roman economy', *JRA* 7: 5–21.

Jones, A. H. M. (1964), *The Later Roman Empire, 284–602: A Social, Economic and Administrative Survey*, 4 vols (Oxford).

—— (1974), *The Roman Economy: Studies in Ancient Economic and Administrative History*, edited by P. A. Brunt (Oxford).

Kehoe, D. P. (1988), *The Economics of Agriculture on Roman Imperial Estates in North Africa* (Hypomnemata, 89; Göttingen).

—— (1992), *Management and Investment in Estates in Roman Egypt during the Early Empire* (Papyrologische Texte und Abhandlungen 40; Bonn).

Lo Cascio, E. (1982), ' "Modo di produzione schiavistico" ed esportazioni italiche', *Opus* 1: 389–98.

Mattingly, D. J. (1994), Review of W. V. Harris (ed. 1993), *The Inscribed Economy*, in *JRS* 84: 233–5.

—— (1997), 'Beyond belief? Drawing a line beneath the consumer city', in H. Parkins (ed. 1997), pp. 210–18.

Morley, N. (1996), *Metropolis and Hinterland: The City of Rome and the Italian Economy, 200 BC–AD 200* (Cambridge).

—— (1997), 'Cities in context: urban systems in Roman Italy', in H. Parkins (ed. 1997), pp. 42–58.

Osborne, R. (1996), 'Pots, trade and the archaic Greek economy', *Antiquity* 70: 31–44.

Parkins, H. (ed. 1997), *Roman Urbanism: Beyond the Consumer City* (London).
Purcell, N. (1990), Review of W. Jongman (1988), *The Society and Economy of Pompeii*, in *CR* n.s. 40 (1): 111–16.
Rathbone, D. (1991), *Economic Rationalism and Rural Society in Third Century AD Egypt: The Heroninus Archive and the Appianus Estate* (Cambridge).
Rich, J. and Wallace-Hadrill, A. (eds 1991), *City and Country in the Ancient World* (London).
Rodriguez-Almeida, E. (1984), *Il Monte Testaccio* (Rome).
Rowlandson, J. (1996) *Landowners and Tenants in Roman Egypt: The Social Relations of Agriculture in the Oxyrhynchite Nome* (Oxford).
Tchernia, A. (1986), *Le Vin d'Italie romaine: essai d'histoire économique d'après les amphores* (Paris).
—— (1989), 'Encore sur les modèles économiques et les amphores', in *Amphores romaines et histoire économique: dix ans de recherche* (Collection de l'École Française de Rome, 114; Rome), pp. 529–36.
Tomber, R. (1993), 'Quantitative approaches to the investigation of long-distance exchange', *JRA* 6: 141–66.
Wallace-Hadrill, A. (1991), 'Elites and trade in the Roman town', in J. Rich and A. Wallace-Hadrill (eds 1991), 241–72.
Whittaker, C. R. (1990), 'The consumer city revisited: the *vicus* and the city', *JRA* 3: 110–18.
—— (1995), 'Do theories of the ancient city matter?', in T. Cornell and K. Lomas (eds 1995), 9–22.

2

The Old Assyrian merchants[1]

Amélie Kuhrt

Introduction

It seemed to the organisers of the symposium and the editors of
the resulting volume that the topic of trade in the ancient world
would benefit from some consideration of commercial practices
in the ancient Near East. As I reflected on the request to
contribute such a piece, I realised rapidly that this is an almost
impossible task. The term 'ancient Near East', as it has come to
be conceptualised by scholars over the years and enshrined in the
curricula of our universities, embraces an immense time span of
c. 3,000 years (from the fourth millennium to Alexander the Great)
and covers an equally immense territory inhabited by many
different peoples and socio-political groups. The very long period
of traceable history down to Alexander's conquest of the Persian
empire saw great changes on the social, economic, political and
cultural planes, which make it meaningless to speak broadly about
ancient Near Eastern trade as a definable aspect of that region's
life. Given that a particular emphasis of this colloquium is the city,

---

[1] I must stress that this chapter is a short summary of the work of the
many specialists to whom I refer. My own period of research is much
later (Achaemenid and Seleucid). It is intended to do no more than draw
the attention of Graeco-Roman historians to the potential importance of
this material.

I have therefore thought it most useful to concentrate on one period and area where, for the space of about 70–80 years, scholars are in a position to trace in considerable detail an extremely complex trade mechanism run by an ancient Near Eastern city-state, namely the city of Ashur in northern Iraq, between *c.* 1900 and 1830 BC.

The Old Assyrian trade is now a well-studied phenomenon, because some of the leading scholars involved in Assyriological studies have devoted themselves to analysing it (for a recent conspectus, together with a full bibliography, see Veenhof 1995); as a result, students are in the unusual position of having, for once, several excellent monographs and a spate of articles discussing details of the trade. It is the very sophisticated nature of this Old Assyrian mercantile system which served as an important stimulus for Susan Frankenstein's characterisation of Phoenician trade and colonisation (Frankenstein 1979), although the modalities of that, determined as they were by large states and empires, differ in detail. So although the material is a great deal earlier than the general focus of this volume, it has a relevance in breaking down established notions: first, about what kinds of commercial activities were possible in the ancient Near East; second, about the complexity and levels of sophistication that can exist in very early societies.

General background

Before looking at some of the Old Assyrian evidence, the material must be set into a context. Between *c.* 2100 and 2000 BC all of the region of south Iraq formed part of a highly centralised, bureaucratic state centred on the city of Ur ('Third Dynasty of Ur'). The rulers extended their sway northwards and eastwards to dominate territories in the Zagros mountain chain, south-west Iran and parts of northern Iraq and Syria, including the city of Ashur. Around 2000 BC this tightly organised structure fell apart and was succeeded for about two hundred and fifty years by a period of decentralisation. This phase is marked by the development of a pattern of city-states locked in competition with each other under their individual rulers. Any attempts by city kings to extend power beyond their city's immediate environs met with varying, usually fleeting, success. The one exception was Hammurabi of Babylon (1792–1750) who, at the end of the period, was able to impose control for a time over a region broadly comparable in extent to the earlier Ur state. The time of the Old Assyrian merchants (1900–1830) thus falls right into the middle of a period where the political norm was the city-state.

Although the available documentary evidence is fullest for the Mesopotamian region, the rich documentation preserved from this period (in Akkadian, written in cuneiform on clay tablets) has allowed scholars to deduce that a broadly similar political pattern existed in contemporary Syria-Palestine, central Anatolia and western Iran. The written material also allows one to see that, despite fierce rivalries and intercity wars, the small states of the entire area (and beyond) were linked to each other in a series of wide-ranging trade circuits: the cities of southern Iraq maintained regular maritime trading links with the Arab-Persian Gulf and Indus Valley; Susa, in south-west Iran (Khuzestan), was part of a network that extended into central Asia (Afghanistan and further north) in the east and fed into the cities of south Iraq in the west; the southern Mesopotamian cities in turn linked up to the north-west with states lying along the mid-Euphrates which, in their turn, connected up with neighbours to the west, south-west and north. Another very important nodal point in this dense mesh of routes and relationships was the small city of Ashur on the Tigris in north Iraq, which had close commercial ties with regions to the east (Iran), south Mesopotamia and central Anatolia.

The site of Ashur

Ashur lies at a point where it can dominate natural routes moving north to south, as well as east to west. It was not, and never became, an immense city.[2] In the period between 2000 and 1750 it was of modest size, small by comparison with the very large cities of southern Mesopotamia. Population estimates are notoriously difficult and unreliable, but most scholars agree that Ashur

---

[2] For the site of Ashur and its archaeology, see *RLA* I s.v. Ashur and Andrae 1938. For a useful recent survey of the site and finds in the Old Assyrian and Middle Assyrian periods, see Harper *et al.* 1995.

cannot have accommodated more than 15,000 inhabitants. It controlled some stretches of the surrounding countryside, but again the territory seems not to have been large and it was limited in its agricultural potential. Ashur lies at the edge of the zone where rainfed farming is possible; it did not, therefore, have access to great tracts of land suitable for good grain production with high yields (of the type possible in the south, cf. Powell 1985); the land in its environs was best suited for the herding of sheep and goats (cf. Oates 1968). Not much archaeological or written evidence survives from the city itself in the first half of the second millennium BC. Part of Ashur's city wall can be traced (on which the population estimates are based), the early levels of the Ishtar temple have been explored going back to the proto-historic period at the end of the fourth millennium, and royal building inscriptions show both that the city was ruled by a king and that there was also a temple to the local god Ashur. The dearth of evidence is to be explained in large part by the fact that much of Ashur was extensively developed and built over in the later, much more famous phases of its existence, when it was the centre of a large empire (Middle Assyrian and Neo-Assyrian periods, *c.* 1400–*c.* 1050 and 934–610 respectively).

The evidence

The bulk of the information for understanding Ashur and its economic base comes from documents found about 1,200 km to the north-west near ancient Kanesh, a site in central Anatolia. It lies near the Halys river, about 20 km north-east of the modern city of Kayseri on the Anatolian plateau, where the great circular mound of Kültepe rises about 20 metres above the surrounding plain. Late in the last century explorers recognised Kültepe as the probable source of many of the cuneiform texts, written in the Old Assyrian dialect of Akkadian, which appeared on the antiquities market. Attempts to locate the precise find spot of the tablets remained fruitless until the Czech scholar Bedrich Hrozný discovered, in 1926, that the tablets were actually being dug up at a much smaller site about 90 metres to the north-east of the main mound. This smaller site turned out to be the settlement of merchants from Ashur. Since 1948 the site has been thoroughly excavated by the Turkish archaeologist Tahsin Özgüç (see Özgüç 1959, 1986) with the result that perhaps 12,000 tablets have been added to the 3,000 or so available earlier, and the stratigraphy of the site has been clarified. It is now plain that the main site of Kültepe consists of a large circular city area with a palace building on the citadel, which was the centre of the important Anatolian principality of Kanesh, while the quarters of the adjacent settlement consisted of sizeable, but not lavish, typically Anatolian houses and were quite separate from the city of Kanesh.

Most of the texts held in museums before the start of the thorough Turkish excavations have been published, but only a tiny handful of the many found more recently have been made available. This means that deductions based on the published material, which probably represents less than a quarter of all the texts, will only be validated when the texts found more recently are studied. Apart from this, at present insuperable, difficulty, other factors complicate the picture. One is that two levels of the merchant settlement at Kanesh have produced tablets: level II, conventionally dated between 1900 and 1830, and Ib, which dates to somewhere around 1800. As matters stand at the moment, the bulk of published written material comes from the earlier level II period, and the later phase of the merchant settlement is very under represented. The political situation in Anatolia presents another problem: it can only be inferred from references in the Assyrian merchant documents themselves. The local Anatolian rulers at this period seem to have used the Old Assyrian dialect and the cuneiform writing system to communicate among themselves, but finds of texts on the city mound have so far been slight.

The chronology of the Kanesh colony has provoked some differences of opinion among scholars in the past. But at present there is a broad agreement: the levels of the city mound extend from the early third millennium right through to *c.* 1200, but the four levels of the colony are generally considered to have flourished in the period between *c.* 2000 and 1600. What we should note is that the quarter existed already well before the Assyrians, as far as we know, became such prominent traders there. It is thus possible that a local Anatolian trading station existed here earlier, of which the Assyrians became the dominant members. But even in the level II phase, the settlement was by no means exclusively inhabited by Assyrians (as the documents show), and the archae-ological material is entirely Anatolian in type. Were it not for the texts, we would have no inkling that any Assyrians were present at all.

The establishment of the trading centres

How did the small city of Ashur, with its modest resources but strategic location, come to play such a dominant role in the economic activities of a region many hundreds of miles away to the north-west?

Texts of two Old Assyrian kings, Ilushuma and his son Erishum I, who reigned in the fifty years before 1900 (i.e. the inception of the Old Assyrian presence at Kanesh, as far as we can tell), give a hint as to how Ashur established itself in this position. The longer one (that of Ilushuma) is extant in numerous copies on bricks from Ashur itself and runs as follows:

> Ilushuma, vice-gerent of Ashur, beloved of the god Ashur and the goddess Ishtar, son of Shallim-ahhe, vice-gerent of Ashur, son of Puzur-Ashur, vice-gerent of Ashur: Ilu-shuma, vice-gerent of Ashur, built the temple for the goddess Ishtar, his mistress, for his life. A new wall . . . I constructed and subdivided for my city house plots. The god Ashur opened for me two springs in Mount Ebih and I made bricks for the wall by the two springs. The water of one spring flowed down to the Aushum Gate, the water of the other spring flowed down to the Wertum Gate.
>
> The 'freedom' (*adduraru*) of the Akkadians and their children I established. I 'purified' their copper. I established their 'freedom' from the border of the marshes and Ur and Nippur, Awal and Kismar, Der of the god Ishtaran, as far as the City [i.e. Ashur].
>
> (Grayson 1987, A.0. 32. 2)

Contrary to an older view, according to which this related to a campaign of conquest in the south by Ilushuma (*CAH* i, ch. 25), Larsen (1976) has argued persuasively that the text reflects an attempt by Ilushuma to attract traders from south Mesopotamia to the Ashur market by giving them certain privileges. Ashur had managed to seize a controlling position in the tin trade with the east, and so served as an entrepôt where south Mesopotamian traders could go to buy tin and probably also to sell some of their copper (which came mainly from the Gulf). Following Ilushuma's decree, they preferred to do this as they could now get a much better deal in Ashur than in other centres. The places mentioned in the text, it is argued, may refer to the three major caravan routes from the south: one ran from Ur (the point of entry for copper from the Gulf) to Nippur then up to Ashur; the second ran perhaps along the Tigris; and the third went from Elam through Der, east of the Tigris, and then across to Ashur. If this proposition is accepted and added to the statement by Erishum, Ilushuma's successor (1939–1900), that he: 'made tax-exempt silver, gold, copper, tin, barley, wool . . .' (Grayson 1972, §62), it is possible to argue that the Assyrian kings deliberately introduced a policy intended to maximise the potential profits of their nodal position in trade.

The city-state of Ashur

Is it possible to define any of the institutions of the city of Ashur? The material from the Old Assyrian trading quarter at Kanesh provides some insights. The king was entitled simply 'vice-gerent' (*iššiʾakum*) of the god Ashur', which probably relates to his role in a cult, where he was conceived as acting on behalf of the god, as illustrated by the statement, found in some inscriptions, that 'the god Ashur is king, X (= royal name) is his vice-gerent'. The title is only used in the formal royal inscriptions, which shows its ceremonial nature. The usage in day-to-day documents is quite distinct: here the ruler was always called simply *rubāʾum* or *bēlum* meaning, respectively, 'prince' and 'lord'. These terms seem to define his position within the community as head of the royal family and so occupying a pre-eminent position *vis-à-vis* other families. They do not depict the king as an autocratic, all-powerful ruler.

The Old Assyrian documents also reveal the working at Ashur of 'the City' (*alum*), which appears to designate a kind of city assembly, probably made up by the heads of the great merchant families there (Larsen 1976). All important matters of policy seem to have been in the hands of 'the City': it was the city that took decisions binding on the community (*awat ālim* = 'the word/command of the city') and passed legal decisions (*dīn alim* = 'the judgement of the city'). It controlled the diplomatic relations with the Anatolian principalities on, or near, whose territories the Assyrian merchant settlements were located. Through the agency of the city herald (*šipru ša ālim*), it enforced general commercial policy; it also fixed the general export tax, which was levied on all trade caravans by the city at a specified rate, and their bales were sealed by the city. It is possible, though not certain, that this important body met in a specially designated building called the 'house of the city' (*bīt ālim*).

The other extremely important political institution (for the whole of Assyrian history) was the *limmum*. This was the title of an official, chosen annually by lot, after whom each year was named and, at this period, the office seems never to have been held by the king (in contrast to the Middle and Neo-Assyrian periods). Those eligible for the *limmu*-ship probably came from a select group, perhaps constituted by the heads of the major families of Ashur. It is possible that the chairman of the city assembly was the current *limmum*; so the office rotated annually among a small, but powerful, group of citizens who effectively counterbalanced the powers of the king (Larsen 1976). The picture of the Ashur community that emerges from this piecemeal evidence is that of a highly complex civic structure, largely run by a powerful group of businessmen, representing their family interests. The position of the ruler was largely restricted to that of acting for the community within the cultic and ceremonial spheres, undertaking public building projects and overseeing the exercise of justice. That is the picture of the city of Ashur as it can be gleaned from the Kanesh documents and the royal inscriptions.

The trading network in Anatolia

The Kanesh texts further show that two distinct types of trading establishment existed in Anatolia. The main one, and the best known, is the *kārum*, a term that in origin means merely a quay, but, because most trade in Mesopotamia was waterborne, it came by extension to mean the harbour and trading quarter of a city, where merchants gathered to transact business. When the Assyrians established permanent trading quarters far from home they simply applied the term to such settlements although they were now, of course, no longer located necessarily on river banks. The other type of trading centre was called *wabartum*, a term unique to the Old Assyrian merchants in Anatolia. The word seems to be linked to a term for 'guest'; it is therefore suggested that it may originally have designated a caravanserai, which eventually expanded into a more permanent residential and trading centre, although smaller and less autonomous than a *kārum*. Some evidence exists to suggest that *wabartum* settlements were usually located adjacent to cities either less economically important or more difficult of access and so off the beaten track. The residents of a *wabartum* seem to have come under the administrative authority of the nearest *kārum*. But it must be admitted that some uncertainty exists in understanding fully this type of commercial settlement.

The numbers and the density of the trading centres can be recovered, more or less, from the documents. The situation in the *kārum* II period is more certain than in the Ib phase. In the earlier period there was probably a total of eleven *kārum*s and ten *wabartum*s; in level Ib the number of *kārum* establishments increased to fourteen, and there is evidence that some of the settlements that earlier on had been smaller *wabartum* stations developed at this time into fully organised *kārum* centres. The most important *kārum* was the one at Kanesh (at least in level II), which formed the hub of the network of trading settlements, with routes radiating northwards as far as the Halys mouth on the Black Sea, north-east to the region of modern Sivas and south-west to the important Anatolian political centres of Purushhattum and Wahshushana. A further group of colonies was located in the area to the south-east, along the routes leading into north Syria and Mesopotamia, and some were set at the northerly crossing points of the Euphrates. These were the routes along which goods coming from the Arab-Persian Gulf, Carchemish and Mari were transmitted to Anatolia.

Ashur's relations with Anatolia

Two important questions that need to be answered before describing the Old Assyrian trading network are: how did the Assyrian colonies relate to the Anatolian principalities in which they were located, and whose agreement did they need in order to carry on their profitable business? In order to answer these central questions, it is necessary to try to reconstruct a picture of the political structure of Anatolia, which can only be done by using incidental references in the Old Assyrian texts (cf. Garelli 1963; Liverani 1988, 366–71). Independent city-states seem to have been the norm. They controlled the surrounding stretches of countryside and, in some instances, smaller urban centres. The majority of the population seems to have been 'Hattian' (the term used to describe the indigenous non-Indo-European population of Anatolia). Three political units, Purushhattum, Kanesh and Wahshushana, were much more powerful, and controlled quite extensive areas defined in each case as a 'country' (*mātum*). The rulers of both the smaller states and the 'countries' were (as far as the evidence goes) all called *rubā'um* (= 'prince'), except for the ruler of Purushhattum who was called 'great prince'. This suggests that this westerly state may have been recognised as wielding some kind of greater power than the others.

It has been argued in the past (see, for example, *CAH* i, ch. 24) that the whole region where Old Assyrian colonies are found was politically subject to Ashur. This view was based on the fact that a few texts demonstrate that the Anatolian states were linked to the city of Ashur by oaths, administered by envoys from there. But recent reconsiderations of this hypothesis make it much more plausible that the city of Ashur simply regulated its diplomatic relations with the Anatolian rulers through the city envoys, and that the oaths almost certainly related to the precise agreements under which the Assyrian traders could operate within the territory of the Anatolian centres. This conclusion is strengthened by other evidence, which shows that Assyrians could be clapped into prison by the Anatolian princes for smuggling restricted goods, that all Assyrian caravans were subject to a tax from the local ruler, that he may have had first pick of the goods and could impose restrictions on the trade in certain materials. The idea that Ashur wielded political control over Anatolia has now become untenable and is to be rejected (Orlin 1970; Larsen 1976).

The trading mechanism

The organisation of this astonishingly complex and far-flung Assyrian commercial system has been painstakingly recovered from the texts (at least for level II: Larsen 1976), although a certain number of uncertainties persist. It seems that the smaller *wabartum* settlement came under the authority of the nearest *kārum*, which deferred to *kārum* Kanesh, which in turn came under the direct supervision of Ashur with its city-assembly. Kanesh was thus of central importance in the system, and some documents reveal that its own institutions were modelled on those of Ashur, with an assembly and officials, mirroring those of 'the City'.

The most striking feature of the Assyrian trade in Anatolia is the fact of permanence: merchant families (*bītum*: lit. 'house', hence also 'family') in Ashur sent some of their male relatives to settle in one of the Anatolian colonies, where they directed and promoted the family trading business by selling consignments of goods, sending the profits back home and also adding to them by engaging in trade internal to the Anatolian principalities. Sometimes a merchant in Ashur might make use of someone outside his family for a time in order to complete a particular transaction. In spite of the fact that business was basically a family matter, some of the capital funding for the trade came from shared, long-term investments which financed a particular trader over a period of several years; at the end of the time specified the investors received equal shares of the profit; the trader also gained a share, and provisions were made for cases of early withdrawal. These agreements were called 'sacks' (*naruqqu*), which derives from the original practice of placing actual goods in a trader's carrying sack (Veenhof 1987). Only one of these important contracts has been published so far (Landsberger 1940, 20–6; cf. Larsen 1976), but it seems likely that it represents a regular practice, which cut across the normal family ties and united the interests of the great merchant houses of Ashur.

The caravans of donkeys by which the goods were actually transported on the five- to six-week journey (cf. Hecker 1980) were generally fairly small. Each donkey usually carried a load of textiles and a small amount of tin. The donkey loads were standardised: a regular full load of tin consisted of 130 minas (*c.* 65 kilos) of tin; a donkey load of textiles consisted of 30 pieces plus accessories. Goods were loaded in standardised half-packs – two half-packs either side and a whole pack on top. The rate at which the caravans were taxed in Anatolia was computed on the basis of two minas per half-pack. Crucial at this time for the local Anatolian rulers was the Assyrian import of tin, which was needed to produce bronze. Ashur played a major role at this time in the acquisition and distribution of this metal from the east (probably central Asia). On arrival in Anatolia everything, including the donkeys, was sold, and the main import back to Ashur was silver and some gold. Within Anatolia itself the Assyrians, given their sophisticated and developed system of trading stations, were able to increase their profits by playing the dominant role in the internal carrying trade. They probably also organised the Anatolian inter-state trade in copper (Larsen 1967), which may have been mined at the rich deposits of Ergani Maden (near Elaziğ, Turkey). The tin was, bulk for bulk, more valuable than the textiles, but it was the textiles which provided the main volume of the trade (Veenhof 1972; cf. Larsen 1987), and the documents show that they were centrally important to Assyrian commerce and highly valued in Anatolia. The texts refer to special kinds of garments and certain types of cloth as being more popular at this or that moment, and the merchants were careful to watch the market and work out where their best chances for profit lay. Some, though not the majority, of the textiles were produced in Ashur itself by the female members of the merchant houses, as shown by this letter written to a woman in Ashur by her merchant husband in Kanesh:

Thus Puzur-Ashur, speak to Waqqurtum:
With 1 pound of silver – levy separately added, pay over completed – sealed by me, Ashur-idi is on his way to you. [Concerning] the fine cloth that you sent me: you must make cloth like that and send it to me via Ashur-idi, then I will send you [as payment] half pound of silver [per piece]. Have one side of the cloth combed, but not shaved smooth: it should be close-textured. Compared to the textiles you sent me earlier, you must work in 1 pound of wool more per piece of cloth, but they must still be fine! The other side [of the cloth] must be just lightly combed: if it still looks hairy, it will have to be closeshaved, like *kutānu*-cloth [a very common textile, possibly a kind of sheet]. As for the *abarnê*-cloth [originally named after the place, Abarne, which became the name of a type of cloth, cf. 'tweed'] which you sent me, you must not send me that sort of thing again. If you do want to do so, then make it the way I used to wear it. But if you don't want to make fine textiles as I have heard it they can be bought in quantity over there [i.e. where you are]; buy [them] and send them to me. One finished [piece of] cloth, when you make it, should be nine ells long and eight ells wide [4.5 × 4 m].

(*TCL* 19: 17; cf. Veenhof 1972, 103v)

Conclusion

This has of necessity been little more than a rough sketch of some of the salient points of the Old Assyrian trade; many more details of this richly documented trade network exist and are emerging more clearly as Assyriologists analyse more texts. It is possible, for example, to estimate the quantities of tin imported over a 40–50 year period (at least 80 tons, sufficient to produce 800 tons of bronze over the same period). A conservative assessment of the number of pieces of textile imported in this period comes to at least 100,000. These must have been highly specific, high status types of cloth, as indicated in the quoted letter. The profit for the Assyrians (well-attested) on tin was 100 per cent, on textiles 200 per cent. Control of the continuing profitability of this trade was paramount: when the merchant-bosses in Ashur heard that some Assyrians in Anatolia were trading in locally made, cheap imitation cloth, they issued strong warnings against this practice through the city-assembly in Ashur and fined those proven to have been involved in it heavily. The trade bore such rich fruits that it is quite feasible to call some of the participants that surface in the documentation 'millionaires'. There is even an interesting hint of the kind of tensions the unswerving pursuit of profit could provoke occasionally within families: a letter written to a million-aire merchant in *kārum* Kanesh (probably) by his wife and his sister in Ashur contains the following statement:

> Here we ask the women who interpret oracles, the women who inter-pret omens from entrails, and the ancestral spirits and the god Ashur sends you a serious warning: 'You love money! You hate life!' Can't you satisfy Ashur here in the city? Please when you have heard the letter then come, see Ashur's eye and save your life!
>
> (*TC* I: 5; Larsen 1982, 214)

This, as has been suggested by Larsen (1982), sounds very much like a heartfelt plea to the merchant to stop devoting himself to money and return to the bosom of his family.

The Old Assyrian material is unbelievably rich and deserves to be better known among Graeco-Roman historians in their endless battles about the 'ancient economy'. This debate seems to me to have run its course and it has not got a lot more to offer. Instead it might be more profitable if scholars of the ancient world looked more carefully at *all* the available evidence (including non-Graeco-Roman texts), in which the Old Assyrian material should by rights hold pride of place, as an example of the kinds of sophisticated trade structures that could and did exist, and which would never have been suspected from the purely material remains. It might be fitting to end this brief presentation with a particularly thought-provoking quote from one of the scholars who has worked intensively on the Old Assyrian material:

> The expertise built up (in Ashur) in the field of commerce formed one of the basic elements in the trade towards the west. The construction of elaborate systems of accounting, of investment and partnership structures, and of an administrative system of great elegance and efficiency led to a commercial organisation which in its complex details is paralleled only millennia later by the traders of the Mediterranean cities. The famous 'commercial revolution of the thirteenth century' in Western Europe, which was characterised by a major shift in business organisation away from the travelling, itinerant trader towards the sedentary businessman seated behind his desk is paralleled in many details by the material from Kanesh.
>
> (Larsen 1987, 54)

Bibliography

Andrae, W. (1938), *Das wiederstandene Assur* (Leipzig).
Frankenstein, S. (1979), 'The Phoenicians in the far west: a function of Neo Assyrian imperialism', in M. T. Larsen (ed.), *Power and Propaganda: a Symposium on Ancient Empires* (Mesopotamia 7; Copenhagen), 263–94.
Garelli, P. (1963), *Les Assyriens en Cappadoce* (Paris).
Grayson, A. K. (1972), *Assyrian Royal Inscriptions*, vol. i (Wiesbaden).
—— (1987) *Assyrian Rulers of the Third and Second Millennium BC* (RIM, Assyrian Periods 1: Toronto).
Harper, P. *et al.* (eds 1995), *Discoveries at Ashur on the Tigris: Assyrian Origins* (Metropolitan Museum of Art, New York).
Hecker, K. (1980), 'Der Weg nach Kanis', *ZA* 70: 185–97.
Landsberger, B. (1940), 'Vier Urkunden von Kültepe', *TTAED* 4: 7 ff.
Larsen, M. T. (1967), *Old Assyrian Caravan Procedures* (Istanbul).
—— (1976), *The Old Assyrian City-State and its Colonies* (Mesopotamia

30 Amélie Kuhrt

4; Copenhagen).
—— (1982), 'Your money or your life! A portrait of an Assyrian businessman', in M. Dandamayev *et al.* (eds), *Societies and Languages of the Ancient Near East: Studies in Honour of I. M. Diakonoff* (Warminster), 214–45.
—— (1987), 'Commercial networks in the ancient Near East', in M. Rowlands, M. T. Larsen and K. Kristiansen (eds), *Centre and Periphery in the Ancient World* (New Directions in Archaeology; Cambridge), 47–56.
Liverani, M. (1988), *Antico Oriente: storia, società, economia* (Rome).
Oates, D. (1968), *Studies in the Ancient History of Northern Iraq* (London).
Orlin, L. L. (1970), *Assyrian Colonies in Cappadocia* (The Hague).
Özgüç, T. (1959), *Kültepe-Kaniš I: New Researches at the Center of the Assyrian Trade Colonies* (Ankara).
—— (1986), *Kültepe-Kaniš II: New Researches at the Trading Center of the Ancient Near East* (Ankara).
Powell, M. (1985), 'Salt, seed and yields in Sumerian agriculture: a critique of the theory of progressive salinisation', *ZA* 75: 7–38.
Rathbone, D. (1991), *Economic Rationalism and Rural Society in Third Century AD Egypt: The Heroninus Archive and the Appianus Estate* (Cambridge).
Veenhof, K. (1972), *Aspects of Old Assyrian Trade and its Terminology* (Leiden).
—— (1987), ' "Dying tablets" and "hungry silver": elements of figurative language in Akkadian commercial terminology', in M. Mindlin, M. Geller and J. Wansbrough (eds), *Figurative Language in the Ancient Near East* (London), 41–75.
—— (1995), 'Kanesh: an Assyrian colony in Anatolia', in J. M. Sasson, J. Baines, G. Beckman and K. S. Rubinson (eds), *Civilizations of the Ancient Near East* (New York), 859–71.

3

Traders and artisans in archaic central Italy

Christopher Smith

Introduction

This chapter is concerned with the role of traders and artisans in central Italy from the ninth to the end of the sixth century BC.[1] I hope to be able to indicate the central importance of these figures in and for the society and economy of this region at this time, and through two particular crafts, pottery and terracotta decoration of buildings, to show the originality of central Italian artisans, and the sources of the ideas which they transform. In the course of this discussion I hope also to show how these creative arts serve the purposes of the ruling elite.

In this chapter, I wish to draw particular attention to the role of artisans in the emerging urban communities of central Italy. It is striking how little attention the artisan receives; creator, initiator, servant, supplier, the artisan's role is indispensable, and yet much of the focus in discussions of the ancient economy is given to a class which, although it may overlap significantly with that of the artisan, is nevertheless functionally distinct from it: the class of the trader or merchant.

[1] I am grateful for comments from the conference participants; I remain responsible for any errors. This article is dedicated in gratitude to †Mr J. Creed, and to Mr T. Rhodes.

Whilst it is undoubtedly the case that the movement of goods is a great stimulus to social, political and economic development, there is a serious problem with omitting the artisan from our accounts of such developments. In the first place, artisans are not necessarily static individuals, constrained to remain forever in their workshops. Quite the opposite; certain crafts are necessary in any community, and therefore the great colonising movement from the eighth century in the Mediterranean requires the movement of artisans. At Pithecusa, we have indisputable evidence for metal-workers and potters (Ridgway 1992, 83–103).

There is clearly a problem here, for it is equally true that artisans do not have to move in order for their products to move. La Rocca believed that he had identified a group of itinerant Greek potters from a hoard in Rome; an idea not only unlikely since much of the pottery has since been shown to be local imitation, but also unnecessary, since from other evidence we can show quite clearly that there was a considerable movement of goods around the Mediterranean at precisely the time that this pottery was being produced, and that the end-point of some of this production was in central Italy (Smith 1996, 80; La Rocca, in Vallet ed. 1982; Bartoloni 1987, 45). It is largely impossible to distinguish between the movement of goods and the movement of artisans since archaeologically there is no difference to be discerned. Nevertheless, on occasions we can prove the movement of artisans, and on occasion we can hope to be able to spot the difference between imitation and original, a particular issue for Etruscan painted pottery. A rigid principle in favour of the movement of artisans only or the movement of goods only is certain to be misplaced, given the diversity and energy of the ancient Mediterranean at this time.

The economy of central Italy in the archaic period

The economic structure of central Italy may be briefly sketched; thanks to the archaeological discoveries of the past century or so, we are now relatively well-informed about the position of the region in the larger Mediterranean context and can fit this pattern into a methodological framework (cf. Cornell 1995; Smith 1996).

In essence we find throughout central Italy an elite which was engaged in conspicuous consumption of wealth on a grand scale, in funerary behaviour and daily life. Hence we find that Etruria and Campania boast significant finds of jewellery and other expensive imports, some of which are found in burials, and others (the more scarce because of the more difficult conditions of survival) in settlements. The wealth required to support this activity presumably came from the extraction of a surplus from a dependent labour force; the point at which slavery replaced tied free labour is unknown, though there have been suggestions that slavery was being introduced to Etruria as early as the fifth century, and the Roman practice of *nexum*, known from the Twelve Tables, indicates a form of debt-bondage (Cornell 1995, 280–3).

The sources of these luxuries were in southern Italy and the east, and thus the process whereby the elite of central Italy demonstrated their social status is indissociable from the great colonisation movement that brought Phoenicians and Greeks to Pithecusa and then to other parts of Italy. Whether the elites pre-existed the arrival of these new opportunities for display is somewhat disputed, but I personally believe that social stratification may be identified in Italian society from the tenth century BC (Smith 1996, 106–25), and that the elite were perfectly situated to exploit the new opportunities which trade and colonisation brought, and moreover, that this was one factor in the success of the Greek colonisation process.

Specifically, we can identify two major areas of influence. One is the Levantine culture of Phoenicia and Syria, which both directly and indirectly (through the orientalising culture of the Greek world) had a major impact; the other is the Hellenic civilisation of mainland Greece and its offshoot in southern Italy. In art and in life, there were models here which the Italians followed. On occasion we can be quite specific about the origin of a certain artistic motif or cultural practice, but on the whole the influence is diffuse and pervasive. For instance, the cults of Hercules and Demeter and Persephone seem at present to have stronger roots in southern Italy than in mainland Greece (Bayet 1926; Zuntz 1971; Cazenove 1990), whilst Etruscan pottery owes much if not all to the influence of orientalising Euboean, Corinthian and later Attic pottery (Brendel 1995), but practices like the banquet have too broad a range of predecessors in mainland Greece, Magna

Graecia and the east to permit any conclusive attribution of origin (Murray 1990; Murray and Tecusan eds 1995).

There are three major regions in the central Italy of this chapter: Etruria, Latium and Campania. Less is known of the Sabina, or of Umbria. The developments of the three major regions which I have mentioned depended on their exposure to influxes of foreign populations and foreign goods, and also on their own resources. Campania was most nearly affected by the presence of the Greeks with the trading post of Pithecusa on the island of Ischia, and the colony of Cumae in the eighth century, together with the later colonies in the south. At the same time however, Campania was for a while subjected to the Etruscans, and maintained its own regional identity, so that artistically and culturally Campania was a complex hybrid. Its great asset was its agricultural wealth, as in later times (Frederiksen 1984).

Etruria developed more quickly than either of the other two regions, and became a major political power as well as an artistic centre of cultural excellence, whose goods were found across the Mediterranean and more particularly in southern Gaul (Ridgway 1988). Why this should be so is unanswerable; in terms of language, religion, and possibly ethnic origin, the Etruscans were different from all other Italian peoples. In addition, their region possessed considerable mineral resources, which were exploited from the very beginning of the colonisation period, as iron ore from Elba found on the island of Ischia attests (Ridgway 1992, 105, 108).

Latium, sandwiched between the two, had neither the great agricultural resources nor the mineral wealth of its neighbours, and is in general the least wealthy, to judge by the patchy and fragmentary archaeological record, though its political development, first under the Etruscans and then Rome as an independent power, was remarkable.

Although there are clear regional identities and different trajectories of development, it still makes sense to see this as some sort of unit. One can see that certain areas were favoured as the places where contact with non-Italians was closest. For instance, the ports of Pyrgi and Gravisca in Etruria, and the towns of Cales and Capua in Campania, and Rome in Latium, are particularly significant.[2] There are a number of centres or cores, and a number of

---

[2] See Ciaghi 1993 for an account of the terracotta production of Cales.

peripheries, and they overlap with each other, so that Rome for instance may have received some foreign visitors but must also have relied heavily on trade with Etruscan cities to provide the imports which were then redistributed through Latium, thus enhancing Rome's own position within the region. Trade between Campania and Etruria was probably quite intense in both directions. This kind of system has been described as 'dendritic', and is typical of a society with an elite but also some sense of the market (Smith 1996, 114–22; Smith forthcoming). As we shall see, the conditions of archaic Italian trade were by no means primitive, and although it is easy to see that the economy remained firmly embedded in the social relations of competitive hierarchies, both supplier and consumer had quite accurate and clear ideas of the sorts of goods which were needed to fulfil the attendant requirements. Recently, the strikingly limited range of iconography preferred in central Italian imports of Greek pottery has led some to suspect the identification of favoured mythological scenes and their production to order (Arafat and Morgan 1994). Without pursuing this too far, such attention to detail rather gives the lie, in my opinion, to the idea that even in the foreign markets Greek pottery had a strictly limited value (Gill 1994; Small 1995).

On one thing we are not and will never be clear. There is no satisfactory archaeological indicator in any non-colonial site for the numbers of immigrants from outside Italy at any one time. The number of imported pots gives no indication whatsoever, nor does the depth of artistic influence of one region on another. The literary sources are notoriously silent on issues of population and proportion. The few inscriptions which we have are not a representative sample, and are too few in number. Short of expensive petrographic analysis, only the eye can spot the difference in style of painting between an imported Corinthian pot, and a pot painted by an Etruscan imitating a Corinthian pot (which is what we mean by an Etrusco-Corinthian pot), and the stylistic ascriptions do not necessarily map directly onto ethnic distinctions; if a Corinthian potter settles in Etruria and marries an Etruscan woman will his son paint in the Corinthian or the Etruscan style, and what will his identity be? If in this chapter I have tried to say something about artisans and the movement of craftsmen between regions, it is in response to the indications of the sources, which I shall discuss in the next section, and to some current thinking on artisan activity and ancient workshops, which I shall turn to in the section after that.

Roman accounts of traders and artisans

When one begins to consider the issue of the artisan in early Italy, it is surprising to discover how many records there are in the sources. Together with priests, warriors and kings, the artisans loom large both in the historians, and also in the invaluable chapters of Pliny the Elder. How much weight can we place on such frail evidence?

I suspect that we should not be surprised to discover a kernel of truth behind the stories, so even if the man who made the terracotta *quadriga* for the Temple of Jupiter Optimus Maximus on the Capitol was not called Vulca, he may yet have come from Veii (Pliny, *HN* 35. 157). What the sources preserve is either real names and facts, or a structural pattern of events which was familiar to the writer, and which he could therefore extrapolate backwards – and there is of course a good deal of possibility for a bit of both. If we are dealing with a structural pattern, is it a pattern that makes sense in the time of the author, or one that might make sense at the time of the events recorded? Let us swiftly review the evidence.

The evidence refers to statues, painting and architectural terracotta. Pliny the Elder is in two minds about the earliest Roman statuary and painting, for there was clearly a strong tradition that the Romans did not engage in such activities during the earliest period, and that it was only the arrival of the Greeks that brought them to work in clay and paint. He gives the palm in bronzework to the Romans in one passage, however (Pliny, *HN* 34. 33, 35. 152, 35. 6–8; Pollitt 1983, 6–8).

There are two different things going on here. First, Pliny is engaging in the endless debate about the impact of the Greeks on the Romans that is so heavily immersed in a moral discourse. Plutarch says that Numa prohibited the making of images of the divine: 'during the first 170 years of their history, though they built temples and established holy shrines, they did not undertake to make a holy image, since it was not holy to liken exalted things to baser things nor to come into contact with the divine by any other means than the intellect' (Plut. *Numa* 8). This philosophical objection is wholly anachronistic, but it can be explained by the other issue which Pliny is having difficulty with here and elsewhere, and that is dating the objects which he can see or has report of. If we consider the issue of painting, Pliny reports that a Corinthian named Ekphantos was said to have invented painting, but that he himself had seen paintings at Ardea, Lanuvium and Caere which were much older. These were found in the first two cases in temples. Since the advent of stone-built temples does not precede the sixth century, and few of these survived without serious refurbishment, it looks as if Pliny's claim to have seen paintings which predated the middle of the seventh century is implausible. Presumably, however, Pliny is making a case for an indigenous tradition here, as he does for bronzeworking, and one must wonder whether Pliny felt he could spot the difference between Greek artistry and Italian artistry.

Central to the debate is the figure of Demaratus of Corinth, apparently one of the casualties of the collapse of the Bacchiad reign at Corinth (Ampolo 1976/7; Ridgway and Ridgway 1994). He was a trader, and it appears a successful one, for he brought with him from Corinth, according to some traditions, both Ekphantos the founder of painting and Eucheir, Diopos, and Eugrammos who brought the art of clay modelling into Rome. The names are suspicious, and so is the story; Demaratus of course was the father or grandfather of Tarquinius Priscus, first Etruscan king of Rome. Yet when the great terracotta roof decoration for Capitoline Jupiter is required, it is the Etruscans who provide the skill, as we have seen.

All in all, the sources seem to give a slightly confused picture, on the one hand proclaiming the significance of the Greeks and on the other the flourishing native tradition. When speaking of the Greeks, we hear only of the first founders of a skill or technique (a tradition of reporting which is of course a favourite in antiquity), and there is a close association with one man, a trader. If one were to take the story of Demaratus seriously, we would be thinking of a man wealthy enough to engage in the movement not only of goods but also of workshops, or sufficiently desperate, and suffi-ciently optimistic about the market that he paid for at least three craftsmen to accompany him out of the tumultuous days of Cypselid Corinth into the new horizons of Etruria.

Is the tradition acceptable? In terms of the first-founder rhetoric it is not, and in a recent article, David and Francesca Serra Ridgway (1994) have shown that by the time Demaratus and his *fictores* had arrived in Italy, there was already a developed knowledge of stone statuary, and terracotta roof decoration which included at least head antefixes and possibly larger-scale seated or standing statues as well. Of course dating is difficult in this early and unrecorded period, but we shall discuss this in more detail later. Crucially however, the arrival of Greeks does not fit archaeologically with the invention of central Italian art, and if the Roman artistic development is later, it is not the Greeks but the Etruscans who are making the difference.

What though of the association between Demaratus the trader and his three *fictores*? We know enough of later Roman practices to realise that workshops could be alienated with their staff attached, so that what really changes hands is the skilled labour. Supposing that we are looking at something similar here, does it still make sense to see the movement of artisans as part of the complex economic exchanges of the time? We need to look closer at current thinking about workshops in the archaic period.

Artisans and workshops

Much work has been done recently on the nature of artisan activity, largely as a result of the ever increasing amount of evidence (Bonghi Jovino 1989, 1990, 1993; Carafa 1995). Although this is necessarily speculative, certain general trends can be identified. First, it is clear that no branch of artistic activity in central Italy was happening in complete isolation from the others. We shall see later evidence for the influences of one art form on another; here I wish merely to point out that the use of the mould is common to both terracotta decoration and to bronzeworking through the lost wax method which was prevalent at this time. We should not be surprised therefore to see parallels between the two. There is, I believe, even more reason to assume these sorts of connections if one begins to move away from any conception of ornamentation as being idle and devoid of ideological message.

Second, we have begun to see more and more instances of the movement of decorative motifs, particularly in terracotta reliefs, which require explanation other than simple imitation. Ever since Andren the clear similarities between friezes at Rome and Velletri have been explained by the re-use of the same mould with some alterations, and such examples are multiplying. How can we explain this in terms of what actually occurred (Rystedt *et al.* 1993)?

Andren believed at one stage in wandering craftsmen, but found the idea less attractive later in his life. The idea of artisans wandering through central Italy hawking their terracotta friezes is implausible, since there is a considerable amount of material and equipment which was essential to any such activity. The story of Vulca's difficulty with the kiln in which he created the great *quadriga* for the Temple of Capitoline Jupiter may reflect an understanding of the sheer technical complexity of moulding and firing large-scale statues (Plut. *Popl.* 13). What seems to be clearer now is that the decoration of public and domestic architecture was a large-scale and programmatic affair; that one did not simply add bits and pieces, but rather built up a relatively coherent order of decoration. A roof for instance requires the gables, simas and ridgepoles to be planned, especially if standing or seated figures are to be added on the top. So a single man, carrying a couple of decorative moulds, will not go far to explain both the inventiveness and the complexity of Italian architectural decoration.

Bonghi Jovino (1990) has therefore suggested a different approach. She introduces the concept of a small and rather mono-functional workshop for the earlier period, tracing the move to a polyfunctional workshop which produces more standardised material in larger quantities to some time in the sixth century.[3] Certainly we shall see reasons to accept a major change in archi-tectural terracotta decoration in the sixth century. I wish here to focus on the idea of workshops built around a master-craftsman, at first serving a very specific and limited set of needs, perhaps at the top end of the market, and later broadening their production.

---

[3] Carafa 1995, in a detailed study of the pottery found in the Palatine excavations at Rome, comes to similar sorts of conclusions about the development of workshops from domestic adjuncts to diverse polyfunc-tional workshops, and this was accompanied by a greater standardisation of forms again.

Bonghi Jovino suggests at one point that we could imagine the master-craftsman moving between different workshops, given temporary hospitality in a different city, or actually owning or running operations across a wide area. This fits well with the account in the sources of Vulca being called from Veii to participate in the construction of the Temple of Jupiter, and it also seems to me to fit well with another feature of early Latin society which Carmine Ampolo has described as its horizontal mobility – that is, the movement of members of the elite into different areas, most clearly seen in the arrival of Tarquinius Priscus in Rome (Ampolo 1970/1). Other examples are less easy to pinpoint, though inscriptions suggest Latins in Etruria (Smith 1996, 238), and the very precise material parallels between the grave-goods found in Cerveteri and Praeneste, if they do not indicate the movement of an aristocrat from the one place to the other, do indicate close links between the areas (Smith 1996, 93–7). The goods may have moved as part of gift exchange.

Latin society at the upper level at least seems open; the elite is a permeable structure. If patronage operated in the sixth century, as would seem plausible if not readily demonstrable, then it makes sense for artisans to follow their patrons' movements around central Italy, and this is perhaps the most significant aspect of the Etruscans' domination down to Campania.

Thus Bonghi Jovino's intuition would seem valuable, not simply on the grounds of the practicalities but also in terms of the political and economic relationships of the time. She is also correct, I think, in identifying two different kinds of activity: that of the master-craftsmen engaged in specific tasks for specific patrons, and that of the more general and standardised production which will have required more labour. Thus the production of roof-tiles demands a single pattern to be followed repeatedly, whilst the crafting of the statues that adorned the ridgepole requires the hand of the master.

One aspect of this division is that the more basic operations are relatively value-free, for whilst one does not expect all roofs to be tiled so that possession of such a durable roof is a mark of status for building or owner, there is little else of ideological value in the tiles themselves. It is the other parts of the roof, the painting and particularly the statuary, or the friezes, or the decoration of

pottery, which carried the loaded messages of superiority or difference. Hence the master craftsman was not simply an artist; he
was also the conveyor of a political message (Colonna 1988). In
this he inherited some of the roles which his predecessors as far
back as the ninth century BC had fulfilled, and it is to this that
I now turn.

Pottery

Pottery is ubiquitous in central Italian archaeology, since the focus
on burial grounds has left us with a huge collection of ceramic
pieces from the whole area. Whilst the arguments rage about the
value of Greek pottery, Italian archaeology indicates some rather
precise functions for the different styles of pottery, and suggests
that pottery and its decoration were not idly undertaken, but
produced for specific markets.

Let us take first the instance of Osteria dell'Osa, a burial ground
in Latium which was in use from the end of the tenth century to
the early sixth century (Bietti-Sestieri 1992b for full publication).
The excavator, Anna Maria Bietti-Sestieri, has identified two
ninth-century groups in this burial population at its outset;
they surround a group of four or five cremations. Each group
has a consistent set of burial characteristics and there are clear
differences between the two groups. One group has pottery
with particular forms of incised and/or moulded decoration that
remains constant for a period much longer than the life of any
individual (Bietti-Sestieri 1992a, 141–98).

This is the clearest example of a more general feature of Latin
life, the presence of a set of objects which are thought suitable
for burial with a deceased person for a period of some centuries.
Although the goods change in material and the technique becomes
more elaborate, the major features remain much the same. In the
early period in particular, the decorative traditions are relatively
standard across the region – it is this standardisation that permits
us to speak of a Latin culture.

The place of the artisan in this culture is therefore not merely
that of a craft specialist, for in fact pottery may have been a task
which many people could have participated in. Since the early
incised decoration has been likened to the sorts of patterns which

one might find on textiles, clearly a major feature of Latin production as the amount of weaving equipment in female burials in particular shows, it may even have been a task which was not confined to men. The standardisation does however suggest that there was a tradition for burial goods at least, and that this tradition was carefully preserved for a considerable length of time. The evidence from Osteria dell'Osa shows that local differences may have had considerable significance as a means of differentiating between groups. The potters then are preservers of a tradition with specific local and perhaps religious connotations.

If we turn to another major burial ground in central Italy, Pontecagnano in Campania, we can find evidence of the politicisation of this tradition (D'Agostino 1977; D'Agostino and Gastaldi 1989; Cerchiai 1990; de Natale 1992 for reports). In a recent article Cuozzo has speculated on the impact of the Etruscan domination of the area as indicated by the bucchero production of the seventh and early sixth centuries (Cuozzo 1993). Cerchiai had already noted two different traditions in the Etrusco-Corinthian production of this site. One tradition is strongly related to the workshops of Vulci, the other to the workshops of Caere and Veii. Bucchero and impasto production also shows two different traditions, one of which is close in terms of size and shape to the Caere/Veii group. The other tradition is represented by some rare large bucchero pieces, which follow examples in metal rather than any ceramic pattern.

What is significant about this evidence is that the major bucchero pieces come from a site called the Scarico Granozio off the Via Sicilia, an area which had not been used for burials before the end of the seventh century, and were in a necropolis which also produced Etrusco-Corinthian ware. So the emergence of important new forms of pottery coincides with the reshaping of the necropolis area and the arrival of the Etruscans in force in the area, and there seems no doubt that one should connect all these features. The new elite of Pontecagnano brought with them the goods, the skills and quite possibly the artisans of their homeland, and in at least one instance it would appear that they commissioned a special set of bucchero pieces for use in a new burial ground which has a high proportion of infant burials. Once again, we can see the use of artisan skills in the context of political and social display.[4]

Terracotta roof decoration and friezes

The study of terracotta architectural decoration has become of immense importance for the study of central Italian society as more fragments have been unearthed, and attention revived after the pioneering work of Andren (see Rystedt *et al.* 1993, 306–10 for a bibliography). We are beginning to be able to make tentative steps towards a history of the craft and to identify areas of production and innovation.[5]

Of all the crafts of the period, this is the one which most readily lends itself to the idea of travelling artisans, as we have seen, in particular because of the presence of friezes which seem to come from the same mould though found in quite different areas. In this section I wish to focus on the iconography of the friezes and the ideology which seems to underlie them, and as we shall see in the following section, this iconography draws in a number of other crafts as well.

The purpose of terracotta coverings of wooden roofs is to provide protection against the rain, and a more durable covering than natural material would permit. It has been suggested that it may have originated from a simple clay covering to wooden beams which the sun would naturally bake dry, though this might have cracked more easily. Once in use, certain features of the roof can be highlighted. Around the ends antefixes can conceal the runoffs from the guttering, and channel water away from the walls and the revetment friezes beneath. Simas can be added which project above the roof, and these have a clear development in the sixth century, as has recently been shown, from the lateral and raking simas to the torus sima, which eschews figural decoration for floral

[4]   Carafa 1995, 259 speculates on the possibility that there may have been a workshop attached to one of the high-status houses on the slopes of the Palatine; there was a kiln there from the second quarter of the fourth century BC, and the suggestion is that it may have had a predecessor. Given the high status of these buildings (which await full publication), the link between potter and patron is here suggestive, though not proven.
[5]   Downey 1995, for instance, observes that the architectural decoration of the third Regia (first half of the sixth century) is uniquely Roman, but that by the time of the fourth Regia (second half of the sixth century), 'Rome is no longer isolated . . . but is part of a central Italian unit' (1995, 71). This again suggests polyfunctional workshops, and exchange of ideas.

decoration and achieves greater height. The torus sima develops under influence from southern Italy in response to the increased size of the buildings of the sixth century, and requires greater elevation in order to fit the new proportions (Wikander 1994). The provision of a strong and stable roof allows for acroterial decoration and figures along the ridgepole; one of the important aspects of the Etrusco-Italic temple is the attention to sculptural decoration on top of the roof, not just in friezes around the pediments. The effects are quite different.

The ridgepole *acroteria* are so important because they come early, and reveal similarities with depictions of Villanovan period housing in hut urns from the tenth century onwards. There is in fact no need to posit a Greek origin for the *acroteria*, though in the course of time Greek influence on both the *acroteria* and the nature of roof decoration as a whole increases, with the south Italian colonies being crucial.

One of the elements of the acroterial sculpture is seated figures. We now know that the so-called Murlo cowboy was seated, and we find other such figures at an early period (later on they stand, under the influence perhaps of Greek kouros sculpture) (Edlund-Berry 1993). Colonna and von Hase have attempted to demonstrate that the true predecessor of the seated statue was not Greek but Syrian (Colonna and von Hase 1984). The context for their assertion was the discussion of a seated stone statue in an early seventh-century tumulus tomb just outside Cerveteri. The parallels they sought to draw were with seated rulers in Alalakh and Carchemish, several centuries earlier. There are missing links in the argument, especially since not all of the Syrian examples which are given were intended to be seen, but one can perhaps accept a generalised influence from the east.

The iconography of the seated individual is of tremendous significance in the Etruscan world. There are in fact a number of instances in tombs. They also exist as we have seen in *acroteria* such as that at Murlo (Poggio Le Civitate), and in the so-called canopic urns, cremation urns with a figure of the deceased on the top (Nielsen 1994; Damgaard Andersen 1993). Finally we may note their presence on numerous frieze plaques, together with scenes such as hunting or banqueting or procession (Sinos 1994 for Murlo; Bruun 1993 for Velletri; Downey 1995 for Rome (Regia); Rystedt *et al.* 1993 for further examples).

For Colonna and von Hase (1984), and Ridgway and Ridgway more recently (1994), these seated statues represent the impact of Syrian craftsmen on the Etruscan world, possibly coming through the northern Adriatic rather than through southern Italy as the Greeks were to do; the Mediterranean may be too much of a cultural melange to permit such close national identifications. The development of clay examples of a sculpture, executed either in free-standing or relief form in stone in Syria, adapts the new ideas to a new material, and one which was easier to use in a variety of contexts, and closer to bronzeworking in which the Etruscans were pre-eminent.

What the figures actually represent is of course rather harder to define. Interpretations move uneasily between political elites and gods, and in some cases try to combine the two by suggesting a deliberate blurring of the boundaries, an idea which I think is particularly attractive given the religious authority of, say, the king at Rome.

Let us return for a moment to the story of Demaratus' three *fictores*. If it is true that they contributed to terracotta work, they cannot have been the initiators since the dates do not match up, and we have seen other influences at work. Ridgway and Ridgway suggest that the Greeks contributed to the standardisation of the decoration, so that we find roof tiles on a number of the buildings at Acquarossa which cannot all have been elite dwellings (Ridgway and Ridgway 1994, 7). The pattern which they propose is of an entrepreneur importing and maintaining artisans who can exploit the needs of the communities of central Italy. There are other possibilities; the floral decoration of the seventh- and sixth-century simas does reflect the patterns found on Corinthian pottery, and the tradition may be a more generic connection between central Italy and Corinth, if it has any validity at all. The parallel that they draw, which is a very significant one, is of two Corinthian workshops or single artisans producing *aryballoi* on the island of Pithecusa. It has been observed that the clear reason for the presence of Potters/Painters X, Y and Z is to exploit the market – 'immigrant potters were needed to supplement supplies'.[6] Although Ridgway and Ridgway make a very good case for the development of central Italian art without the Greeks (a

---

[6]   Ridgway and Ridgway 1994, 12, quoting Williams 1986.

case which, as we have seen, has roots in ancient debates), by the mid-seventh century the Greek impact is already enormous. That Demaratus importing Greek artisans might be compared to his grandson Tarquinius Priscus asking for Vulca from Veii to assist with the Temple of Capitoline Jupiter is an intriguing instance of the variety of political and social experience in the archaic period.

Crossover between crafts

I wish to end this summary of artisan activity with a brief consideration of the concept of ideas crossing over between different metiers. Let us consider the example of the antefix with a head surrounded by a kind of cloak or halo. The image can be found on antefixes, but also on sixth-century bronzes and ceramic ware; there are good examples from Capua. The origin may lie in Laconian bronzes of the seventh and sixth centuries (Minoja 1993).

Similarly, the seated figure appears in stone in tumuli, in terracotta on roofs, and in terracotta reliefs. The scene of the banquet is to be located in terracotta reliefs, in tomb paintings and in vase painting. The hunt occurs in the reliefs and in the imported Syrian gilded bowls found in Cerveteri and Praeneste. The figure of the lion can be spotted on everything from large-scale transverse *acroteria* to tiny *aryballoi*, and again has an eastern origin.

There are other examples, and many have been exhaustively documented, and occasionally tentatively dated. What does this suggest about central Italian art? It seems to me to suggest that the relationships between the crafts became quite close from the seventh century on. It may be that the specialist traditions of the ninth century that we saw operating in the necropolis at Osteria dell'Osa have given way to a different form of artisan activity, one not so particularist, but still at the service of an elite. These motifs are not empty ciphers; the hunt and the banquet are classic elite practices, and even the lion may have more than a decorative function in the visual shorthand of the time. Necessarily, the skills of the artisan have had to become attuned to a broader market, a wider variety of skills, and a different artistic repertoire, removed from familial or gentilicial control, and seated in a different environment. This brings me to the theme of the city, which is part of this volume's concern.

The artisan and the city

Power and ideology go hand in hand. As the nature of a society changes the status and importance of its ideologues also change. In better-documented periods, it is interesting to note that some of the major artistic figures come to the fore in the sources in periods where propaganda is of great significance. So Pheidias is a central character in the history of Athens as a democratic and imperial power; Lysippus and Apelles rank in the history of Hellenistic art through their connection with Alexander. The Roman imperial context is slightly different perhaps, since the major artists were still Greek it appears, but perhaps often in a subservient position.

As I have mentioned, we do have the putative names of some artisans from archaic central Italy. I am personally very struck by one; the man who, according to Plutarch, created eleven shields to copy the one that fell from heaven and was placed in the Temple of Mars in the time of Numa was one Mamurius Veturius (Plut. *Numa* 13. 3). The name is a patrician one. It may be another piece of the jigsaw of evidence that indicates the gentilicial basis of early Roman religion; is it also an indication of a higher prestige for craftsmanship, reflecting perhaps the long-felt awe for the artistic genius, and the worker of metal and fire (Delcourt 1957, 204–22)?

As ideas become replaced by standardisation, the position of the artisan decreases. In the archaic period, some figures seem to have held the keys to the iconography of elite behaviour, and access to their skills was a part of the nature of power as much as access to the traders who brought in prestigious imports like jewellery and perfume.

During the seventh and particularly the sixth century, the shape of the community in central Italy evolved in the direction of urban form. This change is of the utmost significance, and is still, I believe, poorly understood in both the Italian and the Greek contexts. There is no doubt that trade has something to do with this change, in that it helps to provide the goods which are the markers of status. In this context, it encourages the production of a surplus and the increased exploitation of an agricultural labour-force. The arrival of traders from different countries, as well as the possession of easily removable wealth, may have sharpened a sense of identity, which is the basis of an early concept of citizenship.

In sixth-century Latium, the boundaries were being erected haphazardly through the sixth century. We hear of trading arrangements between Rome and the Carthaginians. We see the formation of *jura* or rules of co-operation between Rome and the Latins after the Battle of Lake Regillus at the beginning of the fifth century. At roughly the same time we see more control over the public display of wealth by an elite, and the basis of that elite beginning to broaden – a picture which fits well with Etruscan evidence too (Smith 1996, 130ff.).

The artisan in this context purveys the images of authority that serve the elite in the sixth century. The sources tend to suggest that this period also sees the rise of representative sculpture of individuals like kings. The creation of hierarchical images by craftsmen of recognised and respected skill sets them at the centre of the move away from power as something localised in chieftainship to something at the heart of civic community. It is perhaps no coincidence that early Rome provides evidence for the creation of artisans' *collegia* and a potters' quarter known as the Vicus Tuscus.[7]

The development of an urban settlement requires people to be located and respected for their constructive occupations, and it requires an iconography of authority and community. I do not mean to suggest that artisans held positions of enormous authority or that they invented the city, but rather that they were instrumental in its creation, at least as much as the army for instance. What gave them this potential was first their skill, and second, especially at a time of enormous cultural variety and international contact, their ability to adapt and adopt ideas from elsewhere. One of the most important items of trade in this period was knowledge; it is not only the movement of goods but also the movement of artisans which provides the vehicle.

Bibliography

Ampolo, C. (1970/1), 'Su alcuni mutamenti sociali nel Lazio tra l'VIII sec. e il IV sec.', *DdA* 4–5: 37–99.

---

[7]   Carafa's suggestion of a kiln attached to an elite house (see n. 4 above) fits in well in this context.

—— (1976/7), 'Demarato: Osservazioni sulla mobilità sociale arcaica', *DdA* 9–10: 333–45.

Arafat, K. and Morgan, C. (1994), 'Athens, Etruria and the Heuneburg: mutual misconceptions in the study of Greek–barbarian relations', in I. Morris (ed.), *Classical Greece: Ancient Histories and Modern Archaeologies* (Cambridge), 108–33.

Bartoloni, G. (1987), 'Le comunità dell'Italia centrale tirrenica e la colonizzazione greca in Campania', in M. Cristofani (ed.), *Etruria e Lazio Arcaico* (Rome), 37–54.

Bayet, J. (1926), *Les Origines de l'Hercule Romain* (Paris).

Bietti-Sestieri, A. M. (1992a), *The Iron Age Community of Osteria dell'Osa: A Study of Socio-Political Development in Central Tyrrhenian Italy* (Rome).

—— (1992b), *La Necropoli Laziale di Osteria dell'Osa* (Rome).

Bonghi Jovino, M. (1989), 'La produzione fittile in Etruria ed i suoi riflessi nell'Italia antica', in *Secondo Congresso Internazionale Etrusco* (Rome): 667–82.

—— (ed.) (1990), *Artigiani e Botteghe nell'Italia Preromana: Studi sulla Coroplastica di Area Etrusco-Laziale-Camapana* (Rome).

—— (ed.) (1993), *Produzione Artigianale ed Esportazione nel Mondo Antico: Il Bucchero Etrusco* (Milan).

Brendel, O. (1995), *Etruscan Art* (Yale).

Bruun, C. (1993), 'Herakles and the tyrants: an archaic frieze from Velletri', in E. Rystedt *et al.* (eds 1993), 267–78.

Carafa, P. (1995), *Officine Ceramiche di Età Regia* (Rome).

Cazenove, O. de (1990), 'Les sanctuaires de Cérès jusqu'à la deuxième sécession de la plèbe', in *Crise et Transformation des sociétés archaïques de l'Italie antique au Ve siècle av. J.C.* (Rome), 373–99.

Cerchiai, L. (1990), *Le Officine Etrusco-Corinzie di Pontecagnano* (Naples).

Ciaghi, S. (1993), *Le terrecotte figurate da Cales del Museo Nazionale di Napoli* (Rome).

Colonna, G. (1988), 'La produzione artigianale', in A. Momigliano and A. Schiavone (eds), *Storia di Roma I* (Turin), 292–316.

Colonna, G. and Von Hase, F. W. (1984), 'Alle origini della statuaria Etrusca: La tomba delle statue presso Ceri', *St. Etr.* 52: 13–59.

Cornell, T. J. (1995), *The Beginnings of Rome: Italy and Rome from the Bronze Age to the Beginnings of the Punic Wars (c. 1000 to 264 BC)* (London).

Cuozzo, M. (1993), 'Produzione di lusso, produzione corrente nel bucchero di Pontecagnano: alcune considerazioni', in M. Bonghi Jovino (ed. 1993), 147–65.

D'Agostino, B. (1977), *Tombe 'Principesche' dell'Orientalizzante Antico da Pontecagnano* (Rome).

Damgaard Andersen, H. (1993) 'Archaic architectural terracottas and their relation to building identification', in E. Rystedt *et al.* (eds 1993), 71–86.

D'Agostino, B. and Gastaldi, P. (1989), *Pontecagnano II. La Necropoli del Picentino. 1 Le Tombe della Prima Età del Ferro* (Naples).
De Natale, S. (1992), *Pontecagnano II. La necropoli di S. Antonio: Propr. ECI 2. Tombe della Prima Età del Ferro* (Naples).
Delcourt, M. (1957), *Héphaistos ou la Légende du Magicien* (Paris).
Downey, S. (1995), *Architectural Terracottas from the Regia* (Papers and Monographs of the American Academy in Rome, 30; Michigan).
Edlund-Berry, I. (1993), 'The Murlo cowboy: problems of reconstruction and interpretation', in E. Rystedt *et al.* (eds 1993), 117–22.
Frederiksen, M. (1984), *Campania* (Rome).
Gill, D. W. (1994), 'Positivism, pots and long-distance trade', in I. Morris (ed.), *Classical Greece: Ancient Histories and Modern Archaeologies* (Cambridge), 99–107.
Minoja, M. (1993), 'Breve note sui rapporti tra produzione vascolare in bucchero, bronzistica e coroplastica nell'artigianato capuano del VI secolo', in M. Bonghi Jovino (ed. 1993), 167–70.
Murray, O. (ed. 1990), *Sympotica: A Symposium on the Symposion* (Oxford).
Murray, O. and Tecusan, M. (eds 1995), *In Vino Veritas* (Rome).
Nielsen, E. (1994), 'Interpreting the lateral sima at Poggio Civitate', in R. D. de Puma and J. P. Small (eds), *Murlo and the Etruscans: Art and Society in Ancient Etruria* (Wisconsin), 67–74.
Pollitt, J. J. (1983), *The Art of Rome c. 753 BC–AD 337* (Cambridge).
Ridgway, D. (1988), 'The Etruscans', in *Cambridge Ancient History*, iv (2nd edn, Cambridge), 634–75.
—— (1992) *The First Western Greeks* (Cambridge).
Ridgway, D. and Serra Ridgway, F. (1994), 'Demaratus and the archaeologists', in R. D. de Puma and J. P. Small (eds), *Murlo and the Etruscans: Art and Society in Ancient Etruria* (Wisconsin), 6–15.
Rystedt, E., Wikander, C. and Wikander, O. (eds 1993), *Deliciae Fictiles: Proceedings of the First International Conference on Etruscan Terracottas* (Stockholm).
Sinos, R. H. (1994), 'Godlike men: a discussion of the Murlo procession frieze', in R. D. de Puma and J. P. Small (eds), *Murlo and the Etruscans: Art and Society in Ancient Etruria* (Wisconsin), 100–17.
Small, J. P. (1995), 'New views on Greek artifacts found in Etruria', *JRA* 8: 317–19.
Smith, C. J. (1996), *Early Rome and Latium: Economy and Society c. 1000 to 500 BC* (Oxford).
—— forthcoming, 'Medea in Italy: barter and exchange in the archaic Mediterranean', in G. Tsetskhladze (ed.), *East and West*.
Vallet, G. (ed. 1982), *La Céramique Grecque ou de Tradition Grecque .1au VIIIe siècle en Italie Centrale* (Naples).
Wikander, O. (1994), 'The archaic Etruscan sima', in R. D. de Puma and J. P. Small (eds), *Murlo and the Etruscans: Art and Society in Ancient Etruria* (Wisconsin), 47–63.

Williams, D. (1986), 'Greek potters and their descendants in Campania and southern Etruria', in J. Swaddling (ed.), *Italian Iron Age Artefacts in the British Museum* (London), 295–304.

Zuntz, G. (1971), *Persephone: Three Essays on Religion and Thought in Magna Graecia* (Oxford).

4

Trade on the Black Sea in the archaic and classical periods: some observations

Gocha R. Tsetskhladze

In the specialist literature and even in student textbooks, the Black Sea area and Greek trade with this region are mainly presented in a very simple way: that the Greeks colonised the Black Sea because they lacked food and natural resources and, consequently, imported grain, metals, slaves, etc. from the Pontic region. This can be summarised in the words of J. Fine:

> Greek colonisation of the Black Sea was of great importance for subsequent Greek history. A huge area, rich in metals, timber, grain, fish and many other products, was thus opened to a Greek world, whose resources in raw materials and food products were inadequate for the constantly growing population. The necessity to pay for those imports stimulated the activity of Greek craftsmen – especially the potters and metal-workers
>
> (Fine 1983, 81)

Is all this true? Is it the only conclusion to which the available evidence points? I think not.

From the beginning it must be said that in discussing the colonisation of the Black Sea it is a mistake to consider Greek interest in trade as a major reason. I have already argued this elsewhere (Tsetskhladze 1994). The Black Sea was colonised by Ionians, whose first colonies were established there in the third quarter of the seventh century BC. The reasons for Ionian colonisation are highly complex. For long it was believed that the main impulse for colonising the Black Sea was interest in the metals of its southern and eastern parts and the grain of the north. However, recent studies have shown these regions to be less metal-rich than was thought and alternative explanations have to be sought (Treister 1992, 1995; Tsetskhladze 1995; Tsetskhladze and Treister 1995). Furthermore, the northern Black Sea could not be the main source of grain in the seventh–sixth centuries BC: no evidence exists for it, whilst written, archaeological and palaeobotanical sources show that grain could not be acquired from the Scythians (Sceglov 1990). A simple understanding of the motives and processes of Greek colonisation does not hold water. It was never exclusively agrarian, commercial or connected with the need for metals on the one hand, or a consequence of over-population on the other. Each mother-city had its own reason for sending out colonies and it is essential to analyse the *metropolis* and reasons that might have obliged the Greeks to emigrate. From this standpoint, study of the situation in Asia Minor in the seventh century suggests that enforced emigration was the motive: the consequence of the hostile policy towards Miletus and other Ionian cities of Lydia (and, in the middle of the sixth century, the Persians) was a reduction of their *chorai*, and a grim political struggle within Miletus itself. One of the most radical solutions in these circumstances was emigration. At that time the only region not yet colonised by other Greek cities was the Black Sea, and it was precisely in that direction that Miletus looked (Tsetskhladze 1994, 123–6). With survival at stake, trade was simply not a consideration.

There is a further complex question which we need to examine. Although all the earliest *apoikiai* were settlements probably without their own *chorai* (Tsetskhladze 1994, 115–18), can we consider trade as the main activity of these early settlements? Perhaps trade was simply a means of survival for the first colonists before they organised their own agriculture and craft activity (cf. Graham 1982, 129). Seventh-century Greek pottery was found far inland in the tumuli or settlements of the Scythians – eight sites altogether (Onaiko 1966, 56; Vakhtina 1993). There is no seventh-century Greek pottery in Thracian or Getae sites, but sixth-century pottery was found in about fifteen sites (Vakhtina 1993). Phrygian pottery was found in Sinope, which shows that some relations existed with the peoples of the interior (Boardman 1980, 255).

The answer to my last question lies in what kind of Greek pottery it is that we are finding in the sites of the local population. Furthermore, it is often the case that such pottery is of an earlier date than the Greek settlements themselves. Study of this pottery shows that it comprises luxury objects, which are, as usual, found in the tumuli of the local elite (Boardman 1980, 243–4; Vakhtina 1993). All of the foregoing leads us to the following conclusions. The first colonists arriving in a new land are subject to the whims of local circumstances. It is in their best interest to establish friendly relations with the local population, especially the elite. The pottery found in local sites should not be considered a subject of trade as we now understand the word. 'Many scholars at present hold the view that trade in the Archaic period took the form of gift exchange – which could explain the sometimes unexpected finds of ceramics' (Tsetskhladze and Treister 1995, 24, with literature; von Reden 1995, 209). In this respect, I may cite Strabo, who tells us that the Greeks always sought to have peaceful relations with the local tribes. From the early stages of the colonisation of the Pontus, land for settlements and agriculture was given by local tribal chiefs to the Greeks either by special agreement or for 'the tribute ... which is a moderate one' (7. 4. 6).

The grain trade

When we are talking about trade on the Black Sea in the archaic period this is mostly between colonies and their mother cities in Ionia, chiefly Miletus. To establish what objects were traded is extremely difficult because our main source is pottery and, without doubt, it was not the sole product traded. We have much more evidence for the classical period when, according to the scholarly literature, grain was the principal commodity traded and the trade was now connected with Athens. Of course, this is so, but there are some questions which have to be asked about this trade.

The question of the Athenian grain trade is one of great debate in the literature. It has mainly been considered from the Athenian point of view, with modern scholars seeing the Pontic region as a major source of grain (see, for example, Meiggs 1972, 197–9, 264; Isager and Hansen 1975, 19–29; Garnsey 1985, 67–74 and 1988,

123–40; Gallant 1991; Keen 1993a; cf. Whitby, in the present volume). The other potential sources of grain have been discussed in the literature (see, for example, Isager and Hansen 1975, 19–29; Keen 1993b, 154; Austin 1994, 558–64) but all of the authors have culled their information from the same sources, still much as they were fifty or more years ago. The size of the Athenian population and what quantity of grain it consumed are other matters of dispute (Whitby, in the present volume; Hansen 1986, 1988, 1994). I wish to look at the Athenian grain trade from the perspective of the Black Sea.

Although permanent Athenian settlements on the Black Sea appeared no earlier than the second quarter of the fifth century BC, the early Attic black-figure pottery dates from *c.* 600–550 BC, just at the time of Athenian political expansion reaching the Propontis. It has been found in Berezan, Histria and Apollonia. The most important Athenian foundations were Sigeion and the settlements in Thracian Chersonesus. In the wake of the growing troubles of the Ionians with the Persian empire and the suppression of the Ionian Revolt, the colonial and commercial activities of the Ionians decreased and Athens began turning its attention to the Black Sea market. After the consolidation of the Athenian maritime empire, the amount of fine Attic pottery increases. It was marketed in all parts of the Pontus but the largest share seems to have gone to the Bosporan area, to Olbia and Apollonia Pontica (see, for example, Brashinskii 1963, 11–55; Bouzek 1989, 1990, 42–7, 1994).

We have no evidence at all about the Pontic grain trade for the archaic period. As I have already mentioned, and contrary to the literature, grain was not available from the Scythians. Grain for trade had to come from the *chorai* of the Greek colonies themselves. Only from the middle of the sixth century BC did the first Greek *apoikiai* grow into *poleis* with their own strong state and religious institutions. The main point of interest for us is that the *chorai* of these city-states became massive and corn started to be grown there (Vinogradov 1988, 375–6). If, indeed, grain had started to reach mainland Greece from Pontus this should not predate the second half of the sixth century. But there is no evidence for the Athenian grain trade in the archaic period be it with the Black Sea or elsewhere (Garnsey 1988, 110–13; cf. Noonan 1973).

How much grain, if any, Greece imported from the Black Sea area before the Persian wars is unclear although Herodotus (6. 5, 6. 26) states that in c. 494/493 BC merchant ships were seen sailing out of the Pontus. Initially, Athens' own need for grain may have been satisfied by supplies from Sicily and Egypt but after the middle of the fifth century her interest in the Black Sea lands could, of course, have quickened in the wake of the disastrous Egyptian expedition and the growing enmity with Corinth (Isager and Hansen 1975, 23–6). There were, however, some problems with Sinope and Megarian Heraklea Pontica – which was a potential enemy of Athens. At the same time, it is thought that Heraklea, which commanded one of the shorter crossings of the Black Sea, posed a threat to the interests of Bosporus in her trade with the Athens-dominated Aegean (Hind 1994, 488–95). The Pontus was not very peaceful at a time when Thracians and Scythians were maintaining constant pressure on the Greek cities (Vinogradov 1980; Marchenko 1993; Andrukh 1995, 86–95, 147–61).

Another unresolved question is that of Pericles' expedition to the Black Sea, which is generally presented in the following way. Athens needed the Black Sea market, probably its grain, and as Plutarch states in his biography of Pericles (20), in c. 437 BC the latter entered the Pontus 'with a large, well-found fleet and accomplished everything which the Greek cities had requested of him, and established friendly relations with them'. At the same time 'he demonstrated the greatness of Athenian power ... making themselves complete masters of the sea'. The main aim was to include Pontic cities in the Athenian-dominated Delian League. Pericles banished the tyrant Timesileos from Sinope and sailed thence across to Bosporus. Nymphaeum, which was not at the time part of the Bosporan kingdom, became a member of the League, paying one talent as its annual contribution. Pericles also reached Olbia where tyranny was restored and the Scythians expelled. It is possible that several other cities apart from Nymphaeum (and Histria) joined the League because some fragmentary names in the Athenian Tribute Lists for 425 BC refer to cities north of the Black Sea (Brashinskii 1963, 56–88; Shelov-Kovedyaev 1985, 90–123; Meiggs 1972, 197–8; cf. Avram 1995, 195–8; Angelescu 1992).

Plutarch is our only source of information for this expedition and the search to find his source has occupied scholars for many generations, as yet without result. Nevertheless, there has been a belief in the great importance of the expedition. Although Plutarch speaks only about the southern Black Sea littoral, scholars have wished this expedition upon the other coasts of the Pontus as well (see, for example, Inadze 1982, 134–80) without any supporting evidence. It is hard for me to believe that this expedition took place at all (there are no other sources bar Plutarch); if it did so, it was confined to the southern shore and had no great importance for Athens or the Pontus (Brashinskii 1963, 60–2).[1]

Thus, there is no strong and undisputed evidence for the grain trade between Athens and the Black Sea in the fifth century BC. (Herodotus, for example, makes no mention of ships going to Athens.) The whole edifice of the discussion has been constructed on foundations of uncertain evidence, with ever more rickety floors added to the building.[2]

Only from the fourth century BC do we have direct evidence for the grain trade and this concerns the Bosporan kingdom in the time of Leucon I (389/88–349/48 BC) and Athenian–Bosporan relations (Brashinskii 1963, 118–52; Zhebelev 1982, 150–4; Shelov-Kovedyaev 1985, 140–1; Skrzhinskaya 1994; Vinogradov 1995, 5; Saprykin 1995, 134–5; Burstein 1978). During Leucon's reign Athens enjoyed many commercial privileges in the grain trade with Bosporus. Strabo, for example, tells us that 'Leucon . . . once sent from Theodosia to Athens two million, one hundred thousand *medimnoi* [of grain]' (7. 4. 6). According to Demosthenes (*Against Leptines*, 20. 32–3), Leucon sent to Athens 400,000

---

[1] The article by H. B. Mattingly (1996) appeared after this chapter was written. Its author's approach and evidence are different from mine but our conclusions are very similar: 'in the fifth century Athens' interest in the Black Sea was very limited, apart from the question of the corn trade' (Mattingly 1996, 157). Mattingly's discussion on the Pontic cities in the Athenian Tribute List is very convincing. This frees me from the need to cover the same territory (see also Avram 1995). On the question of the corn trade in the fifth century see below. I am not the first to express doubts about the reality of Pericles' Pontic expedition. See my paper in the Proceedings of the V Simposio Español sobre Plutarco, Zaragoza, 20–22 June 1996; and Mattingly 1996, 153 (n. 9).

[2] It seems that Athenian interest in the Black Sea increased from the end of the fifth century, and that this, not earlier, should be considered the true period of 'Athenian interest' (cf. Mattingly 1996; ML 65; Aeschines 3. 171–2; Xen. *Hellenica* 2. 2. 10, etc.).

medimnoi of wheat annually, but in the year of the great famine (*c.* 360 BC) he sent not only enough for Athens but a surplus which the Athenians sold at a profit of fifteen talents (cf. Lysias, *Against the Graindealers*).

What I mean by Athenian privileges in the grain trade with Bosporus is exemption from duties (*triakoste*) and, according to Demosthenes (*Against Leptines*, 20. 32), this was equivalent in value to an annual gift of 13,000 *medimnoi* of grain. However, the Athenians had, most probably, to pay the harbour dues (*ellimenion*) levied in the Bosporan kingdom (Brashinskii 1963, 118–33; cf. Burstein 1993).

As the above-mentioned sources show, the export of grain from the Bosporan kingdom to Athens was on a massive scale. The main question to be asked is: what did the Athenians export in order to balance this trade? So far, very few Athenian coins are known throughout the Black Sea region, and we have no Black Sea coins in Attica. This is not an indicator that close trade relations were absent: in international commerce Athens used Cyzicenes for payment (Mildenberg 1993/4). Some scholars point out that in the Pontic region Athens paid for its grain not with Athenian silver coins but with manufactured goods (Isager and Hansen 1975, 51–2). According to the reasonable suggestion of the same authors: 'all trade on the Black Sea must ... have been carried out with the Cyzicene stater as current tender' (Isager and Hansen 1975, 165). At the same time, it is believed that Cyzicenes played an important role in the local coin circulation of the Pontic area (Zograf 1951, 112, 148; Shelov 1956, 129). Let me now address the archaeological material:

* *Bosporan Kingdom.* There is information on the circulation of Cyzicenes in the Bosporan kingdom in one of the court speeches of Demosthenes (xxxiv). So far, only two hoards have been found which include several Cyzicenes, plus four individual finds (Kraay *et al.* 1973, 1011–13; Golenko 1977, with literature). From Phanagoria there is a graffito which remarks upon the grain trade. Its publisher concludes that the reference in it to price is measured in Cyzicenes (Vinogradov 1971, 68–70) but the inscription does not indicate what units are being used. Thus, Vinogradov's opinion is not well substantiated by the evidence (cf. Yailenko 1996, 176–9).

- *Chersonesus*. No Cyzicenes were found.
- *Olbia and north-western Pontus*. In this region, exceptionally, many hoards containing scores of Cyzicenes and some individual coins were found (Mildenberg 1993/4, 2, with literature). One of the Olbian decrees (*IOSPE* 1^2: 24) of the first half of the fourth century BC mentions the exchange rate between the Cyzicene and local coins. From Berezan there is a graffito of the second half of the sixth century BC. Like that from Phanagoria, there is a coin measurement but no indication of what coin, and the publisher again thinks that Cyzicenes are meant (Vinogradov 1971, 65–6; cf. Johnston 1979, 209; Bravo 1977, 41–2; Yailenko 1996, 175–6).
- *Histria and the Thracian Coast*. About four coins were found in Histria (*Histria* 1973, 138; Birliba 1990, 40). Forty-seven coins are known from Bulgaria, the vast majority of which were found not in the coastal area but in the Thracian hinterland (Gerasimov 1943).[3]
- *South Pontus*. No coins are known to me.
- *Colchis*. Only four coins have been found (Dundua 1987, 33–4).

The above-mentioned quantities speak for themselves. The region which is of most interest to us from the point of view of the grain trade – the Bosporan kingdom – has provided very few examples of the Cyzicene coins.

Many scholars think that the Athenians exported pottery (Shelov-Kovedyaev 1985, 141, with literature). But how far could this pay for the quantity of grain? It is worth examining some statistics covering the main city-sites of the western and northern Black Sea (very approximate though they be; there are no precise figures to be found anywhere in the literature) which will give some idea of the position. About 180 examples of Attic black-figured pottery have been found and 300 examples of red-figured pottery (Bouzek 1990, 43, and 1989; Lazarov 1990; Reho 1985, 215–26, and 1992; Alexandrescu 1978a; Coja and Gheorghita 1983). In the necropolis of Apollonia Pontica about 850 pieces of Attic pottery

---

[3] Since 1943 the number of Cyzicenes in Bulgarian territory has remained virtually unchanged. I am most grateful to Prof. M. Lazarov (Varna) for this information.

were found inside or outside the 868 graves, dated from the mid-fifth to the beginning of the third century BC (Venedikov 1963, 65–255; Penkova forthcoming; Panayotova 1998).

It is not possible to provide overall statistics for black-glazed pottery and amphorae for the whole Black Sea region. For example, from the Bulgarian Black Sea coast about 300 amphorae from different centres of production of the sixth–first centuries BC are known (up to 1974) (Lazarov 1973, 3–50; 1975, 128–36). From Histria about 1,700 amphora stamps (including examples from the hellenistic period) have been found (Canarache 1957; Coja 1986, 417–50). For three sites I should like to give more detailed statistics:

1   The burial ground of the Elizavetovskoe settlement (this is a very important site because it was the main trade settlement of the Don delta from the fifth to the first half of the third century BC): amphorae, 145 examples; painted and black-glazed pottery, 107 examples; fragments of stamped amphorae from the settlement, 818 (Brashinskii 1980).
2   Pichvnari Greek burial ground (important as belonging to an Athenian settlement or quarter in Colchis): 73 pieces of Attic painted-pottery of the classical period – another three were found in the Colchian burial ground – of which 90 per cent are mass produced works, 80 per cent of which date from the last quarter of the fifth century to the middle of the fourth. They are small lekythoi of neither high quality nor high artistic value (Sikharulidze 1987, 1988, 1991).
3   Vani, the residence of the local Colchian elite: amphorae, including hellenistic ones, 100; painted and black-glazed pottery (sixth–fourth centuries BC), 82 (Lordkipanidze 1983).

The figures speak for themselves. It must be noted that the Thracian aristocracy preferred metal vases to pottery. Attic clay vases seldom appear in Thracian tumuli, with high quality examples being rare. Mainly small fourth-century vases of modest quality were among the offerings of the tumulus burials in eastern Thrace and in the valleys of Tundza (Tonzos) and Marica (Hebros). The burials of Duvanlii are exceptional in having several late black-figured and mid-fifth century red-figured painted vases, but even here, silver tableware was much preferred. The

Thracian share of imported Attic pottery was – outside the *chorai* of Greek colonies – fairly modest (Bouzek 1990, 45).

In Colchis such were the natural conditions – coastal swamps and wetlands (Tsetskhladze forthcoming) – that grain was not grown. The Greeks living there had to import grain (and also salt) from the northern Black Sea littoral (Tsetskhladze 1990, 94–5). A similar situation seems to have existed in Histria, where the terrain was marshy (Alexandrescu 1978b; Avram 1990, 14–30; Bounegru 1988).[4]

The vast majority of Athenian pottery found around the Black Sea is concentrated in the Greek cities and settlements themselves, which again shows that if, indeed, it was the principal form of payment for grain, that grain was grown in the *chorai* of the Greek cities. There is very little Athenian ware found in the local settlements. All trade must have been in the hands of the Greeks themselves, with little involvement of the local population. As D. Braund states, from a Greek perspective, trade itself was a Greek affair (1995, 168). He cites Dio Chrysostom's claim that the Scythians needed a Greek presence in order to trade at Olbia, for 'the Scythians themselves had neither the ambition nor the knowledge to equip a trading-centre of their own after the Greek manner' (36. 5). He characterised the Greek traders who came to Olbia as really barbarous in that they did not engage in trade of a respectable type but in improper trade that rendered them akin to barbarians (Braund 1995, 168).

There is a continuing discussion about how great the contemporary value of Athenian painted pottery might have been (Johnston 1979, 33; Vickers 1985; Vickers and Gill 1994, 4, 13, 85–8, 106, 149; Boardman 1988a, 1988b; Arafat and Morgan 1994, 108–10). But irrespective of the course the discussion takes, and however high the price imputed to the pottery, the above statistics, whatever their imperfections, show that the export of

---

[4] Ancient written sources (especially Demosthenes) describe Thracia as a territory with very low-quality corn whose grain exports were extremely small. Bulgarian scholars have sought to overturn this view (Danov 1967). It is very often difficult to correlate the different kinds of evidence – literary, archaeological, palaeobotanical (*Palaeobotanical Finds* 1980; Bregadze 1982; Shcheglov 1978, 13–28; Yanushevich 1976) – when they point to different conclusions. Even statistics can be used and interpreted in many ways.

Athenian pottery to the Black Sea could not discharge the cost of the grain imported by Athens from there.[5] We must also bear in mind that many of the Pontic Greek cities enjoyed advanced, local pottery production. Even the wine and olive oil transported in amphorae would be insufficient to pay for the grain – and, once again, there were local vineyards.

Another question which must be examined is whether the territory of the Bosporan kingdom was able to produce the astronomical quantity of grain which Demosthenes mentions. I shall address this question in detail at a future date. Here I shall just give the background (cf. Sallares 1991, 330–2; Isager and Skydsgaard 1992, 21–6). The remains of cereal crops have been found during the excavation of several Bosporan sites. Where grain, it is mainly *triticum vulgare* (Kruglikova 1975, 181–3). In one of the sixth-century BC grain pits excavated in Hermonassa the following varieties were found: *hordeum polystichum Döel* (61,525 specimens), *triticum vulgare vill* (33), *triticum compactum Hasyt* (few), *triticum dicoccum Chöbl* (50) and *secale cereale L.* (58) (Kruglikova 1975, 182). Unfortunately, the *chorai* of the Bosporan cities have not been studied in the same detail as the agricultural territory of Chersonesus in order to know what was grown there and in what quantities. The study of the graffito from Zenon Chersonesus (in the north-east corner of the Crimea) shows that the grain yield was 700 kg per hectare. Today, in the same region, the yield per hectare varies from 1,800–4,500 kg depending upon the climate (Maslennikov 1985, 141).

The Taman Peninsula (Asiatic Bosporus) is believed to have been the grain basket of the Bosporan kingdom. To date, there is no hard evidence to support this. The *chorai* of the Greek cities of the Asiatic Bosporus have never been the subject of special study. The study of the region's ancient climate has only just begun and it is too early to make firm pronouncements on natural conditions, whether grain could be grown in quantity and, if so, what varieties were. Recent investigations have indicated that in the

---

[5] 'Pots in Antiquity were ... cheap, and ridiculously so. The highest recorded price for any Attic painted pot is 3 drachmas, or £4.50 [*sic*]. ... A commercial graffito on the underside of a red-figure *pelike* in Oxford ... "Achilles painter" can be read as "four items for 3.5 obols" – 26 pence each' (Shanks 1996, 63).

Taman Peninsula a melioration system was created from the fourth century BC and with it the necessity for irrigation (Gorlov and Lopanov 1995; cf. Kulikov 1995). This is, however, still a working hypothesis and not more. The result of small-scale palaeobotanical study of samples from a limited number of local Maeotian sites in the Kuban region shows that wheat, millet, barley, flax and lentil used to grow there. The chief agricultural product was millet (Lebedeva 1994).

Thus, there is no doubt that grain was exported to Athens from the Black Sea in the classical period. The question is, rather, how did Athens pay for it? Or do the written sources wildly exaggerate the weight of grain received in Athens? Garnsey, writing about the figures given by Demosthenes for the Pontic grain trade, notes: 'Demosthenes had deliberately underestimated the volume of non-Pontic imports. One commentator wrote ... that Demosthenes "was a politician and so was probably not speaking the truth" ' (1988, 97). At the same time Demosthenes was receiving bribes from the Bosporan kings to overestimate the volume of imported grain from the Bosporan kingdom. This is far from unlikely for, as a recent study of the grain trade from Chersonesus in the Roman period shows, authors ancient and modern have both overemphasised and overestimated such trade (Sorochan 1994, 66–72).

I believe that both ancient authors and modern scholars have exaggerated the importance of the grain trade, especially that with the Pontus, in the economy of Athens. Our main sources remain the speeches of Athenian orators on which it is impossible to rely. We must always bear in mind that from the fifth century BC, the Athenians present themselves as a superior nation and the official policy of the empire was to mould the facts to the perpetuation of this image – a subject well treated in recent work (Khan ed. 1994).

The metal trade

The view has been increasingly expressed that the Greeks who founded the colonies in the Black Sea were interested primarily in the supply of raw materials, especially metals (Tsetskhladze 1994, 1995, with literature). Is this so? Did Ionia, which established colonies in the Pontus, need to import metals? Very valuable in the investigation of this question are M. Y. Treister's studies of metalwork in the Pontus and Asia Minor (1988, 1992, 1995).

Treister's study (Tsetskhladze and Treister 1995, 19–25, with exhaustive literature) shows that there is documentary confirmation of the mining and the extraction of gold and electrum in Greece in the eighth–sixth centuries BC. There is also no doubt that the Greeks produced silver and lead objects from the ores of Siphnos and Laurion. A third major silver ore deposit, characterised by high natural concentrations of gold, bismuth and tin, may have been located in either Macedonia or Lydia. The great number of bronze objects of a variety of types and the relatively large number of known bronze workshops of the eighth–sixth centuries BC indicate the use of raw materials most probably from Greece itself. This is shown indirectly by the wide distribution of the Laurion copper ores as early as the Bronze Age.

It must be stressed that the hypotheses put forward by some scholars about the paucity of ore deposits and their poor extraction level in the period of Greek colonisation are without foundation. At the same time, the material to prove the exploitation of mines in the regions of Greek colonisation, and to confirm the presence of the remains of shops for metalworking, is insubstantial and sometimes completely absent. By the sixth century BC iron was sufficiently widespread in Greece for its importation from the Black Sea, especially from Colchis and the southern Pontus, to be unnecessary.

The situation regarding gold sources may have been the following. As well as Thasos, Lydia is considered by scholars to be one of the main sources of gold. Herodotus (5. 101) mentioned the gold from the River Pactolus and the latter passage proves that the Greeks considered Sardis as a market for the acquisition of especially large quantities of precious metals. A new fragment from Heraclitus contains metaphors which describe the process of smelting/refining 'mountain gold'. This is the place to mention that Ephesus was situated near a very rich gold deposit on Mount Tmolus, and the Ionians, judging by Heraclitus' terminology, knew the process of gold smelting in fine detail. In either event, the earliest gold-smelting workshop excavated at Sardis is dated to 620–550 BC. Thus, at the moment of Greek colonisation of the Black Sea littoral, gold was smelted in the direct vicinity of the Ionian centres. In the northern Pontic area there were no gold sources and all gold production was based upon imported raw materials. What remains uncertain is the origin of these imports. The same can be said about the western littoral.

If one refers specifically to Miletus as the mother-city of the Greek colonies of the Black Sea, the following data are at present available. It is maintained that artistic metalwork was not highly developed in Miletus. The identification of a so-called Milesian variant of the deep Achaemenid *phialai* of the second half of the sixth century BC, which probably served as a prototype for Achaemenid bowls, is based on a stylistic analysis of a single bronze vessel, the origin of which is not well documented. Analysis of an early seventh-century BC cast bronze griffin protome and a late sixth–early fifth-century BC casting mould for jewellery, both from Miletus, suggests the work of resident Asia Minor or Syrian toreuts and jewellers there, gradually adapting their products to Greek tastes. The Near Eastern origin of the craftsmen processing metals in Miletus explains, convincingly, the quick adaptation of the craftsmen who migrated to the north Pontic area to the tastes of the Scythian population. Therefore, Miletus had no reason to establish colonies with the aim of supplying the mother-city with raw metals.

One can posit a certain reduction in the supply of precious metals to the Greek world after 546 BC, i.e. following the conquest of the Lydian kingdom by the Persians. Anyhow, this event is supposed to be one of the reasons for the transition from electrum to silver coinage in eastern Greece. Nevertheless, the reduction in the metal supply was not a catastrophe; it led to an orientation on new sources of raw materials – for instance, from the southern Thracian mines which had been exploited at that time by Peisistratos – and to new trade relations. It was the conquest of the Greek cities of Ionia by Cyrus which had a much stronger effect, whose scale it is possible to imagine in the light of the latest archaeological discoveries. It influenced the forced emigration of Ionian craftsmen, including sculptors, bronze-workers and toreuts to other Greek centres, but also to the periphery of the classical world – for example in the context of the 'third wave' of the Greek colonisation of the Pontic area (Tsetskhladze 1994, 120–3).

In the classical period there is a very interesting situation. We cannot talk about trade and local production without considering local society because the trade and production of the Greek cities of the Pontus depended on their relations with newly established local kingdoms. What we now call Scythia was established in two regions by the end of the sixth century – one centre was situated in the Crimea, not far from the future Bosporan kingdom, and the other not far from Olbia (Murzin 1984, 104). In the eastern Black Sea the Colchian kingdom was created (Lordkipanidze 1979, 48–77). In the west, the Thracian kingdom under the Odrysian dynasty came into being (Archibald 1994, 444–50). The tumuli of these local elites contain an enormous quantity of metal objects. Some metal vessels and mirrors, as well as fine jewellery, were brought from Greece itself, but the vast majority was produced in the Greek cities of the Pontus.

It is well known that the Greeks used to establish workshops to produce metal objects and jewellery for the local nobility, adapting their products to local taste. The archaeological evidence clearly shows the existence of very advanced, local metal production in the major cities of the northern Black Sea littoral, for example. But the source of their raw materials is still not clear. One fanciful possibility is that Athens exported raw materials to the Black Sea to pay for the grain it was importing – the complete inversion of the idea that the colonists went to the Black Sea to find raw materials to export to Greece! – but to accept that is to overthrow all our current ideas about trade and colonisation. We should, however, start thinking about these matters from first principles once more.

The question is whether the objects produced by the Pontic Greeks were to be traded with the local nobility or were a form of tribute to guarantee the continuing survival of Greek settlements surrounded by local peoples. To answer this, we must bear in mind several things. The newly established Scythia as well as the Odrysians put pressure on the Greek cities, establishing protectorates over them (Vinogradov 1980; Marchenko 1993). The Greek cities situated on the Kerch and Taman peninsulae united as one state against the Scythians in c. 480 BC (Gaidukevich 1949, 26–42). Written sources tell us that the Thracian kings used to collect tribute from the Greek cities, and these tributes took the form of metal objects (Thucydides 2. 97). Generally speaking, Thracian society was very strongly influenced by Achaemenian culture and customs, even more than by Greek ones (Boardman

1994, 183–92). All fine so-called 'Scythian' metal objects in Animal Style were produced by Greeks in the Greek cities of the northern Black Sea, the vast majority in the Bosporan kingdom (Treister 1998). Although these objects are in Animal Style, which was characteristic for Scythian society, they bear clear Greek features (Boardman 1994, 192–216). The question of how advanced was the hellenisation of the Scythian elite is not the subject of my present discussion. The fact is that Greek craftsmen were either obliged to produce these objects for the local elite or did so to trade with them.

If we turn to Colchis the situation is virtually the same – although it is unlikely that there was political or economic pressure from the local elite. The Greeks established workshops for goldsmiths and for the production of seals and gems to serve the Colchian nobility (Tsetskhladze 1995, 323–5, with literature). One fact is particularly interesting. At the end of the sixth century BC the Greeks began to mint silver coins to serve the Colchian market. In the classical period these coins were found mainly in the Black Sea area – and there are no such finds in the interior, where the local nobility used to live and where the Greek workshops producing for them were located (Dundua 1987, 9–32).

I think that all this shows that the relationship between the local elites and the Greeks living in the Pontic Greek cities was based not on trade but on tribute or gift-giving.

The slave trade

In view of the large number of local peoples around the Black Sea, a healthy trade in slaves could be expected, with the Pontus as a major source of slaves for the Greek world. Strabo (11. 2. 3) and Polybius (4. 38) mention the Black Sea as providing a great number of slaves. Written sources name only one market for slaves in the Black Sea: Tanais, which was not founded until the hellenistic period (Strabo 11. 2. 3). The Black Sea was an area of piracy. Local tribes hostile to the Greeks not infrequently attacked Greek cities and piracy was a matter of concern not just for the colonies but for mainland Greece as well (Asheri 1998; Tsetskhladze 1998). Many local tribes lived from robbery at sea and kidnap for ransom (Diod. 20. 25; Xen. *Anab.* 7. 5. 12;

Plut. *Per.* 50; Aristotle, *Politics* 8. 1338b; Strabo 11. 2. 12; Plin. *HN* 6. 15. 16; Tac. *Hist.* 3. 47; Zos. 1. 28; Ammian. Marc. 31. 5. 15). One of the main motives for piracy has always been to take captives to be sold into slavery. However, it is unlikely that the numbers captured by the local peoples and tribes of Pontus would have had a large impact upon the slave-trading system of the Greek world in general. The largest centres for piracy were Crete and Cilicia (Blavatskii 1954; Velkov 1967; Finley 1962; Braund and Tsetskhladze 1989; Cecchladze 1990).

Attention must be paid to epigraphic sources. In many inscriptions from mainland Greece and Asia Minor tribal names of Thracians, Scythians, Colchians, Cimmerians, etc. are mentioned in use as personal names. Although we have information from Strabo (7. 3. 12) that in Attica slaves were named simply after the names of the countries they were brought from, this custom was not universal. For example, the name 'Persian' was given to Hesiod's brother and the name 'Cimmerian' was common among the citizens of Ephesus and Rhodes (Cecchladze 1990). The special study of Pontic tribal names in epigraphic sources shows that, in most cases, these names do not point to the ethnic background at all (Cecchladze 1990). They are simply the personal names of Greeks, for example: $KOΛXOΣ$ in several variations was a female and male name for the citizens of Cos, Gorgippia. Even the father of one of the *archontes* of Olbia bore this name. There are also epigraphical sources where the tribal name indicates a slave, but these are few in number (Cecchladze 1990). It is a well-known fact that Scythian archers were employed in Athens.

We do not have sources earlier than the fifth century BC for Pontic slaves in Greece. Maybe such slaves reached Greece before then, but there is no information available. It is interesting to note that in the hellenistic period practically all evidence, especially for Colchian slaves, shows that they were females, who were subsequently freed (Cecchladze 1990). Thus, the evidence so far suggests that the Black Sea was not a major source of slaves for the Greek world.

The main aim of this chapter has been to pose as many questions as possible, in order to show how far we are from satisfactorily answering them and how diverse the interpretation of the evidence is. It is time, once again, to rethink our views of trade in the ancient world.

Acknowledgements

I am most grateful to Prof. Sir John Boardman, Prof. A. J. Graham, Prof. S. Burstein and Dr M. Hansen for their comments on an earlier draft of this chapter.

Bibliography

Alexandrescu, P. (1978a), *La céramique de l'époque Archaïque et Classique (VIIe–IVe s.) (Histria IV)* (Bucuresti and Paris).
—— (1978b), 'Notes de topographie Histrienne', *Dacia* n.s. 22: 331–42.
Andrukh, S. I. (1985), *The Lower Danube Scythia in the Sixth–Beginning of the First Century BC* (Zaporozhe) (in Russian, with English summary).
Angelescu, M. (1992), 'Un problème controversé: l'expédition de Péricles dans le Pont Euxin', *Pontica* 25: 45–54.
Arafat, K. and Morgan, C. (1994), 'Athens, Etruria and the Heuneburg: mutual misconceptions in the study of Greek–barbarian relations', in I. Morris (ed.), *Classical Greece: Ancient Histories and Modern Archaeologies* (Cambridge), 108–34.
Archibald, Z. H. (1994), 'Thracians and Scythians', *Cambridge Ancient History*, iii (2nd edn, Cambridge), 444–75.
Asheri, D. (1998), 'The Achaeans and the Heniochi: reflections on the origins and history of a Greek rhetorical *topos*', in G. R. Tsetskhladze (ed.), *Greek Colonisation of the Black Sea: Historical Interpretation of Archaeology (Historia* suppl. vol. (forthcoming)).
Austin, M. M. (1994), 'Society and economy', *Cambridge Ancient History*, vi (2nd edn, Cambridge), 527–64.
Avram, A. (1990), 'Das histrianische Territorium in griechisch-römischer Zeit', in P. Alexandrescu and W. Schuller (eds), *Histria* (Konstanz), 9–46.
—— (1995), '*Poleis* und *Nicht-Poleis* im Ersten und Zweiten Attischen Seebund', in M. H. Hansen and K. Raaflaub (eds), *Studies in the Ancient Greek Polis (Papers from the Copenhagen Polis Centre 2)* (Historia Einzelschriften 95) (Stuttgart), 191–200.
Birliba, V. M. (1990), *Dacia Rasariteana in Secolele VI–I I.E.N. Economie si Moneda* (Iasi).
Blavatskii, V. D. (1954), 'Slavery and the evidence for it in the ancient states of the northern Black Sea littoral', *SA* 20: 40–59 (in Russian).
Boardman, J. (1980³), *The Greeks Overseas* (London).
—— (1988a), 'Trade in Greek decorated pottery', *OJA* 7: 27–33.
—— (1988b), 'The trade figures', *OJA* 7: 371–3.
—— (1994), *The Diffusion of Classical Art in Antiquity* (London).
Bounegru, O. (1988), 'Portul Histriei in antichitate', *Studii Clasice* 26: 67–79.
Bouzek, J. (1989), 'Athènes et la Mer Noire', *BCH* 113: 249–59.

—— (1990), *Studies of Greek Pottery in the Black Sea Area* (Prague).
—— (1994), 'The distribution of Greek painted pottery in the Mediterranean and in the Black Sea region: a comparison', *OJA* 13: 241–3.
Brashinskii, I. B. (1963), *Athens and the Northern Black Sea Littoral in the Sixth–Second Centuries BC* (Moscow) (in Russian).
—— (1980), *Greek Ceramic Imports in the Lower Don* (Leningrad) (in Russian).
Braund, D. (1995), 'Fish from the Black Sea: classical Byzantium and the Greekness of trade', in J. Wilkins, D. Harvey and M. Dobson (eds), *Food in Antiquity* (Exeter), 162–70.
Braund, D. C. and Tsetskhladze, G. R. (1989), 'The export of slaves from Colchis', *CQ* 39: 114–25.
Bravo, B. (1977), 'Remarques sur les assises sociales, les formes d'organisation et la terminologie du commerce maritime grec à l'époque archaïque', Dialogues d'histoire ancienne 3: 32–47.
Bregadze, N. A. (1982), *Essays on the Agroethnography of Georgia* (Tbilisi) (in Russian).
Burstein, S. (1978), '*IG* II² 653, Demosthenes and Athenian relations with Bosporus in the fourth century BC', *Historia* 27: 430–40.
—— (1993), 'The origin of the Athenian privileges at Bosporus: a reconsideration', *AHB* 7 (3): 81–3.
Canarache, V. (1957), *Importul amforelor stampilate la Istria* (Bucuresti).
Cecchladze (Tsetskhladze), G. R. (1990), 'Zu den kolchischen Sklaven in der griechischen Welt', *Klio* 72: 151–9.
Coja, M. (1986), 'Les centres de production d'amphores timbrées identifiés à Istros', in J.-Y. Empereur and Y. Garlan (eds), *Recherches sur les amphores grecques* (*BCH* suppl. 13) (Paris), 417–50.
Coja, M. and Gheorghita, M. (1983), *Vase Grecesti in Muzeul National: Catalog* (Bucuresti).
Danov, Kh. M. (1967), 'Towards the economy of Thrace and its Black Sea and Aegean coasts in the late classical and hellenistic periods', in *Ancient Society* (Moscow), 131–9 (in Russian).
Dundua, G. F. (1987), *Numismatics of Ancient Georgia* (Tbilisi) (in Russian).
Fine, J. V. A. (1983), *The Ancient Greeks: A Critical History* (Cambridge, Mass. and London).
Finley, M. I. (1962), 'The Black Sea, Danubian regions and slave trade in antiquity', *Klio* 40: 51–9.
Gaidukevich, V. F. (1949), *Bosporan Kingdom* (Moscow/Leningrad) (in Russian).
Gallant, T. W. (1991), *Risk and Survival in Ancient Greece* (Cambridge).
Garnsey, P. (1985), 'Grain for Athens', in P. Cartledge and F. D. Harvey (eds), *Crux: Essays Presented to G. E. M. de Ste Croix on his 75th Birthday* (Sidmouth), 62–75.
—— (1988), *Famine and Food Supply in the Graeco-Roman World* (Cambridge).
Gerasimov, T. (1943), 'Finds of Cyzicene electrum coins from Bulgaria', *Annual of the Public Museum VII (142)* (Sofia): 72–88 (in Bulgarian).

Golenko, K. V. (1977), 'Cyzicenes staters found in the Taman peninsula', in M. M. Kobylina (ed.), *History and Culture of the Ancient World* (Moscow), 37–41 (in Russian).

Gorlov, Y. V. and Lopanov, Y. A. (1995), 'The ancient melioration system on the Taman peninsula', *VDI* 3: 121–37 (in Russian, with English summary).

Graham, A. J. (1982), 'The colonial expansion of Greece', *Cambridge Ancient History*, iii, pt 3 (2nd edn, Cambridge), 83–162.

Hansen, M. H. (1986), *Demography and Democracy* (Herning).

—— (1988), 'Three studies in Athenian demography', *Historisk-filosofiske Meddelelser* 56: 1–28.

—— (1994), 'The number of Athenian citizens secundum Sekunda', *Echos du Monde Classique/Classical Views* 38 (n.s. 13): 299–310.

Hind, J. (1994), 'The Bosporan kingdom', *Cambridge Ancient History*, vi (2nd edn, Cambridge), 476–511.

Histria (1973), vol. 3 (Bucuresti).

Inadze, M. P. (1982), *Greek Colonisation of the Eastern Black Sea Littoral* (Tbilisi) (in Georgian, with Russian and French summaries).

Isager, S. and Hansen, M. H. (1975), *Aspects of Athenian Society in the Fourth Century BC* (translated by J. H. Rosenmeier) (Odense).

Isager, S. and Skydsgaard, J. E. (1992), *Ancient Greek Agriculture: An Introduction* (London, New York).

Johnston, A. W. (1979), *Trademarks on Greek Vases* (Warminster).

Keen, A. G. (1993a), ' "Grain for Athens": notes on the importance of the Hellespontine route in Athenian foreign policy before the Peloponnesian War', *Electronic Antiquity: Communicating the Classics*, vol. 1, issue 6 (November): 1–4.

—— (1993b), 'Athenian campaigns in Karia and Lykia during the Peloponnesian War', *JHS* 113: 152–7.

Khan, H. A. (ed. 1994), *The Birth of the European Identity; The Europe–Asia Contrasts in Greek Thought 490–322 BC* (Nottingham).

Kraay, C., Mørkholm, O. and Thompson, M. (1973), *An Inventory of Greek Coin Hoards* (New York).

Kruglikova, I. T. (1975), *Agriculture of the Bosporus* (Moscow) (in Russian).

Kulikov, A. V. (1995), 'On reconstructing the natural conditions of the Kerch-Taman region in ancient times', *Journal of Historical, Philological and Cultural Studies* 2: 97–107 (in Russian, with English summary).

Lazarov, M. (1973), 'Ancient amphorae (sixth–first centuries BC) from the Bulgarian Black Sea littoral', *Bulletin du Musée National de Varna* 9: 3–52 (in Bulgarian, with French summary).

—— (1975), 'Unpublished ancient amphorae and amphora stamps from the Bulgarian Black Sea littoral', *Bulletin du Musée National de Varna* 11: 128–36 (in Bulgarian, with French summary).

——(1990), *Ancient Painted Pottery in Bulgaria* (Sofia) (in Bulgarian, with English summary).

Lebedeva, E. Y. (1994), 'The results of palaeobotanic investigations from Maeotian sites of the Kuban region', *BS* 5: 108–12 (in Russian, with English summary).

Lordkipanidze, O. D. (1979), *Ancient Colchis* (Tbilisi) (in Russian).

—— (ed. 1983), *Vani VII: Archaeological Excavations* (Tbilisi) (in Georgian, with Russian and English summaries).

Marchenko, K. K. (1993), 'On the Scythian protectorate in the northwest Black Sea littoral in the fifth century BC', *PAV* (Petersburg Archaeological Herald) 7: 43–8 (in Russian, with English summary).

Maslennikov, A. A. (1985), 'New data on Bosporan farmers', in *Epigraphy of Ancient Asia Minor and Northern and Western Black Sea Littorals as an Historical and Linguistic Source* (Moscow): 138–47 (in Russian).

Mattingly, H. B. (1996), 'Athens and the Black Sea in the fifth century BC', in O. Lordkipanidzé and P. Lévêque (eds), *Sur les traces des Argonautes* (Besançon), 151–8.

Meiggs, R. (1972), *The Athenian Empire* (Oxford).

Mildenberg, L. (1993/4), 'The Cyzicenes: a reappraisal', *AJN* second series 5–6: 1–14.

Murzin, V. Y. (1984), *Scythian Archaica of the Northern Black Sea Littoral* (Kiev) (in Russian).

Noonan, T. S. (1973), 'The grain trade of the northern Black Sea in antiquity', *AJP* 94 (3): 231–42.

Onaiko, N. A. (1966), *Ancient Imports in the Dnieper and Bug Region in the Seventh–Fifth Centuries BC* (Moscow) (in Russian).

Palaeobotanical Finds (1980), *Palaeobotanical Finds on the Balkan Peninsula* (Studia Praehistorica, 4) (Sofia) (in Russian).

Panayotova, K. (1998), 'Apollonia Pontica: recent discoveries in the necropolis', in G. R. Tsetskhladze (ed.), *Greek Colonisation of the Black Sea: Historical Interpretation of Archaeology* (*Historia*, suppl. vol. (forthcoming)).

Penkova, E. (forthcoming), *Painted Pottery from the Necropolis of Apollonia Pontica* (Oxford, *Colloquia Pontica*).

Reho, M. (1985), 'Diffusione della ceramica Attica a figure nere e rosse nella "Tracia Bulgara" ', *Thracia Pontica* 2: 215–26.

—— (1992), *Athenian Black Figure Pottery in the National Archaeological Museum, Sofia* (Sofia) (in Bulgarian).

Sallares, R. (1991), *The Ecology of the Ancient Greek World* (Ithaca, N.Y.).

Saprykin, S. Y. (1995), 'The struggle for economic zones of influence in the Black Sea region in the sixth–second centuries BC (state policy or private initiative?)', in S. D. Kryzhitskii (ed.), *Ancient Poleis and the Local Population of the Black Sea Littoral* (Sevastopol), 129–42 (in Russian).

Sceglov, A. A. (1990), 'Le commerce du blé dans le Pont septentrional (seconde moitié VIIe–Ve siècles)', in O. Lordkipanidzé and P. Lévêque (eds), *Le Pont-Euxin vu par les Grecs* (Besançon), 141–60.

Shanks, M. (1996), *Classical Archaeology of Greece* (London).

Shcheglov, A. N. (1978), *North-Western Crimea in Ancient Times* (Leningrad) (in Russian).

Shelov, D. B. (1956), *Coinage of the Bosporus of the Sixth–Second centuries BC* (Moscow) (in Russian).

Shelov-Kovedyaev, F. V. (1985), 'History of Bosporus in the sixth–second centuries BC', *Ancient States in the Territory of the USSR 1984* (Moscow), 5–187 (in Russian).

Sikharulidze, T. D. (1987), 'Attic painted vases from Pichvnari burial ground', *Sites of South West Georgia* 16: 51–108 (in Georgian, with Russian summary).

Sikharulidze, T. D. (1988), 'New examples of Attic painted pottery from Pichvnari necropolis', *Sites of South West Georgia*, 17: 60–71 (in Georgian, with Russian summary).

Sikharulidze, T. D. (1991), 'Three lekythoi from Pichvnari burial ground', *Sites of South West Georgia*, 19: 42–51 (in Georgian, with Russian summary).

Skrzhinskaya, M. V. (1994), 'Participation in legal disputes in Athens by Bosporan citizens', *DP* 1994: 125–9 (in Russian).

Sorochan, S. B. (1994), 'Myths and reality of Chersonesian grain export', *Antiquities* 1994 (Kharkov): 66–72 (in Russian, with English summary).

Treister, M. Y. (1988), 'The role of metals in the age of great Greek colonisation', *VDI* 1: 17–42 (in Russian).

—— (1992), 'Trade in metals in the Greek world', *Bulletin of the Metals Museum* 18: 29–43.

—— (1995), *The Role of Metals in Ancient Greek History* (Leiden).

—— (1998), 'Ionia and the North Pontic area. Archaic metal-working: tradition and innovation', in G. R. Tsetskhladze (ed.), *Greek Colonisation of the Black Sea. Historical Interpretation of Archaeology* (*Historia*, suppl. vol. (forthcoming)).

Tsetskhladze, G. R. (1990), 'The northern and eastern Black Sea littorals in the sixth–first centuries BC', *Arkheologiya* 2: 86–97 (in Ukrainian, with English summary).

—— (1994), 'Greek penetration of the Black Sea', in G. R. Tsetskhladze and F. De Angelis (eds), *The Archaeology of Greek Colonisation: Essays Dedicated to Sir John Boardman* (Oxford), 111–36.

—— (1995), 'Did the Greeks go to Colchis for metals?', *OJA* 14: 307–32.

—— (1998), 'On piracy in the Black Sea', in C. Angelova (ed.), *Sea and Civilisation: A Collection of Articles in Honour of M. Lazarov* (Sozopol) (forthcoming).

—— (forthcoming), 'How Greek colonists adapted their way of life to conditions in Colchis', in J. Fossey (ed.), *McGill University Monographs in Classical Archaeology and History: Antiquitates Propontica, Circumponticae et Caucasicae* (Amsterdam).

Tsetskhladze, G. R. and Treister, M. Y. (1995), 'The metallurgy and production of precious metals in Colchis before and after the arrival of the Ionians (towards the problems of the reasons for Greek colonisation)', *Bulletin of the Metals Museum* 24: 1–32.

Vakhtina, M. Y. (1993), 'On the influence of the demographic situation on the development of Graeco-barbarian contacts in the different areas of the north-western Black Sea littoral', *PAV* (Petersburg Archaeological Herald) 6: 53–5 (in Russian).

Velkov, V. I. (1967), 'Thracian slaves in the ancient *poleis* of Greece in the sixth–second centuries BC', *VDI* 4: 60–70 (in Russian).

Venedikov, I. (ed. 1963), *Excavation in the Necropolis of Apollonia in 1947–49* (Sofia) (in Bulgarian, with Russian and French summaries).

Vickers, M. (1985), 'Artful crafts: the influence of metalwork on Athenian painted pottery', *JHS* 105: 108–28.

Vickers, M. and Gill, D. (1994), *Artful Crafts: Ancient Greek Silverware and Pottery* (Oxford).

Vinogradov, Y. G. (1971), 'New data on the early Greek economy', *VDI* 1: 64–76 (in Russian, with English summary).

—— (1980), 'King Scyles' ring (Scythian political and dynastic history in the first half of the fifth century BC)', *SA* 3: 92–109 (in Russian, with English summary).

—— (1988), 'The western and northern Black Sea littorals in the classical period', in E. S. Golubtsova (ed.), *History of Europe*, vol. 1 (Moscow), 373–88 (in Russian).

—— (1995), 'The Pontus Euxinus as a political, economic and cultural unity, and epigraphy', in S. D. Kryzhitskii (ed.), *Ancient Poleis and the Local Population of the Black Sea Littoral* (Sevastopol), 5–55 (in Russian).

von Reden, S. (1995), *Exchange in Ancient Greece* (London).

Yailenko, V. P. (1996), 'Pseudo-epigraphy of the ancient northern Black Sea littoral', in V. P. Yailenko (ed.), *History and Culture of the Ancient World* (Moscow), 175–222 (in Russian).

Yanushevich, Z. V. (1976), *Cultivated Plants of the South-Western USSR According to Palaeobotanic Studies* (Kishinev) (in Russian).

Zhebelev, S. A. (1982), 'The commercial and consular service in the Greek colonies of the northern Black Sea littoral', *VDI* 2: 144–55 (E. I. Solomonik (1982), 'Unpublished article by academician S. A. Zhebelev', *VDI* 2: 140–55) (in Russian, with English summary).

Zograf, A. N. (1951), *Ancient Coins* (Moscow, Leningrad) (in Russian).

5

Ceramics and positivism revisited: Greek transport amphoras and history

Mark Lawall

A frequent topic of debate over the past decade has been the monetary value of archaic and classical Greek finewares and, a related topic, their epistemic value for the archaeology of trade.[1] Considerable attention has been paid to the ancient, commercial significance of the fineware trade, while less attention has been paid to the question of whether finewares, expensive or cheap, ever provided detailed archaeological evidence for the study of trade after *c.* 550 BC.[2] A brief review can highlight why finewares are poor indicators of patterns of trade. The dominance of Athens in exported finewares beginning *c.* 550 limits the visibility of trade involving other cities.[3] The role of Athenians themselves in the process of trade remains uncertain (Johnston 1993, 216–22, 1972, 1985; cf. Gill 1994, 100–1). Furthermore, fineware production

---

[1] Some of the major figures and works in this debate include Gill 1994 (summarising many of his previous remarks and listing many earlier contributions), Vickers 1985, Boardman 1988, Cook 1987.

[2] Vallet and Villard (1963) consider the differing significance of finewares and containers for trade studies; Morel 1989 considers finewares and amphora in the Roman period; now see Osborne 1996 for an argument for a larger scale and complexity of fineware trade than had been assumed before. (All dates BC.)

[3] Hannestad 1988, with references to earlier studies of imports to Etruria; Arafat and Morgan 1994; and Perrault 1986 all illustrate the dominance of Athens after 550.

involved a limited segment of the labour force and resource base of the *polis*.[4]

Archaeological evidence for trade from a different class of ceramics, transport amphoras, responds to many of these short-comings. Amphora types are known from many different cities, and jars from many cities were exported widely.[5] The production of amphoras was closely connected to the agricultural produc-tion of oil, wine, and other products intended for the jars; the amphora trade involved not only potters, distributors, and buyers, but also landowners and their farm labour (Grakov 1935; Garlan 1983; Morel 1989; Whitbread 1995). In addition, the dominance of amphoras in cargoes found in shipwrecks validates their use as indices of commerce (Parker 1992). Amphoras not only serve as valid indicators of patterns of trade, but they can be used to raise and address questions beyond the scope of literary evidence alone.

The study of amphoras as evidence for trade has a long history.[6] Along with the practical necessity of identifying places of manufacture and chronological sequences of jars,[7] studies of amphoras have documented changing sources of imports at a given site through time (for examples see Brashinskii 1980, 1984; Zeest 1960; Onayko 1960; Slaska 1985; Leipunskaya 1981; Buzoianu 1991), and changing access to imports for different segments of a population (for example, Brashinskii 1980; Garlan 1983; Pou-touridze 1990). Studies of production sites have strengthened the connection between amphoras and agricultural production (Gar-lan 1986, 1988; Kats and Monachov eds 1992; Whitbread 1995). The use of amphoras in studies of trade, however, has also encountered

---

[4]   See Arafat and Morgan 1989, 321–9 on the scale and organisation of fineware production at Athens and Corinth.

[5]   For surveys of Greek amphora types, see Grace and Savvatianou-Petropoulakou 1970; Grace 1979a; Brashinskii 1980, 1984; Leipunskaya 1981; Doger 1992.

[6]   For historical surveys of studies of amphoras, see Garlan 1983; Shelov-Kovedjaev 1986 for the history of research in the Soviet Union before 1986.

[7]   Chronological studies of various classical series include Grace 1971 (for Samos); Grace 1953 (includes discussion of Lesbos, Chios, and Mende); and Grace 1979a; Brashinskii 1984 surveys the chronologies of many types; Whitbread 1995 summarises the evidence for the provenance of many known amphora types.

some difficulties.Studies often depend on counts of stamped handles.[8] Direct comparison of numbers of stamps from different amphora types may ignore chronological differences, different stamping practices, different sizes of the jars involved, and the significant numbers of unstamped jars (Empereur 1982; Garlan 1983, 28–30; Whitbread 1995, 24–7). Indeed, studies involving unstamped Greek amphoras tend to document only the presence or absence of a type without more detailed quantitative information.[9]

Such shortcomings of past uses of amphoras can be addressed by exploiting aspects of amphoras that make them suitable alternatives to finewares for studying trade. Research can combine distributions of different types, markings on the jars, changes in fabric, and aspects of the shapes of the jars. Close attention to shapes and fabrics permits the use of unstamped amphoras in quantitative studies, thereby avoiding overemphasis on stamped types, and permitting greater attention to diachronic change in patterns of imports than was practised in earlier studies. Practices of marking amphoras, particularly when considered alongside changes in volume of trade, can be used to explore change in the organisation of trade. By these methods, amphoras can contribute to histories of trade, both its intensity or frequency and its organisation, and the interaction between commercial interests and political events. Amphoras, in this way, become tools for investigating economic and political change at a local, regional, or inter-regional level.

The case study of Chian amphoras of the fifth century BC, presented below, is based on studies of amphoras – chronological and typological evidence, counts, markings – from Athens, Gordion, and other published sites. Data from Athens are drawn from the contents of thirty-six fifth-century well-deposits from the Athenian Agora.[10] Evidence from Gordion was gathered from excavations of 1988–96.[11] Both sites provide useful quantitative

[8]   A sequence of references – Fraser 1972, 165; Sherwin-White 1978, 238; Sarikakis 1986, 122–4 – illustrates how problematic statistics from Alexandria have been taken up in successive historical discussions.
[9]   Exceptions to this situation include some more specific references in Brashinskii 1980 and Buzoianu 1991.
[10]   These data were gathered as part of my doctoral research, see Lawall 1995.
[11]   These data are part of my study of amphoras at Gordion, see Lawall 1996.

data, summarising the frequencies with which Chian amphoras were imported relative to all other types between 525 and 400. Sites throughout the Aegean, Turkey, the Black Sea region, Egypt, and the Near East provide useful comparative material.

Chian amphoras and economic history, 525 to 400 BC

Chios produced two types of amphora during the fifth century. The earlier type has a noticeably bulging neck.[12] The fabric of this type shows some variation but was found through petrographic and x-ray fluorescence analyses to match the local geology and other local pottery types.[13] The type is also recognisably depicted on Chian coinage of the fifth century.[14] The second Chian type has a straight-sided neck,[15] and this type also appears on Chian coins.[16] Some examples of this second type are stamped with a coin-image still depicting a bulging-necked amphora.[17] There may be a difference in fabrics between the bulging-neck and the straight-neck types, and there appear to be developments of the straight-neck fabric as well.[18] Such variation in Chian fabrics requires further study; however, the attribution of both types to Chios is certain.

Development of shape

The bulging-neck Chian type was produced from late in the sixth century to the third quarter of the fifth century. Three stages

[12]   Grace 1979a, fig. 44 is the most accessible illustration of the type.
[13]   For comments on fabric variation see Anderson 1954, 169; Dupont 1982, 198; for the results of x-ray fluorescence study, see Dupont 1982, 198 and 1983, 24, 30–1; for further results distinguishing Chian from other East Greek amphora fabrics, see Seifert and Yalçin 1995, 24–5; for petrographic study see Whitbread 1995, 134–53, 213–29.
[14]   Grace 1979a, figs 48 and 49.
[15]   Grace 1979a, fig. 45.
[16]   See Seltman 1977, pl. 29.13.
[17]   Grace 1934, 202, fig. 1, pl. 1; Talcott 1935, 495–6; Grace 1953, 105; Grace 1979a, figs 48, 49.
[18]   Whitbread 1995, 141–3 did examine samples of the straight-neck type but did not isolate the fabric as significantly different.

of development were labelled by U. Knigge as C/1, C/2, and
C/3.[19] The first stage, C/1, continues from the late sixth century
to *c.* 480.[20] The rim, while rounded as in later stages, is noticeably narrower. The toe is typical of fifth-century Chian amphoras:
the body wall simply flares outward, forming a cylindrical pedestal
with a hollowed underside.[21] The most diagnostic feature of the
C/1 stage is its painted decoration. A pattern of thin, red or brown
lines are found on the handles and body, a curlicue pattern often
appears on the shoulder, the rim is painted, and a circle, dotted
circle, letter, or cross appears on the neck between the handles.

The second stage in the development, form C/2, begins *c.* 480
and continues to *c.* 440 BC.[22] This stage differs from its predecessor in the heavier, more noticeably bulging neck, more robust
rim, and narrower body.[23] The handles compress the sides of the

[19] Knigge 1976, 23–4, though the following chronology departs in places
from Knigge's proposed chronology.
[20] The starting date of the C/1 jars in the late sixth century is supported
by finds at Histria (Dimitriu 1966, 90–1, with pls 52 and 53) and Orphani
(Nicolaïdou-Patera 1987, 344, 351, pl. 9). Continuity down to 480 is
supported by finds published by Onayko 1980, 68 and 123; Voigtländer
1982, 44, nos. 31–33; Johnston 1990, 38–40; Okhotnikov 1990, 19–20, pl.
9 and 'photo 2', nos. 4–6; and in the Athenian Agora (all references to
finds in Agora deposits are presented in greater detail in Lawall 1995
with further references for the dates of the deposits): Deposits D 7:2; D
15:1; C 18:4a; E 14:3; F 14:3; H 12:15; R 12:1; Rectangular Rock-Cut Shaft
(upper fill); Roberts 1986, 66–7, fig. 42 and pl. 18, nos. 419 and 420; and
the Kerameikos excavations include the following graves dated to *c.* 480:
Knigge 1976, 108, no. 82, SW 179 (*c.* 480); 111–12, no. 95, SW 147, pl.
51.6 (480/70); 115, no. 108, SW 120 (480/70).
[21] See Tsaravopoulos 1986, pl. 39, fig. 2; Johnston 1990, 38 n. 5 and 39
fig. 1; Grace 1979b, 121, figs 1–4.
[22] For C/2 amphoras datable to *c.* 480 or slightly later, see Ebert 1913,
12–13, figs 9 and 10; Knigge 1976, 178, no. E 40, pl. 90.6 (to 480); and
Okhotnikov 1990, 20, 'photo 2', no. 7. The general span of 480 to 440 is
supported by Abramov and Maslennikov 1991, 234–7; and continuity to *c.*
440 is supported by graves in the Kerameikos, see Knigge 1976, 146, no.
263, SW 26, pl. 62.5 (to the mid-fifth); 150, 282, HW 24 (450/40); 152,
no. 294, SW 82 (3rd quarter fifth); 154–5, no. 302, SW 129 (3rd quarter
fifth). See, too, Williams and Fisher 1976, 104–5; Williams 1978, 17–19 with
fig. 5; and Munn 1983, 381. The C/2 form dominates deposits from the
Athenian Agora closed before 440: F 19:4 (9 C/2, 2 C/1), N 7:3 (16 C/2, 3
C/1), C18:4b (10C/2, 2C/1), and C 9:6 (6 C/2 and no other Chian forms).
A–B 21–22:1 (1 est. vessel); B 12:4 (1); B 13:6 (2); O 19:4 (1); M17:7 (5).
[23] See Grace 1979a, fig. 44 third from left.

neck, forming an ovoid mouth. Unlike the preceding C/1 form, the C/2 amphoras have little or no painted decoration.

The third stage, C/3, is distinguished both by a higher place-ment of the bulge and by a new form of toe.[24] The bulge of the neck now appears as a thickened band just below the rim. These jars have a more distinctly articulated shoulder than was seen earlier. The flaring, hollow toe of the preceding forms is replaced here with a cap-like toe, still hollowed underneath.[25] The transi-tion from the C/2 stage to this third and final stage in the bulging-neck series seems to be gradual, with the distinctive features of the C/3 amphoras emerging *c.* 440 and continuing in production down to *c.* 425.[26]

The succeeding Chian straight-neck type resembles its prede-cessor in many elements.[27] The rim of the straight-neck type is nar-rower than that of its predecessors. The transition at the outer edge of the shoulder to the body is often even sharper than was seen with the C/3 stage. The lower bodies and toes of the earlier C/3 stage and straight-neck type, however, are quite similar in shape. The straight-neck type itself varies in the bulkiness of the neck and handles. Some of heavier examples have a larger capacity.[28] The shoulder is often flatter on jars of the bulkier form, but this differ-ence is often difficult to judge if only small fragments are preserved. To speak of heavy and light variants, however, may oversimplify the situation; many examples fall between the two extremes.

[24] See Grace 1979a, fig. 44 far right.
[25] See Grace 1979b, 121, fig. 4; Knigge 1976, no. 304; and Anderson 1954, 175, fig. 9g; though cf. Mylonas 1975, pl. 302, no. Z1, a C/3 amphora with the older toe form.
[26] The transition to, production, and decline of use of C/3 jars is shown by three Agora deposits: N 7:3 (closed *c.* 440 with no C/3 jars), M 17:7 (closed *c.* 425 with 5 C/2 and 6 C/3 but no examples of the following straight-neck type), and R 13:4 (closed *c.* 425 with 7 C/3 and 18 straight-neck jars). I suggest that M 17:7 was closed sufficiently before R 13:4 so as not to include the straight-neck jars while still including residual C/2 jars. The range 440 to 425 is supported by other findspots: see Alexan-drescu 1966, 168, 521, pl. 89, tomb 14; Williams 1978, 15–20, esp. 17–19 with fig. 5; Williams 1979, 112; Williams and Fisher 1976, no. 28, pl. 20; Munn 1983, 381 n. 7; and Knigge 1976, 151–2, no. 290, SW 5, pl. 65.4.
[27] Grace 1979a, fig. 45.
[28] Mattingly 1981, 80 suggests a gradual increase in the capacity of this type through time. Known measurements do not support this view as of now.

The date of introduction of the straight-neck type is very problematic.[29] The disappearance of the bulge would seem to indicate a rapid shift in practice, and yet there is evidence for overlap of the two types. They occur together in deposits from the Athenian Agora,[30] Corinth,[31] and Olbia.[32] The two types appear to have coincided in exportation for some time during the third quarter of the fifth century (see too, Munn 1983, 378, n. 7). This evidence for joint exportation correlates well with the apparent differences in fabrics between the two types, raising the likelihood that they were produced initially by different, contemporary workshops.[33] If the two types did in fact overlap in production, the period involved will have lasted, at most, five to ten years. After *c.* 425, the straight-neck type was the only form of Chian amphora.[34]

Developments of markings

A more detailed study of Chian commerce in the fifth century, as is the aim of this case-study, depends not only on knowledge of

[29] For example, see Grace and Savvatianou-Petropoulakou 1970, 259–60; Grace 1979a, text with figs 44–9; Mattingly 1981, 78–80; and Barron 1986, 96–100.

[30] E 19:5 (1–2 C/3 est. vessels, 1 straight neck); R 13:4 (7 C/3, 18 str. neck); C 19:9 (3 C/3, 4 str. neck); and A 20:6 (2 C/3, 1 str. neck).

[31] Corinth pottery lots 1977–87, 1979–75 and –82; 1975–129, –130, and –132 all contain both C/3 and straight-neck fragments.

[32] Pharmakovskyi 1929, 66–9, pls 58 and 59, shows 95 jars arranged around a tumulus; at least 5 jars are clearly C/3s and others appear to be straight-neck Chians. Parker 1992, 287, no. 737 mentions the discovery of 'both types of Chian amphoras found in the mid fifth century BC' at the Neseber A wreck off the Bulgarian coast.

[33] There is a possible transitional piece that could imply a smoother development, though still rapid, from the C/3 stage to the straight-neck type. The fragment is from a well published by Talcott (1935); the piece itself is discussed in Lawall 1995, 92. The piece, however, could be the work of a producer of the older bulging-neck type changing to the already introduced straight-neck form.

[34] Findspots for straight-neck jars from the Athenian Agora include A–B 21–22:1 (2 straight-neck, 1 C/2); B 13:5 (3 straight-neck); B 13:6 (5 straight-neck, 2 C/2); B 15:1 (6 straight-neck); B 19:11 (1 straight-neck); G 12:21 (2 straight-neck); R 13:1 (17 straight-neck). In addition O 19:4 closed sometime in the late fifth century, included 2 straight-neck and 1 C/3.

the development of Chian amphora shapes and fabrics, but also on changes in practices of marking the jars. Indeed, major developments in Chian production are often accompanied by changes in amphora markings.

Markings on the Chian amphoras fall into two patterns, separated by a time when marks are quite rare. From the late sixth through the first quarter of the fifth century, the Chian bulging-neck jars were marked with carefully applied, pre-firing dipinti. This practice rapidly faded from use in the second quarter of the fifth century. In the second half of the century, Chian amphoras were again marked with some frequency, but stamps and numerical graffiti replaced the earlier dipinti.

The C/1 amphoras were often marked by a circle or dotted circle painted between the handles before firing.[35] A narrow repertoire of other symbols can replace the circle: a cross,[36] the letter A,[37] or a single, vertical stroke.[38] In addition to these dipinti, Okhotnikov publishes examples of incised marks in the same position, also applied before firing.[39] The consistency of position and time of application of such marks suggests that all were part of one system; however, the meaning of the marks themselves is uncertain. On the one hand, they may be considered within the general decorative scheme of the vessel (Johnston 1990, 38–9). And yet, the neck symbols are differentiated from the rest of the decoration of the vessels in their variety. Anderson thought the markings might be 'some sort of trademark' (Anderson 1954, 169). An

[35]   For examples, see Kutaysov 1990, pl. 12.1 and 2; pl. 13.1, 2, 4, 5; Roberts 1986, 67, nos. 419 and 420; Knigge 1976 pl. 49.4, no. 48, SW 127; pl. 45.8, no. 17, SW 137; pl. 48.2, no. 34, HW 58; pl. 51.6, no. 95, SW 147; Lambrino 1938, figs 178–81; Alekseeva 1990, pl. 4.10; Okhotnikov 1990, pl. 9.1, 3, and 4; Vallet and Villard 1964, pl. 70.1; Tsaravopoulos 1986, pl. 30.4; and examples from the Athenian Agora are listed by Lawall 1995, 340.
[36]   See, too, Lambrino 1938, fig. 183b; Kutaysov 1990, pl. 14.4, pl. 13.3 and 19 (on toe); Alekseeva 1990, pl. 4.9; Zeest 1960, pl. 3. 10a and 11b; and Okhotnikov 1990, pl. 9.2 and 'photo 2', nos. 4 and 6.
[37]   Tsaravopoulos 1986, pl. 30.4.
[38]   Lawall 1995, 340, ch. 5. This mark may have been accidental; one neck fragment from Gordion has vertical painted lines near one handle where the painter simply missed trying to paint the vertical line along the outer surface of the handle.
[39]   Okhotnikov 1990, pl. 9.5–8.

upward pointing arrow published by Okhotnikov does resemble a symbol for the numeral 10 noted by Johnston on Attic fineware graffiti.[40] Circles or dotted-circles appear to have been used as numerical notations elsewhere.[41] Whatever the precise meaning of the painted symbols, they likely referred to a variable with few different values; the range of symbols used is quite restricted. If, for example, they refer to potters, then there were very few active amphora makers during this time; if they refer to quality or quantity of contents, then the information provided was necessarily vague (e.g. excellent, good, not so good); if they refer to shippers or purchasers, then again the range of symbols would suggest a restricted group of such people. None of these possible meanings seems particularly plausible, but the list is useful for raising, and excluding, some possibilities. At this point, all that can be said with certainty is that if the general decorative scheme and shape of the jar identified it as 'Chian', then the various symbols on the neck should add some further information.

Further markings on the C/1 jars are far less consistent or common. Small circles impressed before firing appear sporadically throughout the Chian series and on many other amphora types.[42] Although certainly applied on Chios, these marks are too simple and widespread to have been part of any organisational system.[43] Johnston mentions some further markings among material from Aegina, 'red dipinti, probably of broad commercial meaning' (Johnston 1990, 39). Perhaps of a related nature, large painted letters are found on bodies of C/1 and later Chian jars along the north coast of the Black Sea.[44] These painted letters tend to be limited to the Black Sea region and should be more related in some way to import practices than to Chios' exporting mechanisms. In addition to these dipinti, there are also examples of

---

[40] Okhotnikov 1990, pl. 9.8; Johnston 1979, 29–30.
[41] Roller 1987, 61–3 discusses a series of circle graffiti from the sixth through to the early fourth century Gordion on non-Greek pottery.
[42] Onayko 1980, no. 35, pl. 3; Lambrino 1938, figs 185b and 195; Okhotnikov 1990, pl. 9.10–11; and Lawall 1995, 340, ch. 4.
[43] For examples on other amphora types, see Garlan and Dougléri-Intzessiloglou 1990, 383–4; Eiseman and Ridgway 1987, 41–2; Mantsevich 1987, 55 and 106.
[44] From sites near Olbia, see Kryzhitskii *et al.* 1989, 58, pl. 18; from Kerkinitis, see Kutaysov 1990, pl. 14.6.

alphabetic and numerical graffiti.[45] A graffito of seven parallel lines, found in the Athenian Agora, was interpreted by M. Lang as standing for seven Athenian choes and would have been incised at Athens (Lang 1956, 3).

Just as the lack of painted decoration characterises the succeeding C/2 amphoras, so too there is a noticeable decline in commercial markings with the shift to the new form *c.* 480. The production-area marks noted on the necks of the C/1 jars are known, but are quite rare, for the C/2 amphoras.[46] Use of the earlier marking system declined rapidly. Extended alphabetic graffiti are also extremely rare.[47] There is no consistent marking system for the second quarter of the fifth century.

Markings are again more common on the C/3 jars, but these markings do not resemble earlier practices. Painted letters appear occasionally on the bulge of the neck including two amphoras found on Chios with the letter E;[48] such labels were certainly applied prior to exportation. One known stamp from a C/3 jar, an incuse A,[49] would have also been applied before firing and shipment. Both the recurrence of painted letters at various sites and the use of stamps suggest the introduction of new production-area marking practices with the C/3 variant. The paucity of known examples indicates the sporadic use of these innovations.

Another innovation accompanying the C/3 amphoras is the increased use of graffiti tallies. Three such tallies on identifiably C/3 amphoras are known from Athens along with a fourth with alphabetic abbreviations for the numbers. A fifth example may belong to a C/3 jar or may belong to a straight-neck jar.[50]

---

[45]   Johnston 1990, nos. 22–7; and Brashinskii 1984, 171.

[46]   Knigge 1976, no. 166, SW 128, 2nd quarter fifth. Brashinskii 1984, 171–2 lists 2 dipinto circles from a total of 28 C/2 amphoras.

[47]   Bingen 1967, 42–3, figs 34–6 has the label *hERIAS* on the shoulder. A fragmentary graffito is found in the Athenian Agora (Lawall 1995, 340, ch. 14).

[48]   Boardman 1967, 179–80, no. 954; *Knigge* 1976, pl. 65.8, no. 304, SW 145; and Tsaravopoulos 1986, pl. 37a. A large X painted on the side of a C/3 jar is found at Corinth, see Williams and Fisher 1976, no. 28, pl. 20.

[49]   This is SS 7805 from the Agora (Lawall 1995, 341, ch. 22).

[50]   Listed by Lawall 1995, 341.

Four of these five marks were found in Agora deposit R 13:4 – a well that contained many similar graffiti on other amphora types.[51] This topographical concentration of tally-marks encourages their classification as importation-area marks.[52]

The subsequent straight-neck type shows an increased use of stamps, thereby building on an innovation in production-area marks from the C/3 jars. An A-stamp, quite similar to the A-stamp seen on a C/3 jar, appears on a straight-neck jar in Athens.[53] Another A-stamp in a circular field was found in the 'Amphora Pit' at Corinth.[54] These stamps provide a direct link between the markings on C/3 amphoras and those on straight-neck amphoras and provide further evidence that the two types overlapped in production. The most common stamp on the straight-neck amphoras, however, is the Chian coin-type stamp of a sphinx seated before what appears to be a C/3 amphora.[55] This stamp can be found either near the lower end of a handle or on the neck near the rim. The use of this coin-type stamp is a practice that begins only with the straight-neck type, even if the act of stamping can be traced to the C/3 type. Other stamps include a kantharos and a plain, small oval impression.

Markings on the straight-neck amphoras are also related to those on the C/3 amphoras by virtue of the frequent occurrence of tally graffiti.[56] As noted before, well R 13:4 and its vicinity accounted for the majority of the examples recovered in Athens. This importation-area marking practice represents a further point of continuity between stage C/3 and the straight-neck type.

[51] Some of these markings from R 13:4 are published by Talcott 1935, fig. 28 and by Lang 1956.
[52] Certain tally-marks are interpreted by Lang (1956 and 1976) as having been applied in Athens (see p. 84).
[53] SS 8083, Lawall 1995, 341, ch. 29.
[54] C 75–121 from the Amphora Pit at Corinth (unpublished). See Brashinskii 1984, 174 for a further letter stamp, this one of a P.
[55] Examples come from Hermonasa (Zeest 1960, 77, fig. 3); from Corinth (C 77–89); and from Athens (Lawall 1995, 342, chs 38–43; and Grace 1979a, fig. 48).
[56] From Athens, see Lawall 1995, 341–2, chs 28–37, chs 39–40 and ch. 42, with references to further publications.

Distribution of Chian amphoras in the late sixth and fifth centuries

Both fifth-century types of Chian amphoras were widely and frequently exported. The bulging-neck type may be more easily recognised, with the result that it may be over-represented in publications. The straight-neck jars, however, are also found outside Chios. A survey of findspots gives a general impression of the extent of Chian exports, while a more detailed view of finds at Athens and Gordion refines the quantitative and chronological quality of the evidence.

Chian jars datable between *c*. 525 and *c*. 400 BC are widely distributed.[57] Sites on the Greek mainland reporting Chian amphoras include Athens,[58] Corinth,[59] Oisyme (Phagris),[60] Aegina,[61] and Olympia.[62] Further east, in the Black Sea region, numerous sites have published Chian jars of this period, including Histria and other sites in Romania (Dimitriu 1966; Alexandrescu 1966; Buzoianu 1991; Sirbu 1993), Olbia and nearby rural sites (Leipunskaya 1981; Kryzhitskii *et al.* 1989), Kerkinitis (Kutaysov 1990), Elizavetovskoe (Brashinskii 1980), and Vani (Poutouridze 1990). Also to the East, imported jars are published from Miletos (Voigtländer 1982), Marion, Salamis and Kition on Cyprus,[63] and Tell el-Maskhuta in Egypt (Holladay 1982). Despite the frequent appearance of Chian jars in the western Mediterranean earlier in the archaic period, few jars are found in that region after *c*. 525.[64] Though incomplete, this selection of findspots includes a wide geographical range of sites and a variety of political affiliations: some are closely tied to Athens, others to Persia, and still others have only tenuous connections with the area generally thought of as

[57]   Findspots of Chian jars are also listed by Sarikakis 1986, 122–4.
[58]   Grace 1979a and 1979b; and Lawall 1995, 88–115.
[59]   See for examples, Williams 1978, 15–20; Munn 1983, 381–4.
[60]   Nicolaïdou-Patera 1987, 344, 351, pl. 9.
[61]   Johnston 1990, 38–40.
[62]   Gauer 1975.
[63]   For jars from the tombs at Salamis and Marion, see Gjerstad *et al.* 1935; for Kition, see Johnston 1981.
[64]   For material from Megara Hyblaia, see Vallet and Villard 1964; for Gravisca, see Slaska 1985, noting the decrease in Chian presence here in the late archaic period.

'the Greek world'. Even with relatively little information published as to quantities found at each site and the dates of finds, a general conclusion may be drawn from this evidence: Chios was an active exporter of amphoras from the late sixth century throughout the fifth century. Despite the general nature of this conclusion, an important point emerges. Although Chian fineware exports decline by 550, the island's amphora production and distribution continues. Without a more detailed view of Chian exports, however, shorter-term, significant fluctuations in exports can disappear, and exports might be too quickly associated with prosperity (i.e. if goods were exported, there must have been an equivalent return in imports). More detailed evidence of the history of Chian exports is available from two very different importing centres: Athens and the inland Phrygian city of Gordion. At Athens, from the late sixth century through 440, Chian jars comprise on average 16 per cent of the amphoras present in selected well deposits. Wells filled between 425 and 410 contain, on average, 28 per cent Chian amphoras. Deposits closed at the end of the century include 12 per cent Chian jars (Figure 5.1).[65] Chian exports to Athens thus appear to remain quite consistent until the middle

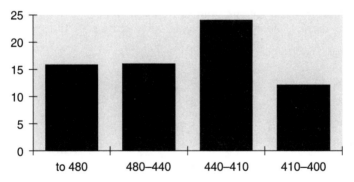

Figure 5.1 Chian imports to Athens represented as a percentage of total imports in each period.

[65] Figures adapted from Lawall 1995, 395–6, table 4. The choices of terminal dates for these periods were made on the basis of discriminant analyses of the content of the deposits in order to find those clusters of deposits (maintaining chronological integrity) that resulted in the most significant changes in the patterns of imports between periods; see Lawall 1995, 284–92.

of the century, at which time there is a significant increase in the proportion of Chian imports compared to others, followed by a decrease in the relative number of Chian jars arriving in the last decades of the century.

The evidence from Gordion is problematic on account of more dramatic changes in the overall importation of Greek amphoras to the site during the fifth century.[66] From the late sixth century to *c.* 475, there are sixty-seven datable fragments at Gordion, of which twenty-three (34 per cent) are from Chian jars. From 475 to 425 the overall number of datable fragments declines to thirteen, of which seven (54 per cent) are Chian. Although, in terms of percentages, this number is substantially higher than in the previous period, the small sample size makes such a figure unreliable. The last quarter of the century sees a slight increase in the total number of datable fragments – twenty – but only one of these is attributed to Chios. These figures may be summarised as follows: from the late sixth century to 425 Chios is one of the dominant exporters to Gordion, though there may be a decline in exports between 475 and 425; there is a definite decline in Chian exports to Gordion after 425 (Figure 5.2).

The interpretation of these figures requires some caution. Reconstruction of actual numbers of imported jars is impossible since there is no way of knowing what portion of the total has

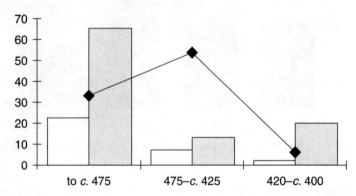

Figure 5.2 Numbers of Chian imports to Gordion (white columns) compared to total datable imports (grey columns) and the Chian imports expressed as a percentage of the total datable imports per period (line).

[66] Figures adapted from Lawall 1996.

been recovered. Estimation of the presence of one type relative to all other imports, however, is more accessible. In the cases of Athens and early fifth-century Gordion, the recovered sample is assumed to represent the original mix of imported types and, for that reason, is expressed as a percentage. An increase in this percentage could result from any of three scenarios: (1) the total volume of imports declined, but the volume of Chian imports remained the same or declined to a lesser extent than others; (2) the total volume of imports stayed the same, but Chian imports increased in volume; or (3) the total volume of imports increased, with Chian imports increasing to a greater extent than the others. In any of these scenarios, an increased Chian proportion requires increased interaction between the importer and Chios relative to other exporters and may even require greater frequency of imports in absolute terms.

These scenarios have the following implications when applied to the data from Athens and Gordion. At Athens there is no indication of change in the overall volume of amphora imports through the fifth century; the proportions of different types change, but at no time are amphoras themselves particularly rare. Given this apparent stability, and given the increased relative presence of Chian jars from *c.* 450/440 to *c.* 410, the actual volume of Chian shipments to Athens must have increased as well during this time and decreased after 410. At Gordion, on the other hand, there seem to be fewer Greek amphoras arriving between 475 and 400 than had arrived between 525 and 475. Between 475 and 425, Chios seems to maintain her strong position relative to other importers, though the sample size is quite small. Given the overall decline in shipments to Gordion, either the actual volume of Chian shipments to Gordion remained roughly constant or decreased, but at a lesser rate than other exporters' shipments decreased. Comparing the periods 475–425 and 425–400, the overall volume of imports to Gordion shows little change; and yet Chios is no longer a major presence at Gordion relative to other exporters. Given the apparent consistency of import volume from 475–400 at Gordion, the Chian loss of relative presence after 425 must translate into an absolute decline in Chian shipments to Gordion. This decline may have begun considerably earlier.

These changes in evidence provided by importing cities can also be used to document changes in Chian production and exportation.

When the indication of declining Chian imports at Gordion *c.* 425–400 is considered alongside indications of declining Chian exports to Athens *c.* 410, a general decline in Chian production and exportation in the late fifth century seems very likely. The increase in Chian imports at Athens *c.* 450–410 should be considered alongside the reduction in overall imports to Gordion between 475 and 425. The declining interaction, however, between Gordion and the Aegean may start well before the time when Chian imports at Athens increase, so the two events are unlikely to have counterbalanced one another. Instead, Chian production and exportation 450–410 (or a bit earlier?) may have increased in scale to account for the increased Chian presence in Athens. Of course, more such data from more sites in different regions would permit greater certainty in this question of changes in the actual volume of Chian production. The possibilities raised thus far, however, provide a useful starting point for considering the economic history of fifth-century Chios in greater detail.

Chian local economic history

Three periods of significant transformation of Chian amphora production and exportation can be proposed using the evidence of shape development, markings, and quantitative data on Chian exports. The first point of change occurs *c.* 480 with the shift away from the C/1 variant to the C/2 and the concurrent disappearance of the C/1's neck-marking system. This point may mark the beginning of a decline in Chian exports towards Persia, but otherwise the change in appearance of the jars is not accompanied by changes in the scale of Chian exports. The second transformation occurs over a longer period, from roughly 450 to 425. During this period, the amphoras evolve from the C/2 to the C/3 variant, the straight-neck type is introduced, and stamps and lettered dipinti begin to reappear. On the basis of the Athenian evidence, Chian exports appear to increase in volume during this period. Finally, the last quarter of the century sees a continued use of the marking systems that have emerged, but, based on evidence from Gordion and Athens, this period sees a decline in the Chian share of the Aegean amphora trade and perhaps a decline in the actual volume of exports. Although the dates of these periods do not coincide precisely with major shifts in the numismatic and textual evidence for Chian political and economic history, the co-ordination is surprisingly close and bears close consideration. A selective survey of Chian local history follows.[67]

Until 499, various pro-Persian activities can be attributed to Chios. The Chians turned over the Lydian Pactyes to Persia in return for the region of Atarneus on the mainland adjacent to Lesbos (Herodotus, 1. 161), and when the Phocaeans fleeing Persia *c.* 540 tried to buy a place of refuge on the Oenussae islands, the Chians refused their offer (Hdt. 1. 165). Late in the 520s, with the accession of Darius and Persia's acquisition of the Phoenician fleet, Chios came under more direct administrative control from Persia and must have paid some portion of the 400 talents tribute levied from 'the Ionians' (Hdt. 3. 90; Aeschylus, *Persians*, 883).[68] Nevertheless, in 513 the Chian tyrant Strattis is attested among those owing their power to Darius (Hdt. 4. 137), and even as late as 499, Megabates seems to have used Chios as a resting place on his way to attack Naxos (Hdt. 5. 33).[69] Chios, however, did come to the aid of Paeonian exiles fleeing Phrygia (Hdt. 5. 98), and then made a substantial and substantive contribution to the Ionian fleet (Hdt. 6. 8–16). After the disaster at Lade, Chios was 'netted' by the Persians (Hdt. 6. 30), and sometime before 479 Strattis was reinstalled as tyrant.

In 479, there was a transition from the often pro-Persian orientation to a more pro-Athenian stance. In that year, a group of Chians, having tried unsuccessfully to assassinate Strattis, tried to convince the Greek fleet to advance beyond Delos (Hdt. 8. 132). After the battle of Mycale, Chios entered the Delian League as

---

[67] For more detailed consideration of many issues glossed over here, see Quinn 1981, Barron 1986, Roebuck 1986; for summaries of debates concerning the epigraphic sources, see Meiggs and Lewis 1989. For a recent study of Chian coinage, with significant revisions to earlier chronologies, see Hardwick 1993.

[68] According to Herodotus (1. 142), the Ionians of the islands did not initially fear Cyrus, since he lacked a fleet. Lateiner (1982, 132) sees this sum as potentially oppressive, contrasting it with later sums from the Athenian tribute lists. If Chios, Samos and Lesbos all contributed to the Persian tribute as they did not in the case of the Delian League, the Athenian demands on the remaining cities would have been higher.

[69] The connection here, however, could be with Miletos (Hdt. 1. 18); Chios was essentially supporting the efforts of Aristagoras.

a contributor of ships rather than cash (Hdt. 9. 107; Thucydides, 1. 19). By 465, Chios had an arrangement with Athens whereby certain cases involving Athenians and Chians would be heard in Athens.[70] The Chian fleet, meanwhile, was an active ally of Athens: in 440 it supported Athens against Samos (Thuc. 1. 116 and 117), in 430 it accompanied Pericles to the Argolid (Thuc. 2. 56), and between 425 and 415 Chian ships are attested at Pylos (Thuc. 4. 13), Mende and Scione (Thuc. 4. 129), Melos (Thuc. 5. 84) and Sicily (Thuc. 6. 31).

In this later period, however, around 425, anti-Athenian sentiments appeared. 'Friends among the Chians' contributed to Sparta's war chest perhaps in 427,[71] while in the same year Sparta executed other Chians (Thuc. 3. 32). Chios built fortifications against Athenian wishes in 425 (Thuc. 4. 51); however, these were soon taken down. Both events suggest the presence of two relatively strong, competing interests in Chios: pro-Athenian and pro-Spartan (and Persian?).

The latter group gained the upper hand after the Sicilian disaster. A Chian envoy joined Tissaphernes' envoy encouraging Spartan action in 413/2 (Thuc. 8. 5). When Chios decided to revolt in 412, it was the oligarchs of the Boule, against the wishes of the *demos*, who made the decision (Thuc. 8. 14). Athenian retaliation for the revolt, however, brought widespread destruction of Chian agriculture accompanied by a slave revolt (Thuc. 8. 40).

While it cannot be argued that each of these events is echoed in Chian amphora exports, certain 'events' in the two records seem related, and a third source, numismatic evidence, adds significance to these relationships. Two periods in particular emerge as especially important in co-ordinating the various sources: the shift to a consistently pro-Athenian position *c.* 480, and the apparent conflict between *demos* and the oligarchs between 430 and 412.

Chian trade with both Persian and Greek regions was extremely active before 480. Pro-Persian interests, perhaps attributable to Chian oligarchs (Balcer 1985), may have facilitated the eastern exports. These sentiments, however, do not seem to have impeded trade with Greek centres. Chian coinage before 480 has a similarly

[70]   Meiggs and Lewis 1989, no. 31; the decree concerns Phaselis, but refers to an existing arrangement with Chios.
[71]   Meiggs and Lewis 1989, no. 67, and discussed by Barron 1986, 101 n. 62.

wide distribution (Hardwick 1993, 220, fig. 2). It seems likely that Chian trade with Persia is attributable in part to the need to raise funds for paying tribute and rents on royal lands. This need would be particularly true after *c.* 520, around the same time that Chian amphoras begin to arrive at Gordion in significant numbers. The extensive Chian trade with non-Persian centres, the apparent continuity of production and exports after the sack of 493, and the continued ability to pay tribute with the reassessments after the revolt (Hdt. 6. 43), all suggest that Persian administration did not adversely affect Chian trade.

Changes that occur *c.* 480 do not, on the whole, involve the scale of amphora exports or the distribution of Chian coins (Hardwick 1993, 221, fig. 3). Instead, the changes pertain to the appearances of the jars and the coins. At the same time Chios shifts political interests more firmly in support of other Greek cities, especially Athens. All of these changes may be related to one another as follows. Chian C/2 jars differ from the preceding form by emphasising precisely those morphological details that advertise the Chian origin of the jars: a heavier rim and a more dramatically bulged neck. In abandoning the C/1 decoration, the C/2 variant drops an attribute that had connected its appearance to other Ionian amphora types, such as the wide-banded Klazomenian amphoras and the so-called ps.-Samian type, which often carried a circle dipinto on the neck. The C/2's appearance may indicate a greater uniformity of meaning, referring to Chios as a single unit, to the island itself as the producer. A similarly specific reference to Chios appears slightly earlier *c.* 490 in both the adoption of an image of the C/2 amphora as a consistent attribute on Chian coins and the abandonment of coin imagery related to other Greek cities (Hardwick 1993, 214).

The importance of this shift away from similarities with other cities' economic artifacts (coins and amphoras) lies in the idea of archaic and classical Greek aristocracies as having created and maintained various connections between cities and between wide-ranging landholdings.[72] If the Chian oligarchs can be seen as part

---

[72] Cook 1961; Balcer 1985; Murray 1980, 192–203; and Bravo 1977 give an impression of the internationalism of the aristocracy; Herman 1987 presents the continuing importance of aristocratic connections through the Hellenistic period.

of a wider Ionian aristocracy, with landholdings on the mainland as well as on the island, and with connections to other cities, then the move away from similarities to other east Greek amphoras and coin types would fit well with a declining political influence of this aristocracy. The aristocrats would have still owned land and controlled agricultural production and exportation, but the iconography of commerce shifted to reflect changing political realities. The *demos*, rather than the oligarchy, was controlling policy, and the amphoras and coins now proclaim their 'Chianness' rather than any additional element of aristocratic connections.

The subsequent period of 'democratic' amphora production continues until *c.* 440, or somewhat later, when new marking systems appear.[73] Late in this period, in the third quarter of the fifth century, exports seem to increase in scale. Such evidence of prosperity is in keeping with Thucydides' comments on the prosperity of Chios just before the revolt of 412. This increased scale of exports may be related to the introduction of new marking systems *c.* 440–430; more complex organisation of commerce often follows increased scale of activity (for example, see Johnson 1982). These changes in the amphoras need not be seen as breaking with past practice. Similarly, a series of coins showing C/3 amphoras, dated by Hardwick to 435–425, may be seen as a continuation of the earlier series starting in the 480s (Hardwick 1993, 214–16).

Such continuity, however, ends *c.* 430. At this point the straight-neck amphora type appears, perhaps overlapping with C/3 production until *c.* 425. Another significant break occurs: Chios ceases minting sometime after 425 until 412; Hardwick (1993, 216) relates this break to the Athenian Standards Decree. At this same time, the pro-Spartan aristocrats re-emerge as a political force, with sporadic success from 427 to 414, but with sufficient power

---

[73] This period in Chian amphora history is the only one that has received extended attention to date. Attention has centred entirely on the effects of the Athenian decree concerning standards, whose date is problematic (Mattingly 1987, 1992, and 1993; Lewis 1987). As I argued earlier (1995, 292–302; cf. Grace 1979a, text with figs 44, 48, 49; Mattingly 1981; Wallace 1984, 1986; Barron 1986, 96–100), the relationship between Chian amphoras and this decree has yet to be demonstrated. Known measurements do not show significantly more convenient capacities for the C/3 jars than for the C/2 jars, and the evidence of tally graffiti found on stamped jars suggests that stamps did not provide a guarantee of capacity.

to guide policy in 413 and 412. The situation is similar to that of
c. 480, but the sequence of events is reversed; now, the aristocracy gains power, markings on amphoras increase in use (despite
the apparent decline in exports), and the shapes of the newly introduced amphoras resemble other Aegean types.[74] Significantly, in
412, the new, briefly used, Chian electrum stater again brings
Chian coin iconography together with other Greek cities (Hardwick 1993, 218). Aristocratic political power is again associated
with more outward-looking commercial iconography.

There is, however, a point of contrast with 480 as well. After
the Athenian attack, helped by Chian slaves, in 412, Chios'
amphora production and exports seem to decline considerably.
Given Thucydides' praise (8. 24) for Chian agrarian prosperity
before the revolt, the decline in exports likely resulted from this
ravaging of agricultural land. The distribution of Chian coinage,
after 412, is quite restricted (Hardwick 1993, 221, fig. 4). Without
the freight of amphoras to distribute, Chios' economic strength
could not be rebuilt simply by increasing the supply of coins.

A new positivism?

Close attention to Chian amphoras has added considerably greater
detail to interpretations of Chian politics and trade in the late
sixth and fifth centuries. Evidence from amphoras helped identify
a period of internal economic change on Chios *c.* 480, even without
significant changes in resulting Chian trade. The evidence from
exports remains generally constant, and would have masked the
extent of internal change without the attributes of the amphoras
themselves drawing attention to internal political and ideological
factors. The economic prosperity of Chios down to *c.* 425 is
attested by textual and numismatic sources, but the amphoras
provided evidence that this prosperity eventually reached such an
extent that organisational changes occurred. With the subsequent
political and economic changes from *c.* 425 to *c.* 410, the connection between aristocratic power and changes in the appearance of
'economic artifacts', amphoras and coins, reappears, just as was

---

[74] The straight-neck amphoras look very much like the Solokha II type,
see Lawall 1995, 234–44; and Garlan and Dougléri-Intzessiloglou 1990.

noted *c.* 480. This iconographic impact of internal political tension could not be noted without close attention to amphoras and should be explored further for other amphora-producing states. Finally, the truly detrimental effects of the Athenian reaction to the Chian revolt becomes clear only through the amphoras, and they also provide needed guidance for interpreting the restoration of Chian minting.

This case-study and the general method employed may be open to similar charges of positivism as have been brought against fineware studies (and many other fields of archaeology): an over-reliance on unreliable quantitative data, and a dependence on unproved correlations between political changes and archaeological evidence. The conclusions presented here may be overly optimistic. However, exploration of how amphoras can contribute to the study of ancient trade is required before significant progress (as opposed to non-constructive criticism) can occur in the archaeology of economic and political history. An initial sense of optimism is, therefore, necessary and forgivable so long as it generates discussion of previously ignored issues and questions and, thereby, encourages gathering of new evidence. As more data are collected, then models and hypotheses can be refined, and initial positivism can give way to realism.

Bibliography

Abramov, A. P. and Maslennikov, A. A. (1991), 'Amfory V b. do n. e. iz raskopok poseleniya na myse Zyuk', *SovArch* 3: 234–48.

Alekseeva, E. (1990), 'Ranneye poseleniye na meste Anapy (VI–V vv. do n.z.)', *KSIA* 197: 19–30.

Alexandrescu, P. (1966), 'Necropola tumulara: Sapaturi 1955–1961', in E. M. Condurachi (ed.), *Histria II* (Bucarest), 133–294.

Anderson, J. (1954), 'Excavations on the Kofiná Ridge, Chios', *BSA* 49: 123–72.

Arafat, K. and Morgan, C. (1989), 'Pots and potters in Athens and Corinth: a review', *OJA* 8: 311–41.

—— (1994), 'Athens, Etruria and the Heuneburg: mutual misconceptions in the study of Greek–barbarian relations', in I. Morris (ed.), *Classical Greece: Ancient Histories and Modern Archaeologies* (New Directions in Archaeology; Cambridge), 108–34.

Balcer, J. M. (1985), 'Fifth-century BC Ionia: a frontier redefined', *REA* 87: 31–42.

Barron, J. (1986), 'Chios in the Athenian empire', in J. Boardman and C. Vaphopoulou-Richardson (eds), *Chios: A Conference at the Homereion* (Oxford), 89–103.

Bingen, J. (1967), 'L'établissement du IXe siècle et les nécropoles du secteur ouest 4', *Thorikos* 2: 25–46.

Boardman, J. (1967), *Greek Emporio* (London).

—— (1988), 'Trade in Greek decorated pottery', *OJA* 7: 27–33.

Brashinskii, I. (1980), *Grecheskiy Keramicheskiy Importy na Nizhnem Donu v V–III vv. do n.e* (Leningrad).

—— (1984) *Metody Issledovaniya Antichnoy Torgovli* (Leningrad).

Bravo, B. (1977), 'Remarques sur les assises sociales, les formes d'organisation et la terminologie du commerce maritime grec à l'époque archaïque', *DHA* 3: 1–59.

Buzoianu, L. (1991), 'Tipuri de amfore de se. VI–IV a Chr. descoperite la Tomis', *Pontica* 24: 75–96.

Cook, J. (1961), 'The problem of classical Ionia', *PCPS* 7: 9–18.

Cook, R. M. (1987), ' "Artful crafts": a commentary', *JHS* 107: 169–71.

Dimitriu, S. (1966), 'Cartierul de locuinte din zona de vest a cetatii, în epoca arhaica: Sapaturi 1955–1960', in E. M. Condurachi (ed.), *Histria II* (Bucarest), 19–132.

Doger, E. (1992), *Antik çagda Amphoralar* (Izmir).

Dupont, P. (1982), 'Amphores commerciales archaïques de la Grèce de l'Est', *PdP* 37: 193–208.

—— (1983), 'Classification et détermination des provenances des céramiques archaïques grecques orientales d'Istros, rapports préliminaires', *Dacia* 27: 19–93.

Ebert, M. (1913), 'Ausgrabungen auf dem Gute Maritzyn Gouv. Cherson. (Süd-Russland)', *PZ* 5: 1–80.

Eiseman, C. and Ridgway, B. (1987), *The Porticello Shipwreck: a Mediterranean Merchant Vessel of 415–385 BC* (College Station).

Empereur, J.-Y. (1982), 'Les anses d'amphores timbrées et les amphores: aspects quantitatifs', *BCH* 106: 219–33.

Fraser, P. M. (1972), *Ptolemaic Alexandria* (Oxford).

Garlan, Y. (1983), 'Greek amphorae and trade', in P. Garnsey, K. Hopkins and C. Whittaker (eds), *Trade in the Ancient Economy* (Berkeley), 27–35.

—— (1986), 'Quelques nouveaux ateliers amphoriques à Thasos', in J.-Y. Empereur and Y. Garlan (eds), *Recherches sur les amphores greques* (*BCH* suppl. 13), 201–76.

——(1988), *Vin et Amphores de Thasos* (École Française d'Athènes Coll. Sites et Monuments 5, Athens).

Garlan, Y. and Dougléri-Intzessiloglou, A. (1990), 'Vin et amphores de Péparéthos et d'Ikos', *BCH* 114: 361–89.

Gauer, W. (1975), *Die Tongefässe aus dem Brunnen unterm Stadion-nord-wall und im sud-ost Gebiet* (Olympische Forschungen 8; Berlin).

Gill, D. W. J. (1994), 'Positivism, pots and long-distance trade', in I. Morris (ed.), *Classical Greece: Ancient Histories and Modern Archaeologies* (New Directions in Archaeology; Cambridge), 99–107.

Gjerstad, E., Lindros, J., Sjöqvist, E. and Westholm, A. (1935), *The Swedish Cyprus Expedition, Finds and Results of the Excavations in Cyprus, 1927–31*, 2 vols (Stockholm).

Grace, V. (1934), 'Stamped amphora handles found in 1931–1932', *Hesperia* 3: 197–310.

—— (1953), 'Wine jars', in C. Boulter, 'Pottery from the mid-fifth century from a well in the Athenian Agora', *Hesperia* 22: 101–10.

—— (1971), 'Samian amphoras', *Hesperia* 40: 52–95.

—— (1979a), *Amphoras and the Ancient Wine Trade* (Agora Picture Book 6) (rev. edn, Princeton).

—— (1979b), 'Exceptional amphora stamps', in G. Kopcke and M. Moore (eds), *Studies in Classical Art and Archaeology* (Locust Valley), 117–29.

Grace, V. and Savvatianou-Petropoulakou, M. (1970), 'Les timbres amphoriques grecs', *EAD* 27: 277–382.

Grakov, B. (1935), 'Tara i khraneniye sel'skokhozyaystvennykh produktov v klassicheskoy Gretsii 6th–4th v. do n. e.', *IGAIMK* 108: 147–83.

Grandjean, Y. (1992), 'Contribution a l'établissement d'une typologie des amphores thasiennes, le matérial amphorique du quartier de la porte du Silène', *BCH* 116: 541–84.

Hannestad, L. (1988), 'Athenian pottery in Etruria *c.* 550–470 BC', *Acta Archaeologica* 59: 113–30.

Hardwick, N. (1993), 'The coinage of Chios from the VIth to the IVth century BC', in T. Hackens and G. Moucharte, *Proceedings of the XIth International Numismatic Congress*, vol. 1 (Louvain-la-Neuve), 211–21.

Herman, G. (1987), *Ritualized Friendship and the Greek City* (Cambridge).

Holladay, J. (1982), *Tell el-Maskhuta: Preliminary Report on the Wadi-Tumilat Project 1978–1979* (Cities of the Delta, pt. 3; Malibu).

Johnson, G. (1982), 'Organizational structure and scalar stress', in C. Renfrew, M. Rowlands and B. Abbott Segraves (eds), *Theory and Explanation in Archaeology* (New York), 389–421.

Johnston, A. W. (1972), 'The rehabilitation of Sostratos', *Parola del Passato* 27: 416–23.

—— (1979), *Trademarks on Greek Vases* (Warminster).

—— (1981), 'Imported Greek storage amphorae', in V. Karageorghis *et al.* (eds), *Excavations at Kition IV, the Non-Cypriot Pottery* (Nicosia), 37–44.

—— (1982), 'Two numerical notes', *ZPE* 49: 205–9.

—— (1985), 'Etruscans in the Greek vase trade', in M. Cristofani *et al.* (eds), *Il commercio etrusco arcaico, Atti dell' incontro di studio 5–7 dicembre 1983* (Rome).

—— (1987), 'Amasis and the vase trade', in *Papers on the Amasis Painter and his World* (Malibu), 25–140.

—— (1990), 'Aegina, Aphaia-Tempel XIII: the storage amphoras', *AA*: 37–64.

—— (1993), 'Greek vases in the marketplace', in T. Rasmussen and N. Spivey (eds), *Looking at Greek Vases* (repr. edn, Cambridge), 203–31.

Kats, S. and Monachov, V. (eds 1992), *Grecheskie Amphory* (Saratov).
Knigge, U. (1976), *Der Südhügel* (Kerameikos. Ergebnisse der Ausgrabungen 9; Berlin).
Kryzhitskii, S., Buiskikh, S., Burakov, A. and Otreshko, B. (1989), *Sel'skaya okruga Ol'vii* (Kiev).
Kutaysov, V. A. (1990), *Antichnyi gorod Kerkinitida, VI–IIvv.do n.e* (Kiev).
Lambrino, M. (1938), *Les Vases Archaiques d'Histria* (Bucharest).
Lang, M. (1956), 'Numerical notation on Greek vases', *Hesperia* 25: 1–24.
—— (1976), *Graffiti and Dipinti* (The Athenian Agora, 21; Princeton).
Lateiner, D. (1982), 'The failure of the Ionian revolt', *Historia* 31: 129–60
Lawall, M. (1995), *Transport Amphoras and Trademarks: Imports to Athens and Economic Diversity in the Fifth c. BC* (Ann Arbor).
—— (1996), 'Gordion: the imported transport amphoras 600–400 BC', Paper delivered at the Annual Meeting of the Archaeological Institute of America, Dec. 27–30.
Leipunskaya, N. (1981), *Keramicheskaya tara iz Ol'vii* (Kiev).
Lewis, D. (1987), 'The Athenian coinage decree', in I. Carradice (ed.), *Coinage and Administration in the Athenian and Persian Empires* (British Archaeological Reports Int. Ser. 343), 53–63.
Mantsevich, A. (1987), *Kurgan Solokha* (Leningrad).
Mattingly, H. (1981), 'Coins and amphoras: Chios, Samos and Thasos in the fifth c. BC', *JHS* 101: 78–81.
—— (1987), 'The Athenian Coinage Decree and the assertion of empire', in I. Carradice (ed.), *Coinage and Administration in the Athenian and Persian Empires* (BAR Int. Ser. 343), 65–71.
—— (1992), 'Epigraphy and the Athenian empire', *Historia* 51 (2): 129–38.
—— (1993), 'New light on the Athenian standards decree (*ATL* II, D14)', *Klio* 75: 99–102.
Meiggs, R. and Lewis, D. (1989), *A Selection of Greek Historical Inscriptions to the End of the Fifth Century BC* (rev. edn, Oxford).
Morel, J.-P. (1989), 'Les amphores et les autres céramiques (sur quelques problèmes amphoriques)', in *Amphores romaines et histoire économique: dix ans de recherche* (Collection de l'école française de Rome, 114; Rome), 523–7.
Munn, M. L. Z. (1983), *Corinthian Trade with the West in the Classical Period* (Ann Arbor).
Murray, O. (1980), *Early Greece* (Stanford).
Mylonas, G. (1975), *To dutikon Nekrotapheion tis Eleusinos* (Athens).
Nicolaïdou-Patera, M. (1987), 'Prota mnimata apo mia poli tis Pieridas koiladas', *To Arkaiologiko Ergo sti Makedonia Kai Thraki* 1: 343–52.
Okhotnikov, S. B. (1990), *Nizhneye Podnestrov'ye v VI–V vv.do n.e.* (Kiev).
Onayko, N. (1960), 'Antichnyi import na territorii Srednego Pridneprov'ya (VII–V vv.do n.e.)', *SovArch*: 25–41.
—— (1980), *Arkhaicheskiy Torik: Antichnyi gorod na severo-vostoke Ponta* (Moscow).

Osborne, R. (1996), 'Pots, trade and the archaic Greek economy', *Antiquity* 70: 31–44.

Parker, A. J. (1992), *Ancient Shipwrecks of the Mediterranean and the Roman Provinces* (BAR Int. Ser. 580).

Perrault, J. (1986), 'Céramiques et échanges: les importations attiques au Proche-Orient du VIe au milieu du Ve siècle av. J.C.: Les données archéologiques', *BCH* 110: 145–75.

Pharmakovskyi, B. V. (1929), *Roskopivannya Ol'vii r.1926* (Odessa).

Poutouridze, R. (1990), 'Les vases céramiques de Vani aux Ve–IVe siècles', in O. Lordkipanidze and P. Lévêque (eds), *Le Pont-Euxin vu par les Grecs* (Besançon), 273–4.

Quinn, T. (1981), *Athens and Samos, Lesbos and Chios: 478–404 BC* (Manchester).

Roberts, S. (1986), 'The Stoa Gutter Well: a late archaic deposit in the Athenian Agora', *Hesperia* 55: 1–74.

Roebuck, C. (1986), 'Chios in the sixth century BC', in J. Boardman and C. Vaphopoulou-Richardson (eds), *Chios: A Conference at the Homereion* (Oxford), 81–8.

Roller, L. (1987), *Nonverbal Graffiti, Dipinti, and Stamps* (Gordion Special Studies, 1; Philadelphia).

Sarikakis, Th. (1986), 'Commercial relations between Chios and other Greek cities in antiquity', in J. Boardman and C. Vaphopoulou-Richardson (eds), *Chios: A Conference at the Homereion* (Oxford), 121–31.

Seifert, M. and Yalçin, Ü. (1995), 'Milet'te arkeometrik arastirmalar', *Arkeometri Sonuçlari Toplantisi Ankara* 1994: 15–38.

Seltman, C. (1977), *Greek Coins* (2nd edn, London).

Shelov-Kovedjaev, T. V. (1986), 'Histoire et état actuel de l'épigraphie céramique grecque (amphores et tuiles) en Union Soviétique', in J.-Y. Empereur and Y. Garlan (eds), *Recherches sur les amphores grecques* (*BCH* suppl. 13), 9–29.

Sherwin-White, A. (1978), *Ancient Cos* (Hypomnemata 51; Göttingen).

Sirbu, V. (1993), 'Nouvelles considerations générales concernant l'importation des amphores grecques sur le territoire de la Roumanie (les 6e–1er sièc. av. n. è)', *Pontica* 16: 43–67.

Slaska, M. (1985), 'Le anfore da trasporto a Gravisca', in M. Cristofani *et al.* (eds), *Il commercio etrusco arcaico, Atti dell'incontro di studio 5–7 dicembre 1983* (Rome), 19–21.

Talcott, L. (1935), 'Attic black glazed stamped ware and other pottery from a fifth-century well', *Hesperia* 4: 477–523.

Tsaravopoulos, A. (1986), 'E archaia poli tis Chiou', *Horos* 4: 124–44.

Vallet, G. and Villard, F. (1963), 'Ceramique grecque et histoire économique', in P. Courbin (ed.), *Etudes Archéologiques* (Paris), 205–17.

—— (1964), *Megara Hyblaea II: la céramique archaïque* (Paris).

Vickers, M. (1985), 'Artful crafts: the influence of metalwork on Athenian painted pottery', *JHS* 105: 108–28.

Voigtländer, W. (1982), 'Funde aus der Insula westlich des Buleuterion in Milet', *IstMitt* 32: 30–173.

Wallace, M. (1984), 'Texts, amphoras, coins, standards and trade', *Ancient World* 10: 11–14.

—— (1986), 'Progress in measuring amphora capacities', in J.-Y. Empereur and Y. Garlan (eds), *Recherches sur les amphores grecques* (*BCH* suppl. 13), 87–94.

Whitbread, I. (1995), *Greek Transport Amphorae: A Petrological and Archaeological Study* (British School at Athens, Fitch Laboratory Occasional Paper, 4; Athens).

Williams, C. K. (1978), 'Corinth 1977: Forum Southwest', *Hesperia* 47: 1–39.

—— (1979), 'Corinth 1978: Forum Southwest', *Hesperia* 48: 105–44.

Williams, C. K. and Fisher, J. (1976), 'Corinth 1975: Forum Southwest', *Hesperia* 45: 99–162.

Zeest, I. (1960), *Keramicheskaya Tara Bospora* (*MIA* 83; Moscow).

6

The grain trade of Athens in the fourth century BC

Michael Whitby

It used to be widely accepted that Athens at the height of its power in the fifth and fourth centuries BC had regularly to import very substantial quantities of grain to provide for the population of Attica. In this respect Athens differed from all other Greek *poleis*, and this abnormal dependency upon foreign production was held to explain aspects of Athenian actions abroad – indeed to build up a notion of an Athenian foreign policy. Scholars might differ about the starting date of this process, whether the imbalance between home production and consumption was already in existence in the time of Solon, because of his ban on the export of produce other than olive oil, and whether the Peisistratid interest in the Hellespont area already demonstrated concern for the Pontic grain route, but there were no serious doubts about the importance of the trade. This traditional view, indeed, still has supporters.[1]

A decade ago, however, in a deliberately provocative article, Peter Garnsey challenged this theory and injected into the debate some justified scepticism and a new set of calculations (Garnsey 1985). Partly because of the force of Garnsey's demolition of the

---

[1] De Ste Croix 1972, 46–9; Davies 1978, 59; Casson 1994, 521. I am most grateful to Michel Austin, Darel Engen, Antony Keen and Graham Oliver for comments on this chapter. See Tsetskhladze (this volume) for further discussion.

more grandiose aspects of the previous consensus, and partly because of the greater sophistication of his statistics, his thesis has proved influential. The work of Gallant and Sallares follows his lead, though it should be noted that some of Sallares's conclusions on agricultural practice may weaken Garnsey's hypothesis (Garnsey 1988; Gallant 1991; Sallares 1991). The discussion has become increasingly technical, with detailed and precise calculations which could convey a false impression of the extent of our knowledge.[2] My wish is to redress the balance and to return the emphasis to the importance of the trade in grain,[3] partly by pointing to doubts about Garnsey's calculations and partly by stressing a factor that is largely ignored in the pursuit of more exact estimates for Athenian grain requirements – namely, the psychology of the market, something which still remains difficult to predict or regulate in modern economies. My discussion will focus on the fourth century, because that is where the bulk of the evidence for the grain trade lies, but my conclusions would also be relevant to the fifth century.[4]

Calculations of Athenian dependency upon foreign grain entail a complex series of assumptions about the carrying capacity, or potential productivity, of Attica, the size of the population to be supported, and the consumption levels of grain within that population: naturally we do not have anything like adequate evidence for any of these variables in the supply/demand equation, and so all reconstructions are necessarily houses of cards, but my feeling is that Garnsey's choice of guesses is not the most plausible – they all tend to support his conclusion that imported grain was less significant than previous scholars had believed.

First, Attic production of grain. To assess this, it is necessary to take views on the cultivable area of Attica, on the fallow regime,

---

[2] Foxhall and Forbes 1982; cf. also Sallares 1991, 1–2, who bemoans the lack of expertise among ancient historians. Bagnall and Frier 1994 preface their study with a useful caveat: 'we consider it essential that the seeming precision of our statistics not of itself induce false confidence in the result'.

[3] The sensible discussion of Austin 1994, 558–64, should be noted.

[4] I am most grateful to Antony Keen for supplying me with a copy of his paper (Keen 1993). I have considerable sympathy for his basic argument that Garnsey has underestimated the importance for Athens of imported grain, especially from the Pontus, in the fifth century.

and the actual productivity of the land that was devoted to grain. The Eleusis First Fruits inscription plays a part in this particular tangle. Garnsey's assessment that 'to inquire into the yield of the land in Ancient Greece is to pursue a phantom' is absolutely correct even when the investigation is restricted to Attica.[5] The total area of Attica in the fourth century was approximately 240,000 hectares. I would be happy with Garnsey's guess, extrapolated from the 1961 census, that somewhere between 35–40 per cent of ancient Attica was cultivable (Garnsey 1988, 92), with the proviso that some of this land was not suited to grain; Sallares concluded that 30 per cent of the surface area of Attica was available for grain, which in places was intercropped with olives, though the actual area sown would have varied from year to year in response to a number of factors (e.g. availability of labour, climate, general security) (Sallares 1991, 303, 309).

How much of this land was actually devoted to grain in any given year depends on the fallow regime, and the competing attractions of other crops. With regard to fallow, the debate concerns the predominance of a two- or a three-year cropping cycle; its inconclusive nature might suggest, unsurprisingly, that there was no single regime practised in Attica in antiquity. Garnsey argued that, because the dominance of the two-year system cannot be proven, it is incorrect to assume that only 50 per cent of cultivable land was available for grain – for him the implication is that up to two-thirds of cultivable land might be available under a three-year system. First, the regularity of fallow has to be defended, since Gallant has challenged the belief that bare fallow was customary because certain agricultural leases stipulate that fallow must be set aside (Gallant 1991, 56). Gallant's negative argument is weak, since a legal contract may well specify what is good normal practice: tenants might have eschewed fallow not because the practice was uncommon but because they were interested in short-term gain rather than the longer-term health of the owner's property. The case for fallow has been powerfully put by Sallares, who observed that the low-rainfall climate of Attica dictates that 'a not insignificant proportion of arable land is still left fallow', in spite

[5] Garnsey 1992. I am most grateful to Peter Garnsey for providing me with a copy of this article, which I would not otherwise have seen, and for other advice on this chapter in spite of its disagreement with his views.

of the improvements in crop rotation practices and irrigation technology (Sallares 1991, 303 (quotation); 385–6). Lack of rainfall meant that Attica was not well suited to growing leguminous grain crops (e.g. broad beans) as field crops, although a three-year cycle of winter wheat, winter legumes and fallow may have been practised in wetter parts of the ancient Mediterranean and tried in Attica (Sallares 1991, 300, 331, 382; cf. also Garnsey 1992, 151). Any attempt to increase production by more regular cropping would exhaust the soil; there was insufficient fertiliser or manure to counteract this decline, and with regard to grain such attempts to enrich the soil in this way might have had a negative impact, since the available types of grain were not capable of responding positively to these stimuli (Sallares 1991, 381, 385). Biennial fallow permitted long-term cropping of poor land in arid conditions by conserving moisture and allowing the recovery of nutrient levels; Sallares's arguments would suggest that in Attica grain was grown on arable land either one year in two or one year in three, probably with a preponderance towards the former.

Another relevant factor for Attic grain production is the impact of the presence of a very large conurbation, a question raised by Garnsey but not answered (Garnsey 1985, 70). This is discussed by Sallares in relation to modern land use in Attica, where the impact of the capital's wine consumption is apparent (Sallares 1991, 296–300); he concluded that ancient farmers with their overriding concern for self-sufficiency would not have responded in the same way. This, however, seems too negative, and the conurbation of Rome, admittedly far larger than the Athens–Piraeus complex, had an impact on farming practices in South Etruria and the Tiber valley. The small farmer in Attica, who for economic reasons had to sell his crop (whether grain or something else) soon after the harvest, and then repurchase food during the course of the year, might well have considered devoting part of his land to crops that produced the highest return. He could do so with some confidence, since the state attempted to ensure the supply of grain at reasonable prices. If neighbouring Megarians could see the agricultural opportunities presented by the Athenian market, an inference from the trading scene in Aristophanes' *Acharnians* 719–835, Athenians are not likely to have ignored the possibilities. Although the evidence is not extensive, there are allusions in the orators and inscriptions to gardens, *kepoi*, which will have been located on good land accessible to irrigation and so been in competition with grain for cultivable land.[6] Furthermore, some suitable land was either left uncultivated, or was poorly cultivated: Ischomachus, and his father before him, had made money from the purchase and improvement of such land (Xenophon, *Oeconomicus* 20. 22–6). Another relevant consideration is the existence of a certain number of rich landowners, men who would tend to own significant holdings of some of the better quality land which they might choose not to devote entirely to food production – or at least not to the production of food for human consumption, since the horse-owning elite will have had to allocate land for the maintenance of its animals.[7] Sheep and goats may have survived entirely through grazing non-arable land, but oxen are likely to have required feeding, so that some leguminous crops might have to be grown as fodder, or some of the barley production allocated to them. There is no point in attempting to quantify these animal needs, but neither should they be completely ignored.

Some of these factors might seem minimal, but overall they are cumulative. The assumption that no more than half the arable land was available for grain production in any particular year is plausible, and in practice rather less would have been sown because of the impact of leguminous crops, market gardening and animal husbandry. Thus, if 30 per cent of Attica is defined as arable, *no more than* 15 per cent of its surface area would be available for grain in any one year, and the actual figure was probably in the range 10–15 per cent. For Garnsey 15 per cent was the lowest of the three estimates used in his production calculations (Garnsey 1985, 72); he also provided calculations on the basis of 20 per cent and 25 per cent under grain, on the assumption that land was available for grain two years out of three, that vines and olives could occupy hill slopes and poorer arable, and that there was some spring or summer planting of cereals and legumes as well as the standard winter sowing (Garnsey 1985, 73 n. 30). These justifications for higher availability of land are dubious: olives and vines could grow on poorer land, and undoubtedly did, but as

[6]   For example, Demosthenes 47. 53. For discussion, see Osborne 1992, esp. 378–87.
[7]   'The useless animal par excellence in ancient Greece': Sallares 1991, 311. Osborne 1992 also notes the cultivation of flowers (385–6), and the existence of uncultivated temple lands (380–1).

Sallares has pointed out the olive is not naturally suited to the dry Mediterranean climate and performs much better on good land with a regular water supply (Sallares 1991, 304–9); certain crops might be planted in the spring, especially in years when the main crop appeared to be failing, but as Gallant has argued this strategy was only available if the landowner had surplus resources of seed and labour (Gallant 1991, ch. 5).

Finally, for this section, the actual productivity of this land. Here the starting point is the work of Jardé on cereals (Jardé 1925), who conjectured normal returns for wheat and barley in Greece in the range 8–12 and 16–20 hectolitres per hectare respectively. Certainly for wheat one would expect Attica to be at or below the lower end of the range since the quantity and distribution of rain was not particularly favourable, but Attica had a good reputation for barley according to Theophrastus: 'At Athens the barley produces more meal than anywhere else, since it is an excellent land for that crop' (Theophrastus, *History of Plants* 8. 8. 2). Jardé also made the point that overall yields in Attica were on the low side because the demand for food led to the cultivation of mediocre to marginal land (Jardé 1925, 53). Garnsey interpreted, or perhaps misinterpreted, this as an indication that Jardé was contemplating an upwards revision of his estimate for cultivated land in Attica (20 per cent cultivable, with half devoted to grain each year), which was much lower than Garnsey's preference (Garnsey 1985, 67–8). In fact it was an explanation for the low overall rate of return, and accords with the conclusions of Sallares that productivity would have been low, albeit from a comparatively high acreage (Sallares 1991, 79–80). The fact, too, that much grain was grown interspersed with other crops, for example olives or vines, would have reduced yields per hectare: intercropping was an insurance strategy adopted to ensure that land gave some return under almost all circumstances, but the price of reliability was an overall reduction in individual yields (Gallant 1991, 38–41).

A brief look at the Eleusis First Fruits inscription cannot be avoided, though its interpretation entails a fresh range of guesses.[8]

---

[8] *IG* II² 1672; Sallares 1991, 394, rightly stresses the limited value of this isolated item of evidence, but see Garnsey 1992, 147–8, for a sensible defence of attempts to exploit this inscription, however problematic it undoubtedly is.

The inscription is dated to 329/8, and by making reasonable assumptions about the relationship of offerings to overall production it is possible to deduce how much wheat and barley was produced in Attica and various dependent territories in this year. What is striking is the imbalance between barley and wheat production within Attica, with about ten times as much of the former – and the importance of the production of the islands of Lemnos, Imbros and Scyros which produced 2.75 times the small Attic crop of wheat and 80 per cent of the larger barley crop – one can understand the determination of the Athenians to regain these islands after the Peloponnesian War, and to retain possession in 392 when the Spartan–Persian peace proposals threatened to remove them again (Seager 1966, 172). Demosthenes could assume that provisions for a fleet would be available on Lemnos (4. 32). How much of the production of the islands, and other areas, could be demanded by the Athenians is unknown: Garnsey cites evidence for a tax on the islands' grain of 8.33 per cent in 375/4 (Garnsey 1988, 101–2), and, though this may have been an extraordinary additional impost, I suspect that the Athenians regularly tried to squeeze as much of the wheat, in particular, as they possibly could.

Notoriously, however, we do not know whether the harvest in 329/8 was good, bad or indifferent, but the harvest in Attica must have been poor unless the area devoted to grain was very small (5–6 per cent of the total area), or the yield very low (less than half the lower figures offered by Jardé), or a combination of the two. Although Garnsey states that 'It is abundantly clear that the harvest of 329/8 BC was inadequate to feed the population' (Garnsey 1988, 99), at Athens 329/8 is not known as a year of food crisis, in contrast to 330/29 and 328/7, so that things were perhaps not critical. Explanations for this might be that 329/8 was the 'on year' for the olive harvest, since Sallares has plausibly suggested that this biennial event would have an impact on shortages of other types of food (Sallares 1991, 308). Alternatively after the crisis of 330/29 the Athenians might have made substantial efforts to secure foreign supplies, and so managed to avoid a crisis in 329/8, but supplies were insufficient to sustain the population through a third poor harvest in succession. Another solution would be that the year was poor, but not disastrous in Attica, and that the overall production of Attica combined with that of the islands was not wildly out of line with the norm.

The second major variable in calculations of Athenian grain requirements is resident population, and for this the guesswork involves the same types of extrapolation from contested items of evidence as for Attic productivity. Garnsey's first working hypothesis was that there were in the range of 200–300,000 residents in Attica between 450 and 320; this he then refined to posit a peak of 250,000 in the fifth century shortly before the Peloponnesian War, with rather lower figures for the fourth century of a peak of 200,000 and 120–150,000 in 323/2 (Garnsey 1985, 70; 1988, 90). My view is that Garnsey's estimates for the fourth century are significantly too low, and that the focus of his discussion of Athenian grain requirements on the lower of these figures tends to obscure the level of need at more prosperous times. For the fourth-century Athenian population, the figures recorded for citizens at the end of the Lamian War in 322/1, and for citizens, metics and slaves in the census of Demetrius of Phaleron about a decade later, are of key importance. These have been discussed at considerable length, in particular by Hansen, who has attempted to incorporate assumptions about the functioning of democracy as a cross check; my views are broadly similar to his, though I would not attempt to calibrate the precise fluctuations of the population during the fourth century.

Adult male citizens provide the starting point. Demetrius' census recorded 21,000 Athenians, though it is disputed whether this represents all citizens, or only those liable to military service, or only those who met the new property qualification of 1,000 drachmas. At the end of the Lamian War (322/1) the citizen population is also put at 21,000 by Plutarch (*Phocion* 28. 7), but at 31,000 by Diodorus (18. 18. 5): both record 9,000 full citizens with property of over 2,000 drachmas, but diverge on the number disenfranchised by the Macedonian settlement – either 12,000 or 22,000. Although superficially Demetrius' figure might appear to corroborate Plutarch's 21,000, the opposite is probably the case since after the Lamian War there were very substantial movements of population around the Aegean world, with many impoverished Athenians being relocated in colonies in Thrace while the emerging Successor regimes in the east would have attracted others. Thus Diodorus' evidence that there were 31,000 male citizens in 322/1 is the more plausible; this is Hansen's conclusion, which Garnsey has conceded to have some force.[9] The level of Athenian casualties in the battles of the Lamian War is unknown, but at Chaeronea 1,000 citizens were killed and this loss would still have had some impact on citizen numbers fifteen years later.[10] Thus it seems reasonable to assess the numbers of adult male citizens at over 30,000 in the third quarter of the century, perhaps even as high as 35,000. This guess is higher than what is currently accepted, but it is worth noting the evidence for Athenian interest in cleruchies and other forms of overseas property owning in the fourth century (Hansen 1985, 70–2; Sallares 1991, 433 n. 72); similar evidence from the fifth century is taken as a sign that there had been a rapid expansion of population, and, if rapid annual population growth is accepted for the fifth century (Sallares 1991, 95–6), there is no reason why the survivors of the Peloponnesian War should not have contributed to quite a rapid population rebound.[11]

Calculations of the numbers of citizens required to run the *boule* and the surviving ephebic lists both lend some support to such a higher figure. For the *boule* Hansen concluded that its legal operation, namely to satisfy the requirement that no one could serve as president (*epistates*) more than once in their life, would entail a new cohort of 375–400 male citizens over the age of 30 each year;[12] it would appear that members of the *boule* tended to be relatively wealthy, of hoplite status, and might be nearer 40 than 30 in age. For ephebes, the combination of ephebic inscriptions with an estimate in Demosthenes (4. 21) produces an estimate of 500 for the average size of the annual age group of future hoplite soldiers.[13]

---

[9]   Hansen 1985, 28–36 for discussion of the problems of the figures, with a defence against further challenges in Hansen 1994; Garnsey 1988, 136.
[10]   Sallares 1991, 53, though noting the impact of casualties, nevertheless concludes that male citizens numbered fewer than 30,000 in the fourth century.
[11]   Sallares 1991, 95, who postulates a very high rate of growth in the fifth century to a citizen peak of 50–60,000, opts for a much more static situation in the fourth century; he does, however, also assert (p. 70) that stability of populations in the Mediterranean is not normal or to be expected.
[12]   Hansen 1985, 51–64 and 1994, 306–8, argues that these figures are too low and that a cohort closer to 600 is necessary.
[13]   Reinmuth 1971; Sallares 1991, 120–1; fuller discussion in Hansen 1985, 47–50, although he is reluctant to accept that ephebes represented future hoplites; also Hansen 1994, 302–4.

The evidence for the *diaitetai* or public arbitrators, men of hoplite status in their sixtieth year, is also pertinent: an inscription from 325/4 records 103 names from all tribes, while the fragmentary list from 330/29 suggests a total of 100–150.[14] By coincidence these respective age cohorts for men of hoplite status, of 500 aged 18, 400 aged about 35–40, and a few over 100 aged 59 produce a very respectable age profile for the population, one that accords with demographic tables derived from better-attested more modern populations.[15] These figures would suggest that the resident hoplite element in the fourth-century Athenian population numbered 15,000, or perhaps a bit more. The relative balance of thetes to hoplites in the fourth century is unknown, but there are likely to have been at least as many so that this series of calculations results again in a total adult male population of 30,000 or over. Extrapolating from adult males to total citizen numbers entails guesses for numbers of wives and children; the standard multiplier to apply is 4, which means that one can reach a citizen total of 120–140,000.[16]

Similar calculations have to be made with metic numbers, although the evidence is even less helpful.[17] In the census of Demetrius 10,000 metics were recorded; this presumably represents those metics who paid the metoikion tax, so that independent women were included as well as men, although the numbers of such women are likely to have been small (Whitehead 1977, 97;

[14] *IG* II[2] 1926, 2409, with Lewis 1955, 27–36. It might be relevant to the lower numbers on *IG* II[2] 1926 that the *diaitetai* of 325/4 would probably have served at Chaeronea, whereas those of 330/29 would not have been liable.
[15] For example the graph used by Osborne 1985, 196. Sallares is at pains to emphasise that the demography of ancient Greece was qualitatively different from all other demographic patterns, including that of ancient Rome (1991, 11, 42, 107–8), and stresses the problems of applying modern life tables to the ancient Greek world (pp. 112–16). Although I accept the validity of Sallares's argument, it is still of some comfort that the general shape of the Athenian hoplite population does not appear wildly out of line with expectations.
[16] Richard Alston suggested to me that Bagnall and Frier's work on Roman Egypt (1994) might imply that a slightly lower multiplier was applicable (though they accept that their Egyptian census figures probably understate actual family size: 1994, 67 n. 59). On the other hand, Sallares has stressed the distinctiveness of the Greek world (see n. 15). Thus, without great confidence, I apply the traditional multiplier of 4.
[17] 'Meagre and controversial' (Whitehead 1977, 97).

Hansen 1985, 31). This census was taken at a time when the attractions of living in Athens as a foreigner had been very substantially reduced, both by the political instability that followed Athenian defeat in the Lamian War and by the opportunities offered by the emerging Successor regimes – Athens was no longer the economic hub of the Aegean world. Metics were sensitive to such matters: for example, after the Social War in the 350s metic numbers appear to have been at a low level, since Xenophon thought it necessary to offer suggestions about making Athens a more attractive place for them (*Poroi* 2. 1–5). How many metics there were before the Lamian War, or indeed before Chaeronea is a guess, and there will have been considerable fluctuations. For the fifth century the evidence of Thucydides (2. 13. 6–7; 31. 1–2) for numbers of metic hoplites has been used to justify a metic total roughly two-thirds that of the male citizens, but these estimates have, not surprisingly, been challenged.[18] For the fourth century, it is generally accepted that numbers must have been lower than the pre-Peloponnesian War total even though Athens was still a major centre of wealth and trade. We also cannot tell how many of the metics were sufficiently regular or permanent residents of Attica to have established a household and family there, but the numbers were probably significant.[19] My estimate for total metic numbers before Alexander's conquest of the east is 30,000; this is a pure guess on the assumptions that between one-third and one-half of metics had moved away from Athens in the aftermath of the Lamian War and that the combined numbers of metic wives and children roughly equalled male numbers. I suspect that this total is on the low side for actual numbers of metics, but it may represent numbers present in Athens and requiring to be fed regularly. But this is no more than a compilation of guesses.

[18]   Duncan-Jones 1980; scepticism in Whitehead 1977, 98.
[19]   Sallares 1991, 60, bluntly stated that metic numbers did not require a high multiplier as they already included independent women. He also observed that metics were 'unlikely to have been a big drain on the agricultural production of Attica' (loc. cit.) since they had to purchase their food on the market; in a narrow sense this comment is valid if metics largely consumed imported food, but their presence in Attica was still relevant to the carrying capacity of Attica and the extent to which a shortfall in this had to be met by regular imports (an issue to which Sallares chose not to devote attention: 1991, 2).

Slaves are an even more contentious subject because of debates about the extent of slave-ownership in Athens, whether they were widely used in agriculture, how many were required when the mines were in full production, what percentage of Athenian households owned domestic slaves, and how many commercial enterprises there were on the lines of the sword workshop of Demosthenes' father or the shield workshop in Lysias' family. The number preserved for Demetrius' census, 400,000, is too fantastic to be countenanced, and it has been doubted whether slaves were even counted in the census (Hansen 1985, 30–1). So too the proposal of Hyperides (fr. 29), that slaves to the number of more than 150,000, both from the silver mines and from the rest of the country, should be liberated in the aftermath of Chaeronea, is discounted as exaggerated. The current tendency is to estimate slave numbers as being very low, with Garnsey and Sallares both adopting a total in the range 15–30,000, though in the case of Garnsey this relates to 323/2 when the overall Athenian population was at a low level;[20] if such numbers were roughly right, they would have made Hyperides' proposal completely ridiculous, especially since he was only dealing with male slaves. I share the view that slavery was a much more important aspect of many aspects of Athenian life than these low figures would suggest (de Ste Croix 1981, 140–7).

As with metics, slave numbers will have fluctuated very considerably, in line with the wealth and confidence of their Athenian and metic masters, and there is no evidence to indicate how high peak numbers might have been. Xenophon's discussion of a body of state slaves to be hired out in the silver mines (*Poroi* 4. 13–39) envisages the employment of very large numbers: he proposed modest beginnings, with 1,200 being purchased annually at the start to build up a force of 6,000 within five or six years, and 10,000 being the next stage (*Poroi* 4. 23), but his most ambitious suggestion was three slaves for each Athenian (4. 17), which would imply as many as 100,000 male slaves in public ownership. This seems too fanciful, and Xenophon's argument about the scope for

---

[20]   These totals are not explicitly stated by either scholar, but can be inferred from the figures at Garnsey 1988, 90 (applying to 323/2), and Sallares 1991, 60 (the combined total for metics and slaves).

expansion in the mines and his recognition that overcrowding might become a problem (4. 3–7, 11–12, 39) suggest that he was aware that the grander elements of his scheme stretched credibility. On the other hand, bearing in mind the wide range of slave employment, female as well as male, on which his discussion does not touch, I am encouraged to propose a substantially higher figure than that of Garnsey and Sallares – though it should be noted that I am discussing the peak, for which Garnsey does not offer a total: my guess for the slave total would be around 100,000, though I accept that there is no cogent defence for any particular figure.

Combining these various guesses would provide a total resident population of Attica in the mid-fourth century in the range 250,000 to 300,000, (cf. de Ste Croix 1972, 46 n. 88 for the same guess) and at times probably towards the upper end; about half the population were citizens, the remainder metics or slaves. This is right at the upper end of Garnsey's original working hypothesis for the Athenian population, but significantly larger than his subsequent downgrading to a fourth-century range of 120–200,000 (Garnsey 1985, 70; 1988, 90). On my guess the countryside of Attica was perhaps as densely settled as in 1961, when the Eparchy of Attica had a population density of 60 people/sq km (excluding Greater Athens) (Sallares 1991, 84).

The third major variable to be considered is the level of grain consumption. Garnsey proposed an average consumption of 175 kilograms of grain per person per year, which he described as a generous rate (Garnsey 1985, 72–3; 1988, 102–4). In this estimate Garnsey did not distinguish between wheat and barley, but it is clear that much of the grain will have been barley from the relatively large amount of it produced in Attica. Such blurring is not too important if discussions involve wheat and barley meal (*alphita*) by weight, since their calorific values are roughly the same according to modern calculations – though the difference in ancient perceptions of their relative food values was undoubtedly greater, partly because grain was measured by volume and a given measure of wheat is heavier than the same measure of barley or barley meal.[21] But distinctions become crucial when dealing with unprocessed barley, since the milling process whereby the barley hulls were removed would have entailed a weight loss of 30 per cent, or a bit more. While Garnsey's discussion of the food production of Attica naturally deals with quantities of unprocessed barley straight from the fields, his treatment of consumption involves barley meal (*alphita*): he treats the two products as equivalent, whereas on modern calculations the nutritional value of a kilo of barley is only about two-thirds that of barley meal.

In the ancient world, although the evidence is far from conclusive, there would appear to have been a sort of standard notion that 1 *choenix* of wheat per man per day was a proper ration, and that double the quantity of barley meal (*alphita*) might be substituted – barley was regarded as less nourishing, and was of lower status.[22] Slaves, women, children and the elderly would naturally have been allocated less in any notional distribution, although grain probably constituted a higher proportion of the diet of slaves than of citizens; if grain was providing the bulk of the protein requirement for these people, consumption levels would have had to be higher than the straight calorific value of the grain would suggest (Sallares 1991, 301). In terms of weight, these allowances for an adult male represent 0.839 kilo of wheat and 1.4 kilos of barley meal per day,[23] i.e. about 310 kilos of wheat and 510 kilos of barley meal per year (roughly 750 kilos of unprocessed barley). There is no doubt that these quantities provided more food than the normal active man required in calorific terms, assuming that he derived a reasonable portion of his energy require-

[21]   Cf. Rickman 1980, 5. In terms of volume, there is a calorific difference of 18 per cent Foxhall and Forbes 1982, 46 n. 15). Foxhall and Forbes also sensibly observe (1982, 46–7) that ancient milling processes are likely to have caused a significant reduction in the calorific values of the resulting barley meal, so that the modern caloric equivalence between wheat and barley meal must be treated with caution. Petersen 1995, 26, notes that the greater laxative effect of the fibre in barley somewhat reduces its nutritional effect, and, ibid. 32–6, reports the conclusions of a nineteenth-century investigation into the consumption of top-quality bread by the lower classes which decided that it would not be economical or nutritionally effective to encourage them to switch to coarser bread because of its perceived lesser value.

[22]   Foxhall and Forbes 1982, 55, 73; evidence tabulated at 86–9.

[23]   Weights taken from Foxhall and Forbes 1982, 86–7. The figures are more precise than most ancient measuring devices are likely to have been, and the annual figures extrapolated from these calculations are only intended to indicate an order of magnitude.

ments from other sources such as wine or olives; but even the Spartans confined on Sphacteria were supplied with a ration of 2 *choenikes* of barley meal, while their slaves on half rations received 1 *choenix* per day, as well as some wine and meat (Thucydides 4. 16. 1).[24]

At the other end of the scale we have a figure for the starvation ration provided to the Athenian prisoners in the Syracusan quarries, namely 0.5 *choenix* of *sitos* per day (Thucydides 7. 87. 2); although the type of grain is not specified, it was almost certainly barley meal, since wheat would not have been wasted on captives, and the captives could not have coped with unprocessed barley.[25] This prisoner ration has implications for Garnsey's calculations since at an annual rate it converts into about 128 kilos of barley meal, roughly 180 kilos of unprocessed barley.[26] Thus Garnsey's proposition that 175 kilograms of grain from the field, i.e. either wheat or unprocessed barley, was a reasonable average for Athenian consumption looks less than generous. Even the Spartan slaves on Sphacteria were receiving a ration equivalent to an annual figure of 256 kilos of barley meal, or 360 kilos of unprocessed barley. Another approach which suggests the same conclusion is by using the calculations in Foxhall and Forbes for the average wheat consumption of a 'typical household', where,

---

[24]   Petersen 1995, ch. 5, provides interesting comparative information on consumption rates in eighteenth- and nineteenth-century Britain, but direct comparison is virtually impossible because of the significant differences in diet (e.g. consumption of potatoes); his figures suggest consumption of wheat in the range 110–200 kilos per person per year for urban dwellers, with a decided bias towards the upper end of the range; a ration equivalent to 100 kilos of wheat per year was definitely at starvation level, whereas rural inhabitants had a substantially higher rate of consumption, in some cases over 260 kilos per person per year. As a rough estimate of consumption contemporary observers established the product of one Imperial or Winchester quarter of wheat per year, approx. 200 kilos; Petersen regards this as too high a figure for bread alone, but as a reasonable level if other bread products, such as rolls or fancy breads, are included (1995, 145–6).
[25]   Foxhall and Forbes 1982, 61–2; Plutarch, *Nicias* 29. 1, and Diodorus 13. 20 did specify barley, the latter barley meal.
[26]   This is reasonably in line with the nineteenth-century starvation ration of 100 kilos of wheat (see n. 27).

depending upon what assumptions were made, average consumption figures of 212 and 237 kilos of wheat per person per year were produced (Foxhall and Forbes 1982, 71–2). Foxhall and Forbes note reasons for believing that these figures are too high – namely, that the postulated consumption rate for children is too large and that the balance of individuals is weighted in favour of adults.[27] How far the figures should be scaled down is yet another guess, but, when barley is brought into the equation, there would also have to be a substantial countervailing increase in weight of grain per person to take account of the difference in nutritional value (real as well as perceived) between unprocessed wheat and barley.

It would be possible to present these calculations in tabular form with allowances for the different variable factors, but that would lend a spurious authority to what is no more than a collection of guesses, a very fragile house of cards. To my mind it would be more profitable to imagine the way in which the ordinary Athenian in the assembly might respond to speakers who stood up to debate the food supply: even the orators would not have access to such detailed knowledge,[28] while their audience would be influenced by much more basic considerations such as the prices in the market or their awareness about their own stocks and those of their neighbours and relatives. A 'feel good', or 'feel hungry' factor will have been a powerful influence, but one that cannot be quantified. Foxhall and Forbes make the pertinent observations that, in a society that lacked a ready reserve of grain in case estimates fell short of needs, 'the *most* needed to get by is much more important than the *least* needed to get by', and that estimates of need are likely to be much higher than actual consumption (Foxhall and Forbes 1982, 57 (authors' emphasis)). Garnsey estimated that under normal conditions Attic production could support 120–150,000 residents, with a further 20–25,000 fed from

[27] It is probably the case that the population estimates above also underestimate the number of children per household, since there had to be far more than two children per household to maintain even a stable population.

[28] For example, accurate figures for the total resident population may not have been readily available: Hansen 1985, 13.

the dependent territories such as Lemnos, Imbros and Scyros; this represented 75 per cent of his peak citizen total for the fourth century and almost 100 per cent of his total for 323/2 (Garnsey 1985, 73; 1988, 90 with 104). For Garnsey Athens did need to import grain, but except in a poor harvest the quantities were not enormous. My contention so far is that Garnsey has tended to overstate the productive capacity of Attica, and to underestimate by a significant margin both the resident population and its food requirements. I do not wish to offer precise figures,[29] but it seems that the traditional view holds: in a normal year the production of Attica and its dependent territories would probably not have fed more than half the resident population[30] so that the Athenians did have a substantial and continuing need for imported grain, even after a good harvest.

The Athenians were aware, as Demosthenes reminded them in the speech against Leptines, that they relied on imported grain more than anyone else (20. 31), a fact that made them vulnerable: in the debate on the Syracusan expedition Nicias, at least according to Thucydides (6. 20. 4), pointed out to the assembly that the Syracusans possessed a great advantage over the Athenians in growing their own corn rather than having to import it. At the end of the fifth century an aspiring public figure, Glaucon, could be expected to have knowledge about the main subjects of debate, which included checking on the corn supply (Xenophon, *Memorabilia* 3. 6. 13); later in the century commerce is included among the topics particular to deliberative oratory, in a list which closely parallels the subjects on which Socrates asked Glaucon (Aristotle, *Rhetoric*

[29] To relate my discussion to Garnsey's tables of Attic production and consumption, I would posit the need for estimates based on 10 per cent, 12.5 per cent and 15 per cent of Attica under grain (contrast Garnsey's 15 per cent, 20 per cent and 25 per cent), with consumption levels of 210–250 kilograms per person/year (contrast Garnsey's 175 kilos, which has to be adjusted to take into account the difference between unprocessed barley and barley meal).

[30] This position is not far from that first adopted by Garnsey (Attica narrowly defined could support half its population: 1985, 74), but he subsequently reduced his estimate of resident population so that Attica in 323/2 might have been self-supporting in normal conditions (1988, 104 with 90).

1. 4. 11), and by 330 at least the grain supply was on the assembly agenda once a month (Aristotle, *Ath.Pol.* 43. 4).

Grain was clearly a matter of regular public concern, but it is still unlikely that the Athenians themselves could ever establish their grain requirement with great precision: their best indicator was probably the price level on the markets, which might fluctuate in response to rumours and changes in sentiment. What counted overall were impressions, since a belief that grain was in short supply would rapidly escalate into reality as those who could afford to increased their personal stores, while those with substantial reserves held them back from the market in the hope of yet higher prices.[31] Such behaviour is natural in all societies, as was experienced in Britain during the great toilet paper crisis of 1974, followed by the false rumours of salt and spaghetti shortages. The inefficiencies, or inequalities, of the distribution of grain within Attica should also not be forgotten, since too neat an equation of supply and demand would have condemned numerous inhabitants to shortage while their better-off neighbours enjoyed sufficiency or surplus.

A certain degree of oversupply was essential for the tranquillity of the market, so that Athens will have operated on a skewed version of the Micawber equation:[32] the ideal was that what came onto the market, from home production and imports, had to be well above demand. The Athenians were price sensitive: in the *Knights* (642–82) the *boule* is satirised for responding promptly to the news of cheap sardines, while the Sausage-seller consolidated his good reputation by buying up all the onion and coriander on the market to present to the councillors as an accompaniment for their fish. Such consumers would just as readily panic in response to high prices, and the spiralling decline into hoarding and crisis would be rapid: in his speech against the corn-dealers, Lysias referred to just such a situation (22. 8).

---

[31] Rathbone 1983, 49, suggested that some crises at Athens may have been manufactured to further the ends of benefactors and orators.
[32] Charles Dickens, *David Copperfield*, ch. 12: 'Annual income twenty pounds, annual expenditure nineteen nineteen six, result happiness. Annual income twenty pounds, annual expenditure twenty pounds ought and six, result misery.'

In the fifth century the Athenian naval domination of the Aegean ensured a relatively smooth supply of grain, even though the annual requirement must have been somewhat greater than in the fourth, since it is generally agreed that the population of Attica was larger. In the fourth century the command economy had gone (de Ste Croix 1972, 49; Sallares 1991, 299), and instead Athens had to rely on a combination of protection, legislation and encouragement. Considerable attention was paid to the defence of the Attic countryside, since it was essential to maximise home production, whatever the proportion of the population this could actually feed (Ober 1985). Athenian legislation to stimulate and control the grain trade can be divided into two parts, internal and external, according to its impact. Internally the operation of the grain market was supervised by a board of officials, the *sito-phylakes* or grain wardens: in the *Athenaion Politeia* it is recorded that previously there were five each for the Piraeus and Athens, but that now numbers were fifteen and twenty respectively (51. 3). They were responsible for ensuring that unground grain was sold on the market at a fair price, that the millers sold barley meal in accordance with the price paid for the unground barley, and that the bread-sellers sold bread of prescribed weight in accordance with the price paid for the wheat (Rhodes 1981, 577–9; also Garland 1987, 89). There was also a law to restrict to 50 measures (*phormoi*)[33] the amount of grain that the *sitopolai*, grain dealers, could accumulate by purchase, and another to restrict the dealers' profit to one obol, presumably per measure (Lysias 22. 5, 8); the penalty for infringing these laws was death, and Lysias states that the *sitophylakes* had often suffered for failing to curb the *sitopolai* (22. 16).[34] The supervisors of exchange (*epimeletai emporiou*) had the responsibility to ensure that two-thirds of all grain brought into the grain exchange was conveyed

[33] Of unknown size, but usually equated with the standard grain measure, the *medimnos*.
[34] For interpretation, see the discussion of Seager 1966; the restriction on purchasing may have been a daily limit (Garnsey 1988, 141), but the intention was the same, to avoid stockpiling.

up to the city of Athens (*Ath.Pol.* 51. 4).[35] Thus internally there
was a detailed regime, with considerable supervision, to control
the movement of grain from unloading at the Piraeus, or delivery
to market in the case of home production, to the consumer, but
all this depended upon the wholesale price of grain, and hence
the quantity of grain coming onto the market, over which the
Athenians could have no legal control. This situation has been
described as absurd (Seager 1966, 184), but that is to belittle the
force of the external actions which the Athenians took to ensure
the presence on the market of sufficient grain to produce the best
possible wholesale price level.

Externally, Athenian tactics were to use limited legislation to
reinforce the very considerable economic pull of Athens, the single
most substantial market and source of funds in the Aegean world
(Garnsey 1988, 139), to encourage private traders to go out and
obtain the necessary goods. No resident of Athens was to convey
grain to anywhere other than the Athenian market, and no
Athenian citizen or metic or individual under their control was to
lend money on any ship that was not going to bring grain, or other
specified (but unknown) articles, to Athens (Dem. 34. 37, 35. 50–1;
58. 8–9, 12; Lycurgus, *Leoc.* 27);[36] the penalty for infringement

[35] Garnsey 1988, 140–1, translating *emporion* as 'port', suggested that
this law only required that two-thirds of the grain entering the harbour
had to be unloaded and conveyed to Athens (also Garland 1987, 89);
the remaining one-third might be unloaded and sold in the Piraeus
market, or purchased for re-export before being unloaded. Although I
am sympathetic to the notion of re-export of surplus grain (see below),
this interpretation of the *Athenaion Politeia* seems wrong: the law
applied to grain brought into the *sitikon emporion*, which on Garnsey's
interpretation should mean the 'grain harbour' – but there is no other
evidence for such a specialised area within the harbour complex. I
prefer the view that the Athenians required that grain ships which entered
the Piraeus had to be unloaded and their cargo processed through the
grain exchange: Gauthier 1981. The grain exchange was perhaps one
specific stoa within the larger complex that constituted the Emporion (on
which see Garland 1987, 83–95). The law only applied to 'grain brought
in by ship', since it would have damaged the interests of Athenian
producers if it had applied to any home grown grain brought to the
Piraeus market.
[36] The wider scope of the lending law is obviously intended to reflect
current banking practice, where slaves or ex-slaves might control lending:
see Millett 1991, 206–7.

was death. The effectiveness of these laws is unknown. We naturally hear most about their infringement, but that simply reflects
the nature of our legal evidence; on the other hand, traders were
primarily concerned for profits and, as the speech against
Dionysodorus shows (Dem. 56. 8–10), were capable of quite rapid
commercial adjustments in response to price fluctuations at Athens
– a syndicate of dishonest traders is alleged to have redirected
ships in response to changes in the grain price.

Athenian laws, obviously, could only apply to residents, but it
is clear that the conveyance of grain to Athens was a multina-
tional operation and other means had to be used for those outside
Athenian jurisdiction. Athens possessed considerable attractions
as a destination, as Xenophon noted (*Poroi* 3. 1–2): a safe harbour,
and a wide variety of goods available for export, with the option
of the export of silver if a return cargo was not desired.[37]
Xenophon, however, also recommended various improvements to
benefit traders, including rapid settlement of disputes, honorific
treatment, better accommodation and other facilities in the
Piraeus (*Poroi* 3. 3–5, 12–13). It is likely that some changes to
the legal system were introduced about the mid-fourth century
which resulted in quicker justice being available to traders,
especially in the winter months (Aristotle, *Ath.Pol.* 52. 2, with
Rhodes 1981, 582–3, 664–5). The public works carried out during
the Lycurgan 'regime' in the 330s and 320s may have been
intended to help Athens preserve its attractiveness at a time when
its pre-eminence was being challenged by developments further
east, and it is also from this period that inscriptions are preserved
in honour of traders, and others, who had provided gifts of grain
(Garnsey 1988, 139; *IG* II² 360, 398, 408). Special honours were
accorded to reliable suppliers, in particular to the rulers of the
Bosporus kingdom who were granted Athenian citizenship and
the privilege of recruiting *hyperesia*, specialist rowers. In return
traders whose destination was Athens received from the Bosporan
dynasty preferential treatment in loading and exemption from

---

[37]   The agreement quoted in Demosthenes 34. 10–13 provides an example
of such flexibility: the borrowers received a loan of 3,000 drachmas on
condition that they sailed to Mende or Scione, where they were to take
on 3,000 jars of wine; they were then to sail to the Pontus where they
would take on a return cargo.

the normal duty of one-thirtieth on the export of grain from the kingdom.[38]

This combination of regulations and incentives reflects the importance which the Athenians attached to the management of their grain trade; not surprisingly it was a subject that was brought to their attention once a month in the assembly; if the trade was disrupted, the navy was deployed or the Athenians faced starvation (e.g. Demosthenes 50. 4–6). Although the size of the annual requirement cannot be determined, and it will have varied considerably from year to year, it was always large. Some notion of scale can be gained from evidence about supplies from the Black Sea. Demosthenes, in his attack on Leptines, stated that the grain imported to Athens from the Black Sea was equal to the total from all other places, and that about 400,000 *medimnoi* came from the Bosporus, a figure that could be verified in the records of the grain wardens (20. 31–3). Gomme prudently observed that Demosthenes 'was a politician and was probably not speaking the truth', and, concluding that Demosthenes was belittling the significance of non-Pontic imports, proposed an annual total of 1,200,000 *medimnoi* (Gomme 1933, 32–3). Garnsey has exploited the orator's uncertain credibility in the opposite direction, to urge that no conclusions about the scale of non-Pontic imports can be drawn and the figure of 400,000 might represent an exceptional quantity imported in a bad year (Garnsey 1988, 97). Although caution is in order, Garnsey seems too sceptical: Demosthenes presents Leucon of Bosporus as a perpetual benefactor of Athens, and strongly implies that the level of exports was a regular one that would be maintained in the future, and perhaps indeed increased through the opening of another grain depot at Theudosia (20. 32–3). I share the suspicion that Demosthenes was overemphasising the importance of Leucon, but would note that one possible deception in his argument is the suggestion that exports from the Bosporus kingdom are synonymous with exports from the Black Sea, as if there were no other grain-exporting areas there: it is possible that imported grain from the Pontus did roughly match that from other sources, and that substantially more than Leucon's

---

[38] Demosthenes 20. 29–31; Tod 1948, no. 167 = Harding 1985, no. 82. Mytilene was also granted some reduction in the grain duty: Tod no. 163.

annual export, whether 400,000 *medimnoi* or not, came from the Pontus as a whole.

A rough cross-check on the size of the Pontic contribution may be provided by the figures for the grain fleet which Philip of Macedon detained in 340, an action which precipitated an Athenian declaration of war. The fleet is variously recorded as 180 by Theopompus (*FGH* 115 F 292) and 230 by Philochorus (*FGH* 328 F 162); a possible explanation of the different figures is that, out of the total number of ships detained at Hieron at the entrance to the Bosporus, only 180 counted as 'enemy ships', in the sense that they were carrying grain towards Athens.[39] The size of the ships is then a guess, but the example of the grain trade for Rome might suggest that ships tended to be larger rather than smaller for such a round trip (Rickman 1980, 17, 123–4). The Hellenistic harbour regulations from Thasos provide a definition of small, medium and large: ships of 100–150 tons appear to have been common (2,500–3,750 *medimnoi*), while those of 300–350 were large (7,500–8,750 *medimnoi*); the minimum size of ship allowed into the first part of the harbour was 80 tons (2,000 *medimnoi*), and 130 tons for the second part (3,250 *medimnoi*) (Casson 1971, 171 n. 23). In his discussion of ship sizes, Casson also exploited the figures for gifts of grain for which benefactors received public thanks, of which most fall in the range 2,300–4,000 *medimnoi* (eight instances), though with one of only 500 *medimnoi* and one of 8,000. Casson postulated that traders were presenting a complete shipload of grain, and concluded that the commonest size of ship was 120 tons (3,000 *medimnoi*) (Casson 1971, 183–4). This assumption is possible, but not necessary, since a sensible trader might sell part of his cargo and then, if business had been particularly profitable, use the remainder to purchase public goodwill:[40] thus the ships could have been substantially larger. Be that as it may, if the grain fleet detained by Philip numbered about 200 at an average of 120 tons, it would have been carrying 600,000

[39]   See the discussion of Bresson 1994, esp. 47–50. It should be noted that these figures do not necessarily record the total number of grain ships sailing from the Black Sea into the Aegean in 340, but merely those which had collected at Hieron at the time that Philip attacked.

[40]   This practice would parallel that of other donors of grain, who clearly combined the roles or profiteer and benefactor: Garnsey 1988, 82–3; Gallant 1991, 183–5.

medimnoi; if the ships averaged 160 tons, the cargo would have been 800,000. This provides some sort of perspective to Demosthenes' comments on Leucon. The Hellespont was always the crucial bottleneck on the Athenian supply line, as shown in 405/4 and again in 387. Demosthenes claimed that mastery of the Hellespont would have put Philip in control of the food supply of the Greeks (18. 241); once the Macedonians controlled the Hellespont, diversification was essential for Athens and there are signs of interest in the west with a colonial expedition being dispatched to the Adriatic, as well as evidence for contacts with Egypt and Alexander's unscrupulous local controller Cleomenes.[41]

So, my contention is that Athens regularly attempted to import very substantial quantities of grain, even though precise figures cannot be established. In most years it was probably the case that not all of this grain was needed for internal consumption, since it would have been in Athenian interests to encourage a certain amount of oversupply: the presence of a significant surplus in the markets of Attica ensured that prices remained relatively low for the Athenian consumer, but also enabled the Athenians to benefit from the re-export of grain. Although there is no evidence that Athens anticipated Rome as a consumer city where provision of basic commodities might be spectacularly in excess of needs,[42] it must have been good for Athenian esteem to know that their city was better supplied with food than their neighbours. There is, indeed, limited evidence for re-export: Demosthenes records that one of Leucon's grain gifts in a year of shortage was sufficiently large for the Athenians to make a profit of 15 talents, presumably from resale by Callisthenes, the food controller (20. 33).[43] In some years it is possible that the Piraeus was the largest single grain exporting port in the Aegean,[44] an activity that would have

---

[41]   Tod 1948, no. 200 = Harding 1985, no. 121; Demosthenes 56. 5–8.

[42]   Sallares 1991, 393, notes some prestige waterworks at Athens, but they do not compare with the scale of Roman aqueducts.

[43]   The fact that Leucon supplied grain in excess of Athenian needs suggests that Callisthenes sold some grain abroad – though money might also have been generated by sales to Athenians at less than the inflated current prices (cf. Dem. 34. 39 for this).

[44]   A parallel would be Britain's status, in some years, as the largest exporter of olive oil in the European Union, a point I owe to Helen Parkins.

brought considerable profit to Athens from the 2 per cent harbour tax on grain and the whole business of unloading, handling and reloading surplus grain. Athenian residents were prohibited from participating in, or lending money for, such re-export activity, but the Piraeus as a commercial hub naturally attracted traders of all nationalities, and it likely that local movements of grain, perhaps in small or modest-sized ships, were much less dependent on borrowed money than the larger-scale long-haul traffic.[45] The benefits to Athens from the presence of large numbers of traders are stressed by Xenophon (*Poroi* 3. 5, 12–13).

These foreign traders would primarily have purchased grain at the corn exchange in the Piraeus, but even the regulation that two-thirds of imports be transported to Athens need not have removed that grain from the re-export market. Without this requirement there could have been a considerable difference in price between the Piraeus and Athens itself, to the detriment of a larger portion of Athenian inhabitants, so the movement of grain in bulk to the city kept matters relatively stable and ensured that grain did not leave Attica too quickly. But if the supply in the city was adequate there was nothing to stop the grain being purchased for re-export: the costs would have been greater, but it was foreigners who would have to pay these, whereas the Athenians would have benefited from the cheaper supply and from the employment generated by the movement to and fro. Such activity might sound implausibly cumbersome, but there is a parallel in Edinburgh in the early seventeenth century when Leith acted as an entrepôt for much of south-east Scotland and Fife: manufactured imports had to be unloaded at Leith, hauled uphill to market in Edinburgh, unloaded, reloaded and returned to Leith for shipment to their eventual destination (Makey 1987). This might sound absurd, but Edinburgh was the market, its position was defined in law, and its economic dominance ensured that this arrangement did not operate too heavily against mercantile interests; the position of Athens was comparable.

The Athenian ideal was to be able to command the import of a sizeable surplus of grain every year, to keep prices low internally,

---

[45]   The traders responsible for the benefactions of grain must have been sufficiently wealthy to finance their own long-distance ventures; the foreigner Hermaeus honoured at *IG* II[2] 360 was probably another example.

and to generate revenues from the resale of the surplus. How often the Athenians managed to achieve this is another matter, in that so many different variables were relevant, but their assessment of their requirements was considerable and they were very vulnerable to threats of interference, especially to the northern trade which remained their single most important source of supply until Alexander crossed the Hellespont. If there is any merit in this contention, it would reduce the significance of precise answers to the imponderables of carrying capacity, population and consumption: the Athenians did not possess, or need, accurate information, but like most markets they relied on impressions, rumours and hunches.

Bibliography

Austin, M. M. (1994), 'Society and economy', in *Cambridge Ancient History*, vi (2nd edn, Cambridge), 527–64.

Bagnall, R. S. and Frier, B. W. (1994), *The Demography of Roman Egypt* (Cambridge).

Bresson, A. (1994), 'L'attentat d'Hiéron et le commerce grec', in *Économie Antique, Les échanges dans l'Antiquité: le rôle de l'État, Entretiens d'Archéologie et d'Histoire*, Saint-Bertrand-de-Comminges I: 47–68.

Casson L. (1971), *Ships and Seamanship in the Ancient World* (Princeton).

—— (1994), 'Mediterranean communications', in *Cambridge Ancient History*, vi (2nd edn, Cambridge), 512–26.

Davies, J. K. (1978), *Democracy and Classical Greece* (London).

de Ste Croix, G. E. M. (1972), *The Origins of the Peloponnesian War* (London).

—— (1981), *The Class Struggle in the Ancient Greek World* (London).

Duncan-Jones, R. P. (1980), 'Metic numbers in Periclean Athens', *Chiron* 10: 101–9.

Foxhall, L. and Forbes, H. A. (1982), 'Sitometreia: the role of grain as a staple food in classical antiquity', *Chiron* 12: 41–90.

Gallant, T. W. (1991), *Risk and Survival in Ancient Greece: Reconstructing the Rural Domestic Economy* (Cambridge).

Garland R. (1987), *The Piraeus* (London).

Garnsey, P. D. A. (1985), 'Grain for Athens', in P. Cartledge and F. D. Harvey (eds), *Crux* (Sidmouth), 62–75.

—— (1988), *Famine and Food Supply in the Graeco-Roman World, Reponses to Risk and Crisis* (Cambridge).

—— (1992), 'Yield of the land', in B. Wells (ed.), *Agriculture in Ancient Greece* (Stockholm), 147–53.

Gauthier, P. (1981), 'De Lysias à Aristote (*Ath. Pol.* 51.4): le commerce du grain à Athènes et les fonctions des sitophylaques', *Revue Historique de droit français et étranger* 59: 5–28.

Gomme, A. W. (1933), *The Population of Athens in the Fifth and Fourth Centuries BC* (Oxford).

Hansen, M. H. (1985), *Demography and Democracy: The Number of Athenian Citizens in the Fourth Century BC* (Herning, Denmark).

—— (1994), 'The number of Athenian citizens secundum Sekunda', *Echos du Monde Classique* 38 (n.s. 13): 299–310.

Harding, P. (1985), *Translated Documents of Greece and Rome, 2: From the End of the Peloponnesian War to the Battle of Ipsus* (Cambridge).

Jardé, A. (1925), *Les Céréales dans l'antiquité grecque, I: La Production* (Paris).

Keen, A. (1993), ' "Grain for Athens": notes on the importance of the Hellespontine route in Athenian foreign policy before the Peloponnesian War', *Electronic Antiquity: Communicating the Classics* 1 (6) November.

Lewis, D. M. (1955), 'Notes on Attic inscriptions (II)', *BSA* 50: 1–36.

Makey, W. (1987), 'Edinburgh in the mid-seventeenth century', in M. Lynch (ed.), *The Early Modern Town in Scotland* (London), 192–218.

Millett, P. (1991), *Lending and Borrowing in Ancient Athens* (Cambridge).

Ober, J. (1985), *Fortress Attica: Defense of the Athenian Land Frontier 404–322 BC* (Leiden).

Osborne, R. (1985), *Demos: The Discovery of Classical Attika* (Cambridge).

—— (1992), 'Classical Greek gardens: between farm and paradise', in J. D. Hunt (ed.), *Garden History: Issues, Approaches, Methods* (Dumbarton Oaks), 373–91.

Petersen, C. (1995), *Bread and the British Economy c. 1770–1870* (London).

Rathbone, D. (1983), 'The grain trade and grain shortages in the Hellenistic East', in P. Garnsey and C. R. Whittaker (eds), *Trade and Famine in Classical Antiquity* (Cambridge Philological Society, suppl. vol. 8), 45–55.

Reinmuth, O. W. (1971), *The Ephebic Inscriptions of the Fourth Century BC* (*Mnemosyne* suppl. 14).

Rhodes, P. J. (1981), *A Commentary on the Aristotelian Athenaion Politeia* (Oxford).

Rickman, G. E. (1980), *The Corn Supply of Ancient Rome* (Oxford).

Sallares, R. (1991), *The Ecology of the Ancient Greek World* (Ithaca, N.Y.).

Seager, R. (1966), 'Lysias against the corndealers', *Historia* 15: 172–84.

Tod, M. N. (1948), *A Selection of Greek Historical Inscriptions II* (Oxford).

Whitehead, D. (1977), *The Ideology of the Athenian Metic* (Cambridge Philological Society, suppl. vol. 4).

7

Land transport in Roman Italy: costs, practice and the economy[1]

Ray Laurence

Introduction

Reading the work of ancient historians on the Roman economy, we are presented with a paradoxical situation. All historians recognise that the Roman state was involved in the development of an extensive transport network of roads from the fourth century BC. The purpose of these roads is seen by many historians to have been political and militaristic, and even later as having no significant economic impact (Finley 1973, 126–7). The reason for this explanation is given in terms of the cost of transport by land in comparison to the far cheaper forms of transport by river or sea (Finley 1973, 126–7; Duncan-Jones 1974, 1; Garnsey and Saller 1987, 44, 90). This paradoxical situation of high investment in the transport infrastructure and seemingly high cost of land

---

[1] The theoretical framework for this chapter is drawn from recent geographical thinking. In particular, the work of H. Lefebvre (1991), M. Castells (1972) and D. Harvey (1973) and (1990) has been particularly influential in the development of ideas and concepts that underlie the argument of the chapter. There is not space to discuss these fully here, but a full discussion will appear in due course in R. Laurence (forthcoming), *The City and the Road: Land Transport in Roman Italy*. I would like to thank Helen Parkins for her helpful comments on a draft of this chapter and suggestions drawn from her unpublished Ph.D. thesis. Of course, any errors and misconceptions that remain are my own responsibility.

transportation relative to sea and river transport costs has led many historians to view Roman Italy and the Roman Mediterranean generally as dependent on the sea as the primary form of transportation for most agricultural produce. This generally held view of Roman economic practice is repeated at conferences and seminars with an almost doctrinal regularity, in spite of criticism (notably by Hopkins 1978, 107; and Isager and Skydsgaard 1992, 106). However, no overall reassessment of the role of land transport in the economy has been made and it is with this end in mind that this chapter has been written.

The assertion that land transport was prohibitively expensive can be traced back from very recent scholarship through Finley's *Ancient Economy* (1973) and Jones's *Later Roman Empire* (1964) to an article by Yeo published some fifty years ago entitled 'Land and sea transportation in imperial Italy'. This article set up the nature of the discussion of land transport for the next fifty years – the discussion sought to compare the relative costs of land and sea transport. The basis of Yeo's analysis will be examined to investigate what the evidence suggests about the economics of transportation. In fact, I will argue that Yeo's data suggest, instead, that there was little difference in terms of transport costs in Roman Italy from other better documented societies that had undertaken road improvement schemes with similar gains in transport efficiency. Further, later in the chapter I will suggest in terms of economic practice, documented in the agricultural writers, that Roman Italy from the third century BC was developing a system of agricultural production that could only be maintained by the development of a road system for the marketing of produce, and that owners of villas actively improved the road system to facilitate the transport of produce. Finally, the chapter sets out to understand these developments in the context of change in the space economy in Roman Italy.

Transport costs: figures and calculations

Yeo (1946) presented an account of the relative costs of land and sea transport drawing on the ancient sources, primarily Cato's *De Agricultura* (22. 3) and Diocletian's Price Edict. From these sources he attempted to establish the actual costs of transport for imperial Italy. His analysis was detailed and made frequent reference to other costs in Italy by way of comparison. However, at times, he misses the significance of some of the evidence and certainly decontextualises the evidence to create a standard cost for the transportation of items in relation to cost at the point of purchase. There would seem also to be a number of errors in his calculations that cause the transport costs to escalate. Therefore, at this point, it is worth reviewing the figures again.

To deal with Cato's evidence first, he discusses the cost of buying and transporting an olive-oil mill overland from Suessa a mere 25 miles away and, by comparison, a similar mill from Pompeii some 75 miles distant. He tells us that the mill and 50 pounds of oil purchased at Suessa would cost 425 sesterces, that there was an additional cost of the bar for the press of 72 sesterces, and there would also be a cost of 60 sesterces for assembly. The transport cost for this short journey of 25 miles was estimated by Cato as six days' wages for six men using oxen and carts from his estate, which would amount to a cost of 72 sesterces. Therefore, the total cost of the mill and its assembly would have been 557 sesterces and the cost of transport would have been 72 sesterces. Cato also gives another figure for the cost of a similar mill bought at Pompeii, for which he would have paid 384 sesterces for the mill and 280 sesterces for its transport to his farm and a further charge of 60 sesterces for its assembly.

Cato's information on the cost of transport of an oil mill provides us with two working examples of the proportion of transportation costs from two places over different distances. The transport cost over the 25 miles from Suessa was equivalent to 11 per cent of the total cost of the mill (Yeo 1946, 221–2 gives transport cost as 17 per cent of total cost), whereas the transport cost of the mill from Pompeii, over 75 miles, was more than 73 per cent of the total cost. Yeo (1946, 224) converts these costs for the oil mill into cost equivalents for wheat and other staple goods to create a standard cost for all transport over land. In doing so, he decontextualises the original prices to refer to a different product and universalises the specific data into a general rule of thumb. However, this misses the point of what Cato was attempting to illustrate by giving the two examples. He wanted to compare the different costs of buying a mill for his estate. Interestingly, he considers buying a mill from one local location 25 miles away and another location at some distance, 75 miles away. In terms of total cost, the mill from Suessa was 629 sesterces, whereas that from Pompeii cost 724 sesterces. To buy the mill from Suessa would have made a saving of 95 sesterces. This would mean that the cost of the mill and its transport from Pompeii was only 15 per cent more expensive than the cost of a mill and its transport from a much closer location. This relatively small margin of cost demonstrates a number of economic factors that would have been present in the Roman empire that have been ignored or passed over by historians writing since Yeo (1946). First, prices for goods varied across Italy, and goods from further afield could compete with those produced at a closer location. Moreover, the journey from Pompeii to Cato's farm was three times the journey from Suessa to the farm. However, it must be stressed that the overall cost of the mill from Pompeii was only 15 per cent more than that of the mill from Suessa even though its transport costs were nearly four times greater. Clearly, the costs of mills would vary according to the local geology and whether the mill had been transported prior to its sale. Pompeii was ideally located for such a trade, since it had direct access to suitable stone for mill production (on the petrology of mills in Italy see Peacock 1980, 1986, 1989; Williams-Thorpe 1988).

Yeo (1946) also makes a number of deductions about the speed of transport from Cato's evidence. Cato calculates the transport cost from Suessa based on transport by oxen accompanied by six men. He says that it would have taken them six days to transport the mill a mere 25 miles. It should be pointed out initially that the mill was an unusual load, which would have required exceptional efforts. Yeo stresses that the time taken (six days) was calculated for a round trip, because the men use Cato's own carts for the transport of the mill. Therefore, it should be assumed that the total distance was 50 miles and that it took six days to make this journey. Yeo suggests rightly that the average speed was about 8 miles per day. This is true of this example, but Yeo extends this speed to all land transport. In doing so, he backs up his argument with reference to a journey from Brundisium to Rome recorded by Ovid (*Pont.* 4. 5. 8) as taking a total of ten days, which he suggests must have been done at a speed of 6 miles per day. Here, Yeo has made a mistake in his calculations. The journey by his reckoning would have been a total distance of 60 miles, but the distance from Brundisium to Rome was 360 miles. Therefore this error causes us to underestimate the speed of transport by six times – Ovid would have covered about 36 miles per day to travel from Brundisium to Rome on the Via Appia over a distance of 360 miles. The speed of 36 miles per day would not appear to be that exceptional (Pliny, *HN*, 3. 100; Pliny, *Ep*. 2. 17), but we might wish to take the time allowed for journeys to appear in court of 20 miles per day as a standard speed whether by road or track (*Dig*. 11. 1. 1). The adjustment to Yeo's calculations places a control upon the figures from Cato for the transport of a mill. The transport of the mill was exceptional: it took a particularly long time because oxen were used for the transport of particularly heavy loads (Yeo suggests it weighed 3,000 pounds) and a large input of human labour (six men). The use of oxen is significant, because they travel at 2 miles per hour – about half the speed of a mule (Hyland 1990, 261. The mule would appear to have been the animal most widely used for pulling carts in the Roman empire, see Mitchell 1976; Adams 1993, 1995). Further, we do not know if the transport of the mill was over a road surface or not. This would have made a significant difference to the speed at which the item could be moved. Therefore, Cato's figures need to be regarded for what they are – exceptional in every way and not to be used to estimate a cost for land transport generally.

To turn to the figures for the cost of land transport taken from Diocletian's Price Edict (sections 17 and 35; Lauffer 1971; Giacchero 1974; Crawford and Reynolds 1979). Duncan-Jones (1974, 366–9) summarises the calculation for the cost of land transport from this source. Although these figures have been subject to revision with the discovery of further fragments of the Price Edict (Crawford and Reynolds 1979; Giacchero 1974, 45), the overall interpretation of the relative cost of sea, river and land transport has not significantly altered (DeLaine 1992, 126). The edict informs us that the cost of transporting 1,200 pounds in a wagon was charged at 20 *denarii* per Roman mile. To place a scale upon calculations over distance, such figures have to be comparable. To do this, the figures used tend to be a *modius* of wheat (22 pounds), therefore the wagon would carry 54.5 *modii*. This means that for every mile a *modius* of wheat was carried, the cost would have been 0.4 *denarii* per *modius*. If the wheat cost 100 *denarii* a *modius*, the transport cost of the wheat in proportion to its actual cost would increase by about 40 per cent of the value over a distance of 100 miles (Duncan-Jones 1974, 368 calculates this cost at 36.7–73.4 per cent using the same figures – variation may be accounted for due to *kastrensis modius* being viewed as equivalent to either one or two Italian *modii*; I have viewed it as equivalent to one Italian *modius*). The cost of sea transport for wheat can also be calculated. The journey from Alexandria to Rome of 1,250 miles would have cost 16 *denarii* per *modius*. The cost per mile would be equivalent to 0.013 *denarii*. Therefore, the transport costs of a *modius* of wheat (cost 100 *denarii*) per 100 miles would have been 1.3 *denarii*, representing an increase in cost of 1.3 per cent as compared with about 40 per cent for transport over the same distance by land. These comparative figures can be seen to show the different relative costs of sea and land transport.

However, we need to understand these figures in context before we can be sure of readily accepting their value as economic indicators. First, it should be recognised that the figures do not compare like with like. The figure for sea transport was for a bulk cargo over a long distance, whereas the figure for land transport in the Price Edict refers to the calculation of a journey with a smaller load. The modern literature frequently alludes to the fact that the cost of transporting wheat over a sea journey from Alexandria to Rome was the same as transporting the same wheat over a distance of 100 miles overland. However, this comparison seldom takes into account the transport costs for the wheat from Alexandria which would have already been incurred in transporting the goods to that city. Colin Adams's Ph.D. thesis study of transport in Egypt is now showing that agricultural goods incurred land transport costs prior to their shipment from the river ports of the Nile down to Alexandria. This example illustrates how, in the Roman empire, the transport of wheat involved a complementary system of land, river and sea voyages, rather than suggesting that the lower cost of sea transport precluded the possibility of land transport.

What the figures in Diocletian's Price Edict do show though is a variation in cost according to the form of transport taken. This produces a cost ratio of sea to land transport of 1:31. For comparison, in the first half of the eighteenth century a ratio of 1:23 is recorded (quoted in Duncan-Jones 1974, 368). It may well be that we should view Diocletian's Price Edict as the maximum cost and that often costs could be less than those recorded in the Edict. Equally, the figures may be referring to a very particular form of transportation and to the fact that the sums charged covered wages and expenses for the carters, as well as the hire of the vehicle and traction animals. No doubt costs of land transport would have been lower if the carts, traction animals and labour power were owned by the person with goods to be transported. In Egypt, a cost for the transport of wheat by river over 13.6 miles is given for the year AD 42, which Duncan-Jones (1974, 368) sees as an equivalent of a cost of 6.38 per cent per hundred miles, which he converts into a ratio of transport costs sea:river as 1:4.7 (compare DeLaine 1992, 125–6: 1:3.9 for downstream journey and 1:7.7 for upstream journey). The ratio of river transport to land transport based on these figures would have been 1:5. Significantly, these figures are not markedly different from the early modern period in Europe or the period of the early Industrial Revolution in Britain during the eighteenth century. Therefore, the figures for the cost of land transport in the Roman empire do not appear to be exceptional when compared to those of other societies. Indeed the figures in fact demonstrate costs for transport of a very similar order of magnitude.

These tentative calculations of the cost of land transport have been frequently used to explain features of Roman economic action that they do not refer to. For example, high transport costs have been used to explain why famines in inland areas were not relieved:

> Despite the existence of a comprehensive network of trunk roads, land transport remained so costly and inefficient that it was often impossible to relieve inland famines from stocks of grain elsewhere.
>
> (Duncan-Jones 1974, 1)

Such analysis ignores outside factors, for example lack of transport animals and carts for the purpose or, simply, a lack of political will (see Garnsey 1988, 22–3, and compare famines in Ireland in the nineteenth century). Moreover, the 'high' transport costs of goods by land have been used to determine and explain the ideology of self-sufficiency in Italian agriculture (Duncan-Jones

1974, 38) as a functional means of maximising resources. Spurr (1986, 144–6) is critical of the use of these figures from the Price Edict as deterministic of behaviour in agriculture, since they refer to hired transport. Moreover, Spurr argues that the economics of self-sufficiency in agriculture extended to the field of transport, which allowed costs to be reduced by the use of farm animals and farm slaves, both of which would have undertaken much of the transport of goods to market. However, even if we do accept these figures as typical, it does not imply that land transport was an alternative seldom undertaken. To suggest that land transport was too expensive to undertake reduces human activity in the Roman empire to the rationality of modern cost–benefit analysis (a rationality or ideology alien to the ancient world). True, the transport costs by road were more expensive than those by sea, but this does not imply that land transportation was seldom undertaken (Isager and Skydsgaard 1992, 106; see also Garnsey 1988, 23 for examples of long-distance transport of staples in Thessaly and North Africa). Our current knowledge of transport costs in the Roman empire is limited to the creation of an order of magnitude for prices, which would appear to be closely comparable to those in Britain and Europe from 1700 to 1800, and it is to a comparative example from this period that I now turn.

A comparative example: eighteenth-century Britain

Britain between 1700 and 1800 saw a period of rapid change in the efficiency of road travel with the introduction of maintained toll roads, which provides us with an important parallel to the establishment of a road network in Italy from the late third through to the early first century BC. Both periods would appear to have been accompanied by an increase in the circulation of goods and both periods should be viewed as times of rapid economic change. The dynamics of transport in the eighteenth century demonstrate the significance of improved communications for the economy. Increasingly, we are becoming aware that in the eighteenth century the improvement in transport made by the toll roads and canals of Britain stimulated economic growth and can be linked with the technological innovation and reorganisation of labour that we associate with the Industrial

Revolution (Pawson 1977, 4–7). Generally, in this period the improvement in transport conditions overcame many of the constraints placed upon local economies by the factor of distance. Adam Smith, in *The Wealth of Nations*, summarises a contemporary view:

> Good roads, canals and rivers, by diminishing the cost of carriage, put the remote parts of the country more nearly upon a level with those in the neighbourhood of the town.
>
> (Smith 1904, 148)

This has important implications for the interpretation of land transport in the Roman economy. The action of road-building, canal-building and the improvement of river navigation all reduced the cost of transport. The presence of a sophisticated road system in the Roman empire would have reduced the costs of transport; similarly the construction of canals and the control of rivers would also extend the local economies of Italy (on inland waterways see Boffo 1977; Fernandez Casado 1983, 553–91; Uggeri 1987, 1990a, 1990b; Calzolari 1992; Laurence 1998). Moreover, the road systems of Italy caused distant towns to become less remote (to use Smith's terminology). In effect, just as in Britain in the eighteenth century, the road system of Italy in the second and first centuries BC created a new space economy that linked places together.

Significantly, in Britain during the eighteenth century, the cost of transport by sea, water and land did vary with a clear advantage to water and sea transport purely in terms of cost, but the documentation from eighteenth-century Britain shows that the apparent superiority in cost of sea transport did not cause it to be the dominant form of transportation (Pawson 1977, 22–3). This would seem to contradict the logic of prices established for the Roman empire, where it has been argued that land transport was an inferior expensive alternative to maritime transport. Indeed, Pawson (1977, 27–9) points to the key advantages of land transport. It could be cheaper to transport goods solely by land, instead of a journey to port by land and then a coastal journey, because the latter alternative incurred additional costs of handling the goods. Moreover, land transport on the toll roads was reliable in bad weather and the fear of losing valuable cargoes at sea caused many high-cost items to be transported by road. However, most significant for our understanding of transport economics is Pawson's observation on the integration of the transport network:

> Nevertheless, despite the apparently overwhelming economic advantage of trade by water, a well used transport system existed. This land transport system can be classified in two parts: a *complementary* system, which was interdependent with water transport, and performed a feeder and distribution role for it, and a *competitive, independent* system which did not rely on water transport linkages.
>
> (Pawson 1977, 23)

It was the establishment of these two systems of transport in the eighteenth century that radically altered the nature of the economy of Britain, in terms of both the movement of goods and the circulation of ideas. With this in mind, we now need to establish the nature of the transport system in Roman Italy to see if land transport by road had a similar complementary role and significance as it had in eighteenth-century Britain.

Agriculture and land transportation

The connection of roads with the agricultural systems of Italy in the second and first centuries BC through to the first century AD can be demonstrated with reference to literary sources of the time. The agricultural writers Columella and Varro refer to remarks of Cato the Elder on the subject of the buying of agricultural property in the second century BC. Cato was writing in the period when the major roads of Italy had been established and their effect on the transportation of agricultural produce was beginning to be understood. Therefore these remarks of Cato come from a period of change in the human geography of Italy, which can be seen as having an important implication for the Italian economy. Interestingly, these comments of Cato were accepted and reproduced by Varro and Columella, were regarded as still having significance for the selection of viable agricultural properties in the first centuries BC and AD, and should be seen as a general view of the role of road transport for agriculture throughout the period 200 BC to AD 200.

The texts require some discussion to place the importance of the newly established roads in the selection of agricultural property in context. Columella (1. 3) reports that Cato considered of prime importance the quality of the soil and the nature of the climate. After these two primary considerations, the factors of a similar importance were the road, water and the neighbourhood (*viam, aquam, vicinum*). According to Cato, a road added to the value of land in a number of ways, first by allowing the owner to travel in relative comfort to the property, rather than dreading an arduous journey and, in consequence, seldom visiting. Further, a road aided the bringing in of goods and resources to a property as well as the transporting of produce away from a property: 'a factor which increases the value of stored crops and lessens the expense of bringing things in, because they are transported at a lower cost to a place which may be reached without a great effort' (see also Varro, *RR* 1. 16. 3). Already, in the second century BC, we see a view of the road system as an asset for agriculture. Cato also points to the engagement of agriculture with a wider economy that is often underplayed by modern scholarship on the subject. Much of the modern literature refers to the agriculture of Italy as built upon self-sufficiency but, in Cato, we find that certain needs of the villa were performed by outsiders. Certainly an ideology of self-sufficiency was present in Roman agriculture, yet this did not override a practical necessity to interact with the wider economy.

The integration of the villa economy with that of the town is demonstrated with reference to Varro (*RR* 1. 16. 2–6). He is categorical that it is the ability to transport products from the villa by carts on roads or by river which could make a farm more profitable (*fructuosus*). This would suggest that transport was a major factor in the successful economic integration of the villa into the wider economy. The reasons for a villa needing its transport link are also given by Varro:

> Farms which have nearby suitable means of transporting their products to market and convenient means of transporting from there those things needed on the farm, are for that reason profitable. For many have among their holdings some into which grain or wine or the like which they lack must be brought, and on the other hand not a few have holdings from which a surplus must be sent away.
>
> (Varro, *RR* 1. 16. 2–3)

Further, Varro suggests that the villa should be integrated into the local town or *vicus* (village) economy and, if lacking these, an economic relationship with a large rich villa would have been a practical alternative. These centres were potential markets for the produce of the villa and were also centres of labour and services required by the villa owner (by this I do not intend to imply that these centres were 'service' cities in line with Engels's model: see Engels 1990). In terms of labour provision, these centres were the focus for the provision of specialists, such as physicians, fullers and other artisans; because to own your own artisan was one thing but if that person was to die 'the profit of the farm would have been wiped out' until a replacement was found. Only if the farm was isolated from towns, *vici* and large villas would it be necessary to own specialist craftsmen. Similarly, if a villa was close to a road and had good communications with towns elsewhere, it would have been relatively easy to hire the labour for the transport of goods (Columella, *RR* 1. 3. 4, quoting Cato). Transport, like the harvest of crops, involved additional labour that was cheaper to hire for a short period of time, since it averted the need to own extra slaves for the purpose who might be underemployed for much of the year. It would appear that agriculture was thoroughly integrated into a wider economy, and that a villa's economic viability was increased by a good supply of hired labour, a prospering town, and an adequate transport route for the export of goods either by road or river (Pliny, *HN* 17. 28, referring to Cato). It should come as no surprise that Varro (*LL* 5. 35, discussed by Purcell 1995, 170) made an etymological link between the words 'villa' and 'via'. The villa would simply have been an expensive, but largely non-productive investment without the ability to export goods by road or river.

Villa location and road-building

In terms of the development of Roman agriculture, the location of a villa close to a major artery of the transport system was important. Lacking that location, there was always the possibility of building a road to link the villa to the major transport arteries of Italy. This would seem to have been a relatively common practice. For example in the field survey of the Ager Veientanus in Etruria, selce paving stones were found at sixty-three of the

534 sites (data from Kahane *et al.* 1968). Roads were needed to connect the villa with the wider economies of Roman Italy.

The process of villa development after purchase is well documented in the letters of Cicero to his brother with reference to his brother's properties (*QFr.* 3. 1). Cicero had recently visited his brother's properties and was providing a report on the progress of various building works at these sites. At the first property visited, at Arcanum, a stream had been diverted and was providing water in spite of the drought; at the second property, the architect/builder had failed to align the columns in a straight line but the paving of an area was progressing well; at the recently purchased Fufidian farm (*fundus*), Cicero foresees the irrigation of fifty *iugera*, the construction of fish ponds, a palaestra and a wood. Most interesting for our purposes are Cicero's remarks about the building of roads to the property at Laterium. Quintus Cicero and his neighbours would seem to be improving the local roads around their estates. One of his neighbours, Varro, had built a good road in front of his property, whereas another, Locusta, had not built the section of road that would have adjoined their property. Clearly, some agreement had been made between the neighbours over the construction of this road. In addition, Quintus had built a section of road through his own property avoiding the use of his neighbours' land. This is described by his brother:

> I examined the road, which I thought good enough to be a public road, except for 150 paces (I measured it myself) from the little bridge at Furina's temple leading to Satricum. In that stretch, it had a surface of dry clay instead of gravel [*glarea*] (that will have to be altered), and that section had a steep incline, but I understand that it could not be taken in any other direction, especially as you did not want to take it through either Locusta's or Varro's land.

This new road appears to have led from the estate to Satricum (a local town). It was one of Quintus' major developments to his properties outside Rome and would have greatly facilitated access to the property. Significantly, the road connection was being constructed to the highest standard with a gravel surface, which was the technology used on the public roads of the time. Yet the road was a private one and would only have been utilised by the estate. It would have involved considerable investment, but was deemed to have been necessary in order to improve the viability of this property.

In the cases discussed so far, in which roads were built from villas to the major roads of Italy, we are seeing a pattern that emphasises the ideal position of a villa as close to a road rather than on a road (see also Columella, *RR* 1. 5. 6–7). Similarly, there is an emphasis on location of villas that stresses the need to be close to towns but not just outside the walls. The emphasis in the discussion by ancient writers of the location of villas is always to be *close to* rather than *adjacent to* other features of the human landscape. A villa needed to be close to a road to allow for good access and communications; equally a villa needed to be near a town so that it had access to markets and labour; ideally it would also be near a port or river port for the export of produce. This places the villa in a unique position in the Roman landscape. It appears to be separate from the major areas of settlement and might seem to subscribe to an ideology that emphasises subsistence. However, the villa's proximity to towns and roads caused it to be integrated into a wider economy. Moreover, in terms of the Roman space economy, the villas extended the influence of the town over a wider area that economically was integrated with the economy of the local towns and, through ease of transportation away from the local towns, into a wider economic system beyond them.

These features can all be seen to be playing an important role at the classic villa site – Settefinestre. The location of this villa could be seen to be ideal and conform to the prerequisites of the agricultural writers. The villa was positioned upon a hill and dominated the valley of the Oro (Carandini and Settis 1979, 43–9). It was close to a *diverticulum* (side road) leading to the Via Aurelia a mere 1.7 kilometres away (Carandini 1988, 121–2). Moreover, the villa was close to the Latin colony at Cosa and its harbour – 4–4.5 kilometres away (Carandini 1988, 126–7). Other urban centres were also nearby, within a day's journey by road, including: Orbetello (12 km), Porto Ercole (14 km), Heba (18 km), Talamone (22 km), Saturnia (35 km) and Vulci (38 km). All of these towns would have provided markets for goods, which could have been transported using the vehicles, animals and slaves from the villa (Cato, *RR* 52). The economic cost of this form of transport was negligible since the labour power was available within the villa itself. It was only if the agricultural produce of the villa was transported further afield that any additional outside cost for transport was incurred. The villa was integrated into the wider economic system through its proximity to the port at Cosa, which would have allowed for the shipment of produce by sea at a lower cost (we should include the importation of goods as well as export of produce here). The presence of the road (Via Aurelia) should not be ignored in the context of production and export, because the availability of sea transport would have been affected by the weather and was considered to be impractical in winter (from October to April). It would have been in winter that goods produced at Settefinestre would have been transported by land, rather than by sea. Therefore, land transport complemented transportation by sea when the seas did not permit sailing. Further, for short journeys of less than a day we would not foresee the use of shipping due to an extra need for labour in the transshipment of goods from carts or pack animals onto boats. This brings out the complementary nature of land, sea and river transport. Few journeys, if any, would have been entirely water based, because, ultimately at some point, transported goods had to travel overland to reach their final destination. Thus, to discuss water and land transport as competing systems according to price is to misunderstand the economics of transport in the Roman world. It was true that water transport was cheaper, but that did not mean that land transport for the marketing of produce was not possible. Instead, the implication of water transport being cheaper suggests that on a number of routes this form of transport had an advantage. However, it must be stressed that a large proportion of all goods moved in Roman Italy were moved by road. The reason for this can be seen in the availability of water transport, since in no way did navigable rivers and coastal ports service all destinations within Italy. Instead, these rivers and ports were linked to other places and destinations for goods by a sophisticated network of roads, which facilitated overland transport. For example, Terracina, a colony 60 miles south of Rome on the Via Appia, had its port developed at the expense of the Roman state in 179 BC (Liv. 40. 51. 2). This action caused Terracina to become the closest port to Rome. In terms of the importation of goods to Rome these might have been taken by sea to Terracina and then taken the further 60 miles to Rome along the Via Appia. This example illustrates how land and sea transport complemented one another in the long-distance transport of goods.

The space economy of Roman Italy

The evidence from the second century BC that there was a system of land transport that complemented transportation by river and sea, and, as we have seen, that these forms of transport were not exceptionally costly when compared to other economic systems prior to the nineteenth century, has some important implications for our understanding of the Roman economy. Over the last twenty to thirty years we have been taught to think of the Roman economy as underdeveloped and based upon a peasantry living at a level of subsistence, and of cities being places for the consumption of any surplus wealth. A characteristic of this conception of the Roman economy is the lack of integration between its various parts and, certainly, of the maintenance of a minimal level of trade because there are assumed to have been prohibitive transport costs for most products. However, transport costs were a universal in the ancient world and, as Jongman (1988, 140–2) has argued, the more important question is profit rather than cost. Clearly, produce from farms such as Cato's was transported for sale, and it was seen to have been advantageous for the sale of agricultural produce if the farm was close to a town, a river or a road. Therefore, perhaps what we need is a model of the Roman economy that emphasises the interrelationship of the units of production and consumption. To a certain extent we already have a familiar one to hand in Hopkins's (1978, fig. 1.1) model for the growth of slavery in Roman Italy, but this addresses only part of the problem. In what follows, I wish to view Roman Italy in terms of centres of production and consumption to illustrate the interrelated nature of the economic units as both producers and consumers.

By the early to mid-second century BC, the road system of Italy had been established from the River Po down to Italy's southern coast. It is in this period that we tend to see the development of villa-based agricultural systems similar to those of Cato producing surpluses for sale elsewhere. At the same time, we might wish to identify Rome as the key market for the sale of produce, because the population growth in the city demanded this. Again in the early second century, we find the colonies founded earlier in the third century developing distinctive urban features such as walls, temples and fora, and paved streets (e.g. Liv. 41. 27. 10–11). It appears that these developments in towns and in agriculture follow on from the development of a road system in Italy. Indeed, we might view the development of large estates at a distance from Rome owned by the Roman elite as a reaction to the reduction in the temporal distance travelled to estates further away from Rome. The physical distance from Rome of these estates remained the same, yet the introduction of a substantial road system reduced the time it took to travel to estates physically further afield. It would also have made the journey less problematic in terms of personal comfort and would have allowed the owner to visit more frequently. Similarly, towns in Italy began to develop architecturally at the same time as the idea of what a town should be was circulated to even the furthest flung colony. Spatially, those places (whether towns or villas) further away were integrated with the cultural and political centre (Rome) because a new road system had developed to link them together.

The spatial integration of Italy by the second century BC has a number of important implications for our understanding of the nature of trade and the economy of Italy. Most of the information refers to actions of the most wealthy (i.e. the elite) of a similar status to Cato. The villa, as we have seen, was a centre for agricultural production with a view to the export of a surplus for sale, either locally or further away. The extent of the trade in agricultural surplus is subject to debate, but for our purposes here it is necessary simply to recognise its existence. The villa was not simply concerned with production, it was in itself a centre for consumption. A glance at Settefinestre demonstrates the amount of consumption that took place at the villa in terms of building materials, and the degree of architectural embellishment that enhanced the lifestyle of the owner and his family. However, in addition, goods that were unavailable in the locality may have been brought to the villa for consumption. Even though there existed an ideology of agricultural self-sufficiency, many villa owners may have needed certain products (e.g. imported wines, etc.) from towns or further afield to maintain a lifestyle that we tend to associate with Roman culture in the cities of Italy (see, for example, Stefani 1994; for a brief discussion of the data see Laurence 1996). However, it is clear that the material conditions of the lifestyle of the elite in their villas were not significantly different from those found in the towns of Italy. In fact, the villa in Italy should be seen as a place for the display of wealth through storage, whether produced from the villa or imported from elsewhere (see Purcell 1995 on storage and production in villas). Inevitably, the villa could not produce all its own needs and, as we saw above, interacted with towns or *vici* in order to acquire other resources, whether in terms of labour power or material goods. Equally, the villa depended on the town as a place of sale for the surplus produced. Thus, there was a close economic tie between the villa and the town and, importantly, the villa reflected the consumption patterns of the town – though perhaps we should say that the consumption patterns of towns and villas, because of their economic and cultural interaction, were similar.

Finally, to return to transport costs and the economy, the investment of labour and resources in road construction both with public and private monies cannot be entirely related to the conquest of Italy. As I hope to have shown above, by utilising the evidence of economic practice, rather than simple relative costs of land and sea transport, we can begin to understand the significance and success of road building in the Italian economy. Road building allowed for goods to be moved at greater speed, whatever the season. It is true that land transport was more expensive in terms of cost than transport by sea, but that did not prevent goods being transported overland. In fact, in Roman Italy, transport costs did not prevent the movement of goods; significantly, the construction of roads allowed for the movement of goods and the development of a more productive agriculture alongside urbanism.

Bibliography

Adams, J. N. (1993), 'The generic use of *mula* and the status and employment of female mules in the Roman world', *Rheinisches Museum* 136: 35–61.
—— (1995), *Pelagonius and Latin Veterinary Terminology in the Roman Empire* (Leiden).
Boffo, L. (1977), 'Per la storia della antica navigazione fluviale Padana. Un collegium nautarum o naviculariorum a Ticinum in età imperiale', *RAL* 32: 623–32.
Calzolari, M. (1989), *Padana romana: Ricerche archeologiche e palaeoambientali nella pianura tra il Mincio e il Tartaro* (Mantova).
—— (1992), 'Le idrovie della Padana in epoca romana: il Po e il Tartaro', *Quaderni del Gruppo Archeologico Ostigliense* 2: 85–110.

Carandini, A. (1988), *Schiavi in Italia* (Rome).
Carandini, A. and Settis, S. (1979), *Schiavi e padroni nell'Etruria Romana: La villa di Settefinestre dallo scavo alla mostra* (Bari).
Castells, M. (1972), *The Urban Question: A Marxist Approach* (London).
Crawford, M. and Reynolds, J. (1979), 'Aezani copy of the Prices Edict', *ZPE* 34: 163–210.
DeLaine, J. (1992), 'Design and construction in Roman Imperial architecture: the Baths of Caracalla' (Ph.D. diss., University of Adelaide).
Duncan-Jones, R. P. (1974), *The Roman Economy: Quantitative Studies* (Cambridge).
Engels, D. (1990), *Roman Corinth: An Alternative Model for the Classical City* (Chicago).
Fernandez Casado, C. (1983), *Ingeniera Hidraulica Romana* (Madrid).
Finley, M. I. (1973), *The Ancient Economy* (London).
Garnsey, P. (1988), *Famine and the Food Supply in the Graeco-Roman World* (Cambridge).
Garnsey, P. and Saller, R. (1987), *The Roman Empire* (London).
Giacchero, M. (1974), *Edictum Diocletiani et collegarum de pretiis rerum venalium* (Genoa).
Harvey, D. (1973), *Social Justice and the City* (Oxford).
—— (1990), *The Condition of Postmodernity* (Oxford).
Hopkins, K. (1978), *Conquerors and Slaves* (Cambridge).
Hyland, A. (1990), *Equus: the Horse in the Roman World* (London).
Isager, S. and Skydsgaard, J. E. (1992), *Ancient Greek Agriculture* (Rome).
Jones, A. H. M. (1964), *The Later Roman Empire, 284–602: A Social, Economic and Administrative Survey* (Oxford).
Jongman, W. (1988), *The Economy and Society of Pompeii* (Amsterdam).
Kahane, A., Threipland, L. M. and Ward-Perkins, J. (1968), *The Ager Veientanus*, *PBSR* 23.
Lauffer, S. (1971), *Diokletians Preisedikt* (Berlin).
Laurence, R. (1996), Review of Stefani (1994), *CR* 46: 353–4.
—— (1998), 'Nero's canals', *Omnibus,* 33.
Lefebvre, H. (1991), *The Production of Space* (Oxford).
Mitchell, S. (1976), 'Requisitioned transport in the Roman empire: a new inscription from Pisidia', *JRS* 66: 106–31.
Pawson, E. (1977), *Transport and Economy: the Turnpike Roads of Eighteenth-century Britain* (London).
Peacock, D. P. S. (1980), 'The Roman millstone trade: a petrological sketch', *World Archaeology* 12: 43–53.
—— (1986), 'The production of millstones near Orvieto, Umbria, Italy', *Antiquaries Journal* 66: 45–51.
—— (1989), 'The mills of Pompeii', *Antiquity* 63: 205–14.
Purcell, N. (1995), 'The Roman villa and the landscape of production', in T. Cornell and K. Lomas (eds), *Urban Society in Roman Italy* (London), 181–202.
Smith, A. (1904), *The Wealth of Nations*, E. Cannan (ed.) (London).
Spurr, S. (1986), *Arable Cultivation in Roman Italy, c.200 BC–c.AD 100* (London).

Stefani, G. (1994), *Pompei. Vecchi scavi sconosciuti: La villa rinvenuta del marchese Giovanni Imperiali in località Civita (1907–1908)* (Rome).
Uggeri, G. (1987), 'La navigazione interna della Cisalpina in età romana', *Antichità Altoadriatiche* 19: 305–54.
—— (1990a), 'Aspetti archeologici della navigazione interna nella Cisalpina', *Antichità Altoadriatiche* 36: 175–96.
—— (1990b), 'I collegamenti stradali tra Roma e la decima regio', in *Le Venetia nell'area Padano-Danubiana: Le vie communicazione* (Padua), 31–40.
Williams-Thorpe, O. (1988), 'Provenancing and archaeology of Roman millstones from the Mediterranean area', *Journal of Archaeological Science* 15: 253–305.
Yeo, C. A. (1946), 'Land and sea transportation in imperial Italy', *TAPA* 77: 221–44.

8

Trade and traders in the Roman world: scale, structure, and organisation

Jeremy Paterson

Everyone is aware that as a result of the world being united under the majesty of the Roman empire life has improved thanks to trade (*commercium*) and the sharing of the blessings of peace.

So wrote Pliny (*HN* 14. 2) in his characteristically sententious manner in the preamble to his discussion of viticulture. He was not alone. A notorious passage by the author of the *Revelation of John* (18. 11ff.) gives extraordinary prominence among those he sees as devastated by the fall of Babylon/Rome to

the sea-captains and voyagers, the sailors and those who traded by sea . . . Alas, alas for the great city, where all who had ships at sea grew rich on her wealth.

For an observer in the eastern Mediterranean the constant passage of goods to Rome at the end of the first century AD was one of the most notable effects of Rome's domination and, therefore, in dreaming of Rome's fall the consequences for the local economies of the Mediterranean and for those who traded between them were bound to loom large. The language and sentiments of this part of *Revelation*, of course, belong to the well-known discussions of the deleterious effects of luxury; but it needs to be emphasised that the visible reality which underlay the debate on *luxuria* is itself testimony in great measure to the huge increase in trade as a consequence of the Roman empire. The Mediterranean had become Rome's port, as Cicero dramatically represents it (*On the Consular Provinces* 31):

> iamdiu mare videmus illud immensum . . . ab Oceano usque ad ultimum Pontum tamquam unum aliquem portum tutum et clausum teneri.
> (We have long seen that vast stretch of sea from the Ocean to the farthest shore of Pontus held as it were a single safe and closed harbour.)

(See the allusive and stimulating comments of Purcell (1996), who recognises the close interactions between ports, local regions, and the wider world.)

That Roman imperial expansion, even from its earliest days, should be linked to a major increase in commerce should not be doubted. It deserves far greater emphasis than it is usually given in modern accounts. The evidence is clear and varied. Interference with trade could be a factor in Rome's decision to intervene in an area (as for example in the first Illyrian War of 230 BC: Polybius 2. 8). Despite the fact that there is a strong modern tradition which seeks to play down this sort of evidence, commerce deserves to be reinstated among the major factors involved in imperialism. A complex phenomenon like Roman imperialism is likely to be explained not by some one cause, but by the interaction of a number of factors. Even if the mainspring of Roman imperialism was not explicitly economic, the economic consequences were often immediate and great. Consider the exploitation of Spain, which closely followed its incorporation as a province of the empire (see e.g. Richardson 1976). In these cases it is often presumed that the key factors are the decisions of the governing authorities in Rome. But the real initiative lay with hundreds of individuals who had an eye to the main chance. Traders accompanied armies. Indeed, they were frequently in advance of armies and could be a vital source of information for Roman commanders (so Caesar summoned *mercatores* to pool their knowledge of Britain, 'because no one, except traders, goes there without good reason' (*Gallic Wars*, 4. 20)). Some peoples banned the consumption of Italian wine, because it was suspected that it was a part of the Roman fifth-column, designed to sap the energies of Rome's opponents (the Nervii in Caesar, *Gallic Wars*, 2. 15, cf. 4. 2). But it was surely because this was exceptional behaviour that it came in for comment.

The linkage between empire and commerce is illustrated in detail by Cicero in his discussion of Sicily (*Verr.* 2. 2. 6):

> We have many citizens who are the richer, because they have close at hand a loyal and profitable province, to which they can travel with ease, and where they can carry on their business (*negotium*) freely. To some of these Sicily supplies income and sends them home with profits and their accounts in the black (*quaestu compendioque*). Others she keeps there, so that they may become arable farmers, stock farmers or businessmen (*negotiari*), and in short that they may settle and make their homes there. It is of considerable advantage to the *res publica* that so large a number of citizens should be kept close to their own country, engaged in occcupations so honourable and profitable.

The implication of the last sentence is that by Cicero's day many Roman citizens were seeking their fortunes much further afield. The trading links between those in the provinces and those back home meant that the success or failure of those acting in the provinces had knock-on effects on those in the home ports. So it was not just Sicilians who protested about Verres. Cicero claimed that the people of the Campanian port of Puteoli turned out in a body for Verres' trial (*Verr.* 2. 5. 154):

> The traders (*mercatores*), wealthy and honourable men, have come in great numbers for this trial. They tell us that their partners, their freedmen, or fellow-freedmen were plundered and thrown into prison; some were beheaded ... When I call for the evidence of Publius Granius, so that he can tell how his own freedmen were beheaded by you, and claim back his ship and cargo from you, you shall prove him a liar if you can.

Governors could not afford to ignore the interests of those involved in trade and business in their provinces. Cicero was to boast of his own behaviour in Sicily, when there as quaestor in 75 BC (*On behalf of Plancius*, 64):

> negotiatoribus comis, mercatoribus iustus, mancipibus liberalis, sociis abstinens (I was affable to the businessmen, just in my dealings with the traders, generous with those who had contracts in the corn trade, and displayed self-control as regards the partners in the companies of the *publicani*)

(the reference to *socii* is most likely to the companies of *publicani*, rather than 'allies', because Cicero is comparing himself to

Plancius, and one of the charges against Plancius was his shady involvement through his father with the companies of the *publicani*).

The remark also neatly illustrates the careful observation of social gradations by Cicero. So *negotiatores*, the money men who set up deals, were likely to be Cicero's social equals – hence the open friendly discourse. *Mercatores* were going to be slightly down the social scale, but could still expect Cicero to ensure fairness if, as frequently happened, their dealings were the subject of litigation. *Mancipes* would expect Cicero to promote their interests and, of course, Cicero would be a model governor in avoiding making any demands for a cut from the activities of the *publicani*. The subtle differences in Cicero's approach to relations with each group also reveal why we hear more, and in more detail, of the big *negotiatores* in the literary sources rather than *mercatores* and the like.

Many more examples from literary sources are available. But it will be objected that little of it illuminates the issue of scale. Did the empire make a great difference to the economic lives of a large number of its inhabitants? Other types of evidence, evaluated in their own terms, converge to strengthen the case for a positive answer. So, for example, the archaeological evidence of amphorae from wrecks in the Mediterranean reveals a period of some three centuries, from 125 BC to AD 175, coinciding with the height of Rome's domination of the Mediterranean world, during which the number of wrecked cargoes is at least two to three times higher than the period which precedes it or that which follows. Even if we suppose some sort of bias in the archaeological record, the overall picture cannot change to the extent of ironing out this notable peak. There is not going to be similar evidence of activity on such a scale again until the high Renaissance (Parker 1984, 99–113). (On the problems of this sort of quantitative data see Fitzpatrick 1987, 79–112. But see also Parker's pertinent comments on the interpretation of the archaeological record in Parker 1990.)

It is important to recognise the mechanisms at work here. This peak in activity exactly coincides with the full development of the Roman empire. But it did not emerge from nothing. If we take the example of the trade in Italian wine, then the increase in numbers of Graeco-Italiot amphorae testifies to trade in quantity from at least the early third century BC (Parker 1990, 329; Mana-corda 1986). This involved centres such as Minturnae and the cities of Magna Graecia, particularly in Sicily. But the trade also leads to profound changes in the areas of reception of the wine. For example, in Gaul the luxury goods associated with the drinking of wine, often found in prestige burials, disappear completely as the importation of wine in amphorae and of mass-produced black-glaze pottery increases (Morel 1990). Wine had become a much less rare, and therefore less prestigious good, and was distributed and drunk more widely. What Morel does in his brilliant discussion is to demonstrate that the key changes only become identifiable by considering the totality of archaeological evidence over a long period of time. Then the big changes become much more clear, and this particular one is most naturally interpreted as the result of commerce. The coming of the Roman empire provides increased security, while rising populations and rising expectations create a whole range of new opportunities for those already involved in trade. (I am doubtful about Hopkins's famous model, which argues that the imposition of taxation on new provinces is the key stimulus to trade: Hopkins 1980. See the critique of Duncan-Jones 1990, 30ff.) The archaeological evidence is testimony to the decisions of numerous individuals, based upon self-interest, to take advantage of the new conditions.

The development of Roman commercial law is another body of material, still underexploited, which provides further confirmation of trade great in scale and sophisticated in organisation. The beginning of *Digest* 18 quotes the second-century AD jurist, Paul, who recognises the importance of the introduction of money for easing the exchange of goods and the limitations of a barter system (*Dig*. 18. 1. 1):

> Today it is a matter of doubt whether one can talk of 'sale' (*venditio*) when no money passes.

There had been a lively debate among first-century jurists as to whether such exchanges could be deemed *venditio* or *permutatio* (barter). What is happening here is the Roman law coming to grips with the realities of a monetary economy. Much of Books 18 and 19 of the *Digest* is concerned with the large-scale transactions between producers and middlemen or between one wholesaler and

another, not with the retail trade (*Dig.* 18. 6. 2 *pr.* envisages two
kinds of sale of wine: one by the estate owner, who needs to ensure
that his *dolia*, used to store this year's wine, are emptied in time
for the next vintage; the other by the *mercator qui emere vina et
vendere solet* 'the merchant who regularly buys and sells wine').
The jurists' language reflects what may be dubbed 'mature mercantilism' (Frier 1983) or, perhaps better, 'mature commercialism'
– that is, that the deals envisaged are objective and impersonal
between individuals who have no necessary connection with each
other, other than that created by the contract of sale itself. Indeed,
this is the whole point of the development of the law in this field;
it is how to ensure that the conditions of sale are carried out, when
those involved do not have any other personal, moral, or social
relationship, which might constrain them to respect the terms of
the deal. The jurists also reflect the world of a free market, as it
were, in which it is open to individuals to make contractual agreements on any terms which suit the parties concerned, unencum-
bered by tradition, state legislation, or the like. For example,

> the measures and prices with which the *negotiatores* deal in wine are
> a matter for the contracting parties; no one is obliged to sell, if dissat-
> isfied either with the price or the measures, especially when nothing
> is done contrary to the customary practices of the region.
> (*Dig.* 18. 1. 71, quoting a rescript of the Antonine period)

The measure presumably reflects the conditions of long-distance
trade, where it is necessary to take account of local custom and
practice.

The sale of wine figures greatly in the legal sources, in part
because of its prominence as a product which was traded in quantity and over distance, but principally because the nature of the
product highlighted key issues for the lawyers. In particular, wine's
natural and frequent tendency to go off raised two problems. At
what point in the transaction did the seller cease to have any
liability for the quality and nature of the wine sold? And under
what circumstances might the wholesale buyer have some sort of
comeback for wine which had become vinegar? As Bruce Frier
(1983) showed in a ground-breaking study, which deserves the
widest recognition among economic historians, the ways in which
the Roman jurists tackled these problems reveal much about the
nature and scale of commerce in the Roman empire. Wine which

turns to vinegar could have serious consequences for the wholesale buyer, who, having bought large quantities in good faith, finds
the value of his investment drastically reduced before it can be
disposed of. The legal issues involved were already being dealt
with by the early classical jurists – in itself an indication of the
importance of the wine trade. They exploited the doctrine of *error
in substantia* ('mistake as to substance'), where one of the parties
had entered into the sale agreement under a misapprehension as
to the 'material substance' of what was being sold. But in the
imperial period this doctrine was sidelined in favour of a much
more flexible system based upon the seller's bona fide obligations
to the buyer. Not only did the seller have to be responsible for
any claims he might make for the object of sale, he also had to
protect the buyer against any false assumptions which the buyer
might have about the product. There can be no doubt that the
result was to increase the liabilities of the seller in favour of
the buyer. Those liabilities, of course, were not unlimited. The
process by which the buyer tasted the wine and then either
accepted it or rejected it (*degustatio*) was in the interest of both
parties. Once the buyer had expressed satisfaction after tasting
the wine, then the seller was no longer liable, unless he had made
some specific claims about the quality of the wine and its ability
to last. Equally, the buyer had no case if he complained about the
quality of the wine later but had not taken the opportunity given
to him to taste it (see e.g. *Dig.* 18. 6. 16). Usually these large-scale
deals were between businessmen, who might both buy and sell
wine on different occasions. Even where the seller was a vineyard
owner, it was in his interest to have a balanced and fair set of
principles to govern these transactions, particularly to ensure that
the wine-dealer returned to take his next vintage from him. What
all this reveals is that the minutiae of the Roman law on sale are
not simply esoteric, academic legal quibbles, but are the creation
of jurists attempting to tackle real problems in the real world. In
this case the world was one of mature, large-scale commerce.

All the above is intended to provoke. There seems to me to be
an overwhelming body of different kinds of evidence (literary,
legal, epigraphic, and archaeological) all supporting the conclusion
that during, and to some extent as a consequence of, the Roman
empire the nature, scale and complexity of trade was quite unlike
that in the periods which preceded or followed. The explanation of

this expansion, of course, is likely to be multifactorial; but (to continue the provocation) central prominence deserves to be given to the initiative and entrepreneurship of thousands of individuals involved in attempting to satisfy the growing expectations of the populations of the Mediterranean under Roman rule – in short a market economy. Yet the vast majority of modern scholarship prefers to find alternative explanations, which seek to minimise both the scale and nature of commerce in the ancient economy. So, for example, Peacock and Williams (1986, 55–63) offer a range of explanations of the long-distance movement of goods in amphorae:

- reciprocity – gift exchange;
- redistribution – the state supply of the *annona* and the needs of the Roman armies;
- marketing.

But they play down the role of the market. Whittaker (1985) offers the model of the circulation of goods within the households and between the properties of the senatorial elite, so that a great deal of what was produced on their estates was consumed by their own households, their dependants, and their slaves. Long-distance overseas transport of goods, so it is claimed, frequently represents the transfer of provisions from overseas estates to the senatorial houses in and near Rome. Tchernia (1987) offers a variation on the theme. He interprets the evidence not as the workings of markets, but of the circulation of goods around the networks of friendship and obligation built up by the elite. This sort of approach was worked out in a much more sophisticated way by Manacorda (1989), who recognises the relative complexity of the structure of the wine trade and the numbers involved but argues that the elite producer could cream off the profits of all the stages involved in trade: production, wholesale, distribution, and retail through the use of slaves and freedmen. Underlying all these arguments is the assumption, sometimes unspoken, that the one thing that cannot be happening is a free market. So Tchernia simply states that the existence of a market economy

> presupposes the distribution of information, the spread of a social and material infrastructure (merchants, means of transport), and an entrepreneurial spirit, for which there is no evidence in antiquity. The

market economy is not to be excluded *a priori*, but no more does it constitute the natural model one should automatically turn to to explain the archaeological evidence.

(Tchernia 1987, 329)

The ghost of M. I. Finley is everywhere. It needs to be remembered that his marginalisation of traders and of the scale of their enterprises is based on his studies of archaic and classical Greece, and that at least until late in life he was sceptical of archaeological evidence. All the evidence suggests that trading activity in the Roman empire is not just greater in scale than in the classical Greek world, but that it is different in kind.

The reality is that there is evidence for all the mechanisms suggested for the movement of goods; but the various pieces of evidence, even those which sometimes appear contradictory, apply to different layers or sectors of the economy. They are often parts of the same continuum, but reflect the preoccupations and perceptions of people at different points in the chain. The question then is which mechanism predominated. Direct sale from the farm gate is contemplated, but no one suggests that this is the major way in which goods reached the consumers. Equally the widespread distribution of many amphorae types across many sites of different kinds tells against the idea that this represents principally the circulation of goods within the estate-owner's family and retainers.

One of the more powerful models is redistribution, by which the Roman state seeks to supply its armies and the *annona* for the city of Rome. But it is clear that the redistributive system presupposes the presence of a multiplicity of private *negotiatores* and *mercatores* to enable it to work; Claudius and later emperors had to offer incentives to private *negotiatores* and *domini navium* to be willing to participate in the supply of corn to Rome (Suetonius, *Claudius* 18 and *Dig.* 50. 6. 6. 3ff.). This was extended to *navicularii*, who 'served the *annona*'. But the state supplies provided for only a minority of the population of Rome. Even given that a significant proportion of the rest relied on supplies from their patrons, there is still a large amount left to be provided by the private merchants (see Sirks 1991a, 1991b). In any case, for an important product like wine, there were no state distributions in Rome until Aurelian; so the supply lay largely in the hands of those involved in the wine trade. Traders, merchants, and entrepreneurs are not marginal. They are at the heart of the economic system, which provided for the needs of people, and they under-pinned the state's contribution as well.

A major part of the determination to play down the abundant sources for commerce rests not only upon the indubitable fact that agriculture provided for the lives of the vast majority of the popu-lation of the ancient world but also on a false dichotomy between agriculture and trade. They are not alternatives, but are inextri-cably linked in the chain of production and consumption in the Roman empire at all levels. The concept of the self-sufficient peasant is a myth. All peasants had to go to market for essentials, such as salt, and the evidence from modern peasant societies is that where markets exist then peasants are quite capable of forgoing self-sufficiency in order to devote part of their small prop-erty to the production of goods for that market. Even more instructive are the agricultural handbooks produced for the large landowners in the Roman empire. These handbooks, albeit that they frequently smack more of the library than the farmyard, deal with two distinct and very real concerns of the elite estate-owners. The failure to recognise this has been the source of endless muddle in modern debate. The first need of the *paterfamilias* is to provide for the good running of the household and the estate. In this the aim is self-sufficiency, to minimise the costs of an estate by ensuring that as far as possible the physical and nutritional needs of those working the estate are met from the estate's own resources. Hence the importance of mixed farms, where parts of the estate can be devoted to the production of corn simply to feed the estate-workers. The second concern is with production for profit. The two goals can be neatly illustrated by an example of the different legal outcomes, which depended on the purpose of exploiting a claypit on an estate:

> Such a requirement might exist, for example, if a man has a pottery where the containers used to carry away the produce of his farm are made (just as on some estates it is the practice to carry wine away in amphorae or to manufacture *dolia*) or where tiles are made to be used in building his villa. However, if the pottery is used to manufacture vessels for sale, this will amount to usufruct.
>
> (*Dig.* 8. 3. 6)

The estate-owners expected to profit from their estates. In this they were what modern economists would describe as 'profit-satis-ficing' and 'risk-averse'. That is, they set a level of return with which they would be satisfied – often arrived at arbitrarily, or by comparison with the return from neighbours; above that level other goals might apply – the pursuit of pleasure or leisure, or the avoidance of further hassles. Second, in seeking the expected return, the owners were fundamentally averse to taking risks with their investments. The famous discussion on the profitability of viticulture in Columella, *RR* 3. 3 is essentially an attempt to persuade people who are risk-averse to invest in vines. In this Columella shows himself more adventurous than many of his contemporaries; elsewhere in his work, though, he is as cautious as any of the writers on agriculture. Nevertheless, profits there must be (Columella, *RR* 1. 1. 3: *certam sequi rationem rei familiaris augendae* (to pursue a secure method of increasing one's property)); but the extraordinary thing is that the handbooks on agriculture entirely ignore the issue of marketing. In this they were setting a trend which was to survive to the eighteenth century, in which writers on agriculture are exclusively concerned with the good regulation of agricultural work, which was conceived as the adequate performance of a household without reference to the place of this household in the larger economy. The best explanation of this surprising lack of interest in markets is if the large estate-owner is not directly concerned with the marketing of the products of his farms, because that lay in other hands.

Once again the legal texts, particularly on wine, offer confirmation. We know from anecdotal evidence (e.g. Pliny, *Letters* 8. 2) that it was convenient in many ways for the task of picking the grapes, making the wine, and organising its sale and distribution to be left to middlemen, *negotiatores*, who brought in their own gangs of pickers, but used the estate's equipment, and left the wine to ferment in the estate's *dolia* before removing it within a year in their own amphorae. But this raised the problems of who was responsible for the wine at any part of the stage and, indeed, whose wine it was – as Gaius, *Inst.* 2. 79, wrote: 'If you make wine from my grapes, the question is whether it is my wine' (cf. *Dig.* 41. 1. 7). This sort of situation might have arisen when a dispute occurred over a contract for the sale of grapes on the vine, after the grapes had been pressed. If the dispute was over the original contract, the situation for a settlement could be complicated, since the original grapes no longer existed, but the wine had been made by the *negotiator*, who had paid and provided the labour.

The period during which wine was left in the estate's *dolia* also raised questions, as, for example, when someone had willed an estate with its *instrumentum,* was the heir entitled to wine in the estate's *dolia* which had already been sold and part-paid for (*Dig.* 33. 7. 27. 3)? Finally, what happened when the *dolia* were needed for the next vintage but the *negotiator* had not turned up to take last year's wine away? The jurists were very circumspect, recommending not that the wine be poured away, but that it be transferred to other storage and the cost put down to the buyer (*Dig.* 18. 6. 1). In this the jurists recognise the particular case of the *mercator*, 'who regularly buys and sells wine' (*Dig.* 18. 6. 2).

Nice legal problems can illuminate what happens to the wine once it is in the hands of merchants. Some might store the wine and use some of it for their own purposes, while intending to sell the bulk of it. If the merchant then wills the contents of his store-room (*promptuarium*), the lawyers had to provide a formula ('sufficient for a year's supply for himself and his household') to distinguish between what had been intended for the household's store and what was to be traded: 'This tends to happen in the cases of *mercatores* or whenever a store of wine or oil which was normally sold on is left in an inheritance' (*Dig.* 33. 9. 4. 2).

The sale, transport and marketing of goods could be carried out in a variety of ways with a range of people involved. The *negotiatores* should normally be seen as the large-scale wholesalers who finance the trade. They may, or may not, also play the role of *mercatores* who are directly involved in the transport and sale of the product. There are also the people involved in the financing and organisation of the shipping of goods. Here the *navicularii* seem to play the same role as financiers of shipping as the *negotiatores* do for trade as a whole, although their role may also merge with that of the *mercator*. Then there are the actual masters of the ships. The roles and titles of the various individuals who may be involved are not clear-cut. Almost all combinations seem possible. For example, there is the famous example of Sextus Arrius from the Dramont A wreck. His name appears both on the anchor and stamped on the lids of the amphorae that formed part of the cargo. He presumably both owned the ship and was carrying, as at least part of the cargo, goods in which he himself was trading (see Hesnard and Gianfrotta 1989). The true complexity of the world of trade comes out in the famous inscription recording the honours held by Gnaeus Sentius Felix, a prominent citizen of Ostia at the end of the first century AD. He was senior official, or patron, or co-opted member of the *collegia* of superintendents of sea-going ships, the shippers from the Adriatic, of a guild which met in the wine forum, of the bankers, of the wine-dealers of the city of Rome, of the corn measurers of Augustan Ceres, of the corporation of rowers, and of the ferry-boat men of the Lucullus crossing, of the citizens from the forum and the public weigh-house, of the oil-dealers, of the young cabmen, of the guild of the catchers and sellers of fish – to leave aside a host of other bodies involved in the administration of Ostia, but not directly in trade (*CIL* xiv. 409).

Ostia, of course, was an exceptional entrepôt, but on a smaller scale a similar range of people could be found at any of the many major ports in the Mediterranean. Lower down the social scale were jobs for porters and stevedores on the docks (on the use of free labour in cities see Brunt 1980). In a world of expanding markets there were many niches and opportunities here to be exploited by the ambitious at all levels of society (this is the multiplier effect which Keith Hopkins saw at work in the economies of ancient cities (Hopkins 1978, 107 n. 19)). The legal evidence in particular suggests that they did so.

There is a powerful alternative to this model – it is to emphasise the role of the freedman and the *institor*, the person who manages an enterprise on behalf of another. By means of these institutions the rich landowner might reap the rewards of trade indirectly by creaming off the profits through putting his or her representatives in place at each of the key stages in the trade (Manacorda 1989; Aubert 1994). In this model we should not envisage a free market, with opportunities to be exploited by anyone who can get a niche in it, but rather a relatively closed market in which profits largely return directly or indirectly to the wealthy landowner. No one can doubt that wealthy people did carry on business overseas through their slaves and freedmen. For example, *Digest* 40 deals with the circumstances in which a person frees his slaves at a time when he believes he is solvent, but in fact he is not so:

This often happens to people who carry on business through their slaves and freedmen overseas (*transmarinas negotiationes*) or in regions where they are not themselves living. They are often not aware of the losses incurred over a long period and bestow the favour of freedom on their slaves, manumitting them without intent to fraud.

(*Dig.* 40. 9. 10)

The implication of the passage, it is worth noting, is that such a system carries with it real risks. There can be no doubt that there is ample evidence, particularly in the legal texts, for both main types of organisation of trade:

• commerce carried on between individuals who have no connection with each other and whose transactions are impersonal and have to be moderated simply by the law;
• commerce in which the individuals concerned have connections other than the transaction itself, such as being the slave or freedman representative or client of someone else.

So, for example, at each stage in trade a person involved may very well be dealing not with the principal but with a representative, his slave or freedman acting as an *institor*. But what there is little or no evidence for is the set-up where all the people involved were in some way the subordinate of the original wealthy producer. There is little or no evidence that the whole process of producing a good, getting it onto the market, transporting it, and selling it retail is usually, or ever, kept 'in house'. Slaves, freedmen, business managers, clients, and the like complicate the picture of the organisation of trade, but they do not undermine a model of a dynamic mercantilism, which brought benefits to a wide range of individuals directly or indirectly.

It is gratifying that this model of a relatively dynamic economy in which large numbers of independent operators take part and make their livelihoods is confirmed by the best and fullest body of evidence available for the structure of the trade in a particular good – that is, the trade in olive oil from southern Spain. The amphorae which carried this oil, the well-known large bulbous amphorae, usually designated Dressel 20, frequently have not just stamps on them, but other painted inscriptions, which appear in a largely standard format and reflect the practices used in production and trade (for an admirable summary of a long and complex debate see Liou and Tchernia 1994). The stamps, usually on the handle, are of the producer of the amphorae. Many of the production sites have been identified in the Guadalquivir valley in southern Spain. These areas were occupied by multiple workshops, which to judge from the names on the stamps were owned and operated by different people, who had not connection with one another. One of the painted inscriptions found frequently on these amphorae, the one labelled δ by scholars, gives the estate where the oil in the amphorae was produced, and its owner or his representative. There is no significant overlap between the list of names of the oil producers and the makers of the amphorae. The two parts of the trade lie in different hands. Another painted inscription, identified as β, undoubtedly represents the shipper, the *navicularius* or *mercator*. So, for example, there is the funerary inscription, found near St. John Lateran in Rome (*CIL* vi. 1935 =*ILS* 7489) to L. Marius Phoebus, who in the middle of the second century AD was described as *mercator olei Hispani ex provincia Baetica*, 'merchant in Spanish oil from the province of Baetica'; his name appears in a number of β inscriptions from the great dump of Dressel 20 amphorae in Rome, known as Monte Testaccio (*CIL* xv. 3943–3956) (L. Marius Phoebus is also described on his tombstone as a *viator tribunicius*, that is one of the *apparitores*, who attend and work for magistrates – in this case carry messages; his role as a trader may be important to his obtaining this position, which was one of some social standing). Again, there is no obvious overlap or link with the names which appear at other stages of production. This is a world of diversity, of multiple independent participants, linked only by business relationships, and, in particular with very little concentration of ownership or control, a conclusion which surprised Liou and Tchernia (1994, 152).

A dynamic economy, then, but clearly one with limits. There seems to be considerable growth which particularly accompanied the period of expansion of the empire and the establishment of the Augustan Peace. Contemporaries were aware of the changes: increased urbanisation, greater variety of goods, and changes in taste (much of this comes out in the contemporary debate about the dangers of *luxuria*). This pace of development then levels off during the first century AD. There is no sign of the economy 'taking off' to be transformed into a modern capitalistic economy. Failures of this sort lie at the heart of the contemporary debate about the economics of development (see Todaro 1994). The factors which contribute to economic development are many. Among the most important are the aggregate economic variables: growth of per capita output and population and rates of increase in total factor productivity, above all the productivity of labour. High levels of growth may be necessary conditions, but they are not in themselves sufficient. The pace of structural change in the economy must be high and must be accompanied above all by appropriate social and ideological changes. The growth in output and the rise in population in the Roman world up to the early empire may have been considerable, but they were not accompanied by a transformation in the productivity of labour. Nor were there the changes in thought and practice which could fuel progress. So the growth levels off.

It may be that it is largely inappropriate to think in terms of *the* Roman economy at all. The best model may be that of a network of micro-regional economies (on the complexity even of Roman Italy, see Foraboschi 1994). These micro-economies have their own natural rhythms and structures designed essentially to meet local needs (see Paterson 1991). But at certain periods some of these economies become more closely linked with the wider world and find a wider market for their goods. The key factor in establishing and maintaining these links was the work of the *negotiatores*. This exploitation of more distant markets could have significant effects on the structure and workings of the local economy. For example, the wine-producing area of Monte Massico on Italy's western coast on the edge of Campania for a time in the last two centuries BC found flourishing and extensive markets for its products. This in turn inspired the appearance of extensive areas of workshops to supply the *negotiatores* with amphorae around the main ports, most notably around Sinuessa. As the scale of export levels off and then declines at the end of the first century BC, these workshops disappear. There is still trade; but the amphorae now seem to be produced on individual estates (Arthur 1991). It is important to realise that these local developments are dependent on a much wider picture. They cannot be explained by local factors alone. Similarly, in southern Gaul kilns produced separate series of amphorae – some types for local distribution, and others for the wider export markets.

Somewhere about the beginning of the first century AD we may posit that the large-scale expansion of markets for goods such as wine and oil reaches a peak and then steadies. There are no great new markets to be found. What then happens is the creation of an 'economy of substitution' – in order to create markets for your goods you have to substitute them for the goods of others. So an increase in the exports from one area is normally matched by a decline in similar exports from another area. No new markets are created. The phenomenon was observed by contemporaries:

> So, in Latium and the land of Saturn, where the gods have taught their offspring of the fruit of the fields, we let contracts at auction for the importation of grain from our overseas provinces, so that we may not suffer from famine; and we lay down vintages from the islands of the Cyclades and from the regions of Baetica and Gaul.
>
> (Columella, *RR* 1. pref. 2, mid-first century AD)

This sort of claim has its origins in part in the strong theme of self-sufficiency, which runs through all the writers on agriculture, and on the constant complaints about the import of luxuries. However, archaeology confirms that Columella was right. An increasing percentage of imported amphorae in the early empire is mirrored by a significant decline in Italian amphorae on sites in Italy. But not just that; within Italy itself different regions (the west coast, the Adriatic coast, NE Italy and Istria, Apulia, Bruttium, etc.) competed with one another to claim their share of the market for Italian wine and oil (see Panella and Tchernia 1994). There is no doubt that this sort of model can be replicated for other regions in the Roman world.

The reasons why one region enjoys a period of popularity and expansion in the market of its goods and then declines in the face of competition from another region are bound to be complex and not always clear-cut. But it is difficult to imagine that any mechanism other than the enterprise of individual *negotiatores*, combined with changing tastes and expectations, can explain this phenomenon. Faced with the threat of being labelled 'anachronistic modernisers', historians have been too quick to establish their credentials by playing down the nature, scale and sophistication of trade and commerce in the Roman empire. *Auri sacra fames* is not the guiding principle of just one economic system, but of most. The fact that people exploited opportunities to create or expand markets does not in itself mean that we are dealing with a modern economy. Indeed, it would have been extraordinary if Rome's expanding control of its empire had not had major effects on the economies of the regions which it came to control. The merchants and businessmen who created and took the opportunities which the empire provided lie at the edges of the elite literary tradition. But they left their mark in many other areas: in the legal texts, when the law was adapted to meet and promote their needs; in epigraphy, where they record their achievements with pride; and in the archaeology.

Bibliography

Arthur, P. (1991), *Romans in Northern Campania* (Archaeological Monographs of the British School at Rome, 1; London).

Aubert, J.-J. (1994), *Business Managers in Ancient Rome: a Social and Economic Study of Institores, 200 BC–AD 250* (Leiden).

Brunt, P. (1980), 'Free labour and public works', *JRS* 70: 81–98.

Duncan-Jones, R. (1990), *Structure and Scale in the Roman Economy* (Cambridge).

Fitzpatrick, A. (1987), 'The structure of a distribution map: problems of sample bias and quantitative studies', *RCRF Acta* 25–26: 79–112.

Foraboschi, D. (1994), 'Economie plurali ed interdipendenze', in *L'Italie d'Auguste à Dioclétien* (Collection de l'École Française de Rome, 198; Rome), 215–18.

Frier, B. (1983), 'Roman law and the wine trade: the problem of "vinegar sold as wine" ', *Zeitschrift der Savigny-Stiftung für Rechtsgeschichte* 100: 257–95.

Hesnard, A. and Gianfrotta, P. (1989), 'Les bouchons d'amphores en pouzzolane', in *Amphores Romaines et Histoire Économique, Actes du Colloque di Sienne 1986* (Collection de l'École Française de Rome, 114; Rome), 393–441.

Hopkins, K. (1978), *Conquerors and Slaves* (Cambridge).

—— (1980), 'Taxes and trade in the Roman empire (200 BC–AD 400)', *JRS* 70: 101–25.

Liou, B. and Tchernia, A. (1994), 'L'interpretation des inscriptions sur les amphores Dressel 20', in *Epigrafia della Produzione e della Distribuzione* (Collection de l'École Française de Rome, 193; Rome), 133–56.

Manacorda, D. (1986), 'A proposito delle anfore cosidette "greco-italiche": una breve nota', in J.-Y. Empereur and Y. Garlan (eds), *Recherches sur les amphores grecques* (*BCH* suppl. 13), 581–6.

—— (1989), 'Le anfore dell'Italia Repubblicana: aspetti economici e sociali', in *Amphores Romaines et Histoire Économique, Actes du Colloque di Sienne 1986* (Collection de l'École Française de Rome, 114; Rome), 443–67.

Morel, J. P. (1990), 'Les échanges entre la Grand-Grèce et la Gaule du VIIe au 1er siècle avant J.-C.', in *La Magna Graecia e Il Lontano Occidente, Atti del 29 Convegno di Studi sulla Magna Grecia*, 247–93.

Panella, C. and Tchernia, A. (1994), 'Produits agricoles transportés en amphores', in *L'Italie d'Auguste à Dioclétien* (Collection de l'École Française de Rome, 198; Rome), 145–65.

Parker, A. J. (1984), 'Shipwrecks and ancient trade in the Mediterranean', *Archaeological Review from Cambridge* 3: 99–113.

—— (1990), 'The wines of Roman Italy', *JRA* 3: 325–31.

Paterson, J. J. (1991), 'Agrarian structures on the lowlands: introduction', in G. Barker and J. Lloyd (eds), *Roman Landscapes* (Archaeological Monographs of the British School at Rome, 2; London), 133–4.

Peacock, D. P. S. and Williams, D. F. (1986), *Amphorae and the Roman Economy* (London).

Purcell, N. (1996), 'The ports of Rome: evolution of a "façade maritime"', in A. G. Zevi and A. Claridge (eds), *Roman Ostia Revisited* (London), 267–79.

Richardson, J. S. (1976), 'The Spanish mines and the development of provincial taxation in the second century BC', *JRS* 66: 139–52.

Sirks, A. J. B. (1991a), 'The size of the grain distributions in imperial Rome and Constantinople', *Athenaeum* n.s. 79: 215–37.

—— (1991b), *Food for Rome* (Amsterdam).

Tchernia, A. (1987), 'Modèles économiques et commerce du vin à la fin de la République et au début de l'Empire', in *El Vi a l'Antiguitat: Economia, Producció i Comerç al Mediterrani Occidental, Actes: i Colloqui d'Arqueologia Romana, Badalona, 1985* (Monografies Badalonines, 9), 327–36.

Todaro, M. (1994), *Economic Development* (5th edn, London).

Whittaker C. R. (1985), 'Trade and aristocracy in the Roman Empire', *Opus* 4: 49–75.

9

Trade and the city in Roman Egypt

Richard Alston

Method and problems

The aim of this chapter is to establish a model for trade in the *chora* of Roman Egypt and to ascertain the place of urban communities within that trading system. Such a task raises considerable methodological problems. We have abundant evidence for the activities of traders and for trade routes from Middle Egypt, both papyrological and archaeological. The quality of this evidence is, however, mixed and often anecdotal by nature: one document attesting a transaction may represent an ancient reality of hundreds of such transactions or just one. Quantification of economic activity is not an option. Instead of approaching the problem through statistical analysis, the only available method is to deal impressionistically with the evidence. Yet, the evidence is in such quantities that the only feasible approach is to quantify the material. The reader is cautioned that any figures produced below quantify surviving evidence, not the activity of the 'real economy'. We must have at the forefront of any analysis the knowledge that figures may be questioned both on the basis of the 'generality' of the evidence from which they were derived and on their applicability to the particular problem. *Caveat lector.*

The problem is, however, worth consideration since the sizeable and varied body of data from Egypt offers more evidence than is available for many other ancient economic systems and, of course, the role of the city and other communities in the trade network is as essential for a proper understanding of the nature and function of an urban system as an understanding of administrative and political structures. For the purposes of this chapter, I will limit discussion of economic exchanges between and within communities (trade) to exchanges which were not mainly or wholly administrative – that is, conducted by governmental bodies, including those acting in an official capacity, or related to taxation (which is, of course, of considerable economic importance).[1] The patterns suggested should not, therefore, reflect administrative or political organisation.[2] In the following analysis, I will examine three main themes: economic structures, goods traded, and patterns of communication.

1 Economic structures
   (a) Craft and trade specialisation: trade specialisation is a sign of a developed trade network. Professional traders need a market both to sell their goods and to purchase their food.
   (b) The regulation of craft production and retailing: any developed trade network may be subjected to governmental control. Authorities can act to prevent markets taking place, place pressure on traders and producers to offer goods at a market, or locate specific exchanges in specific contexts, thereby shaping the exchange network.[3]

---

[1] For most periods, with the exception of the archives from the sixth century AD, this is a relatively straightforward distinction to operate, though there may be doubts about individual transactions. On the great estates of the sixth century, the boundaries between public and private, state and estate, tax and rent, seem blurred, at least in our documentation (Gascou 1985).
[2] Tax rolls attesting ownership of estates in the territory of villages by metropolites are excluded from this analysis since these are classified as part of the administrative–political system. For a survey of the importance of urban landholdings see Rowlandson 1996.
[3] De Ligt 1995 usefully discusses the reasons why local authorities might wish to control the location of a local market. See also Shaw 1981 and Kehoe 1988, 216–17.

   (c) Monetarisation: an effective and convenient medium of
      exchange, though not essential, is a considerable advan-
      tage for the development of trade.[4] Extensive use of
      money, either in coin or through paper credits, in itself
      suggests or perhaps demands a certain level of trading
      activity (Hopkins 1980).

2   Goods traded

    Analysis of trade goods will examine those materials which
    can be detected archaeologically and also consider the papy-
    rological evidence for transport of perishables.

3   Patterns of communication

    These are assessed by examining the pattern of movement
    of people, either reflected through change of residence, or
    through the movement of documents. The latter method
    entails an investigation of places referred to in documents
    from two particular sites: Karanis and Oxyrhynchus. The prin-
    ciple of this analysis is very similar to distribution maps of
    archaeological artifacts, but since it is unlikely that documents
    would have had intermediate users, unlike pottery or coinage,
    the documents should attest direct contact between commu-
    nities. Such an analysis poses certain problems. Differentiating
    between communication that is purely administrative and that
    which is related to trade is not straightforward since, for
    instance, a soldier transported to Alexandria for administra-
    tive or judicial reasons may trade while in the city and send
    goods bought back to his family. Also, citizenship of an urban
    community primarily reflected status, not residence. Never-
    theless, since the documentation establishing such status
    normally refers to district of residence, I have tended to
    assume, unless there is evidence to the contrary, that all citi-
    zens of urban communities attested within rural communities
    would have some economic dealings with the city.

A second method of limiting the crippling effect of our imperfect
data is to assess the emergent picture against economic models.
There are many feasible models for Egyptian trade networks from
which I select three.

---

[4] Bohannan and Dalton 1962, 1–26 show that quite sophisticated
exchange can take place in a non-monetarised economy, yet, at a certain
level of economic activity, money becomes extremely useful.

1   Localised trade networks
    (a) Trade is limited to villages and their immediate environs.
        Several villages may trade with each other. Urban commu-
        nities function either outside the system without extensive
        trade relations with villages or as part of a village network,
        but have no special place within that network.
    (b) Trade is limited to the district (*nome*). The trade network
        incorporates villages and the city and probably focuses on
        the urban community. Most goods traded at urban or
        other markets are produced in the district for district
        consumption.
2   Regional trade networks
    Goods are exchanged within the district and across a wider
    region incorporating several urban communities. The network
    will sometimes focus on the urban communities within the
    system.
3   Long-distance trade networks
    Goods are traded extensively outside the region, reaching the
    most distant parts of the province or beyond.

These are ideal-types and any system will almost certainly show
a combination of such structures.

These models will be tested in the outlined areas of discussion
by studying specific village and urban settlements. For villages, I
shall concentrate on Karanis, though I will use material from other
Fayum villages. For urban communities, I will use papyrological
material mainly derived from Oxyrhynchus and archaeological
data from Hermopolis. This composite picture presents obvious
difficulties since there is no guarantee that trade networks were
similar in the Hermopolite, Oxyrhynchite and Arsinoite.[5] Karanis
and several other villages of the north-east Fayum contained an
unusually high proportion of Roman veterans. These distort the
evidence for trading from the village. Nevertheless, as I have
argued elsewhere (Alston 1995, 117–42), the impact of the military settlers in Karanis was not such as to alter materially the
culture and economic status of the village and, although account

[5]   Bagnall 1992 suggests a composite model of a *nome* using material
from Hermopolis and Karanis. The distribution of our evidence forces
such an imperfect approach.

will be taken of the distortions caused by the military settlers, there is no reason to treat the pattern from Karanis as uncharacteristic of that for other villages.

In the final section of the chapter I consider broader economic issues such as whether the model can be applied to communities outside Middle Egypt and the significance of the conclusions for study of the ancient city.

Villages

Karanis, mainly excavated in the period 1928 to 1935, is one of the best attested villages of Roman Egypt (Husselman 1979; Shier 1978; Johnson 1981; Boak and Peterson 1931; Boak 1933; Harden 1936; Haatvedt and Peterson 1964; Gazda 1983; el-Nassery *et al.* 1976). The archaeological and papyrological evidence suggests a large village with a population of 2,000–3,300 (Alston 1995, 229 n. 20), but the economic status of the villagers appears to have been quite low. There is no suggestion of elite residence within the village. Karanis was primarily dependent on grain and most of the land of the village was devoted to grain production. There was, nevertheless, some production of grapes and olives.[6] The archaeological evidence has uncovered several granaries, some seemingly attached to private houses.[7] In addition to these, the frequently attested *purgoi* (Preisigke 1919; Nowicka 1972; Husson 1983) were probably used to store agricultural products and householders could make use of either basements or upper storeys for storage. This suggests that the farmers stored large amounts of agricultural produce rather than selling most of each year's produce at market. There are notable similarities between the economic situation of the farmers of Karanis and that outlined by Gallant (1991, 94–8) for peasant farmers elsewhere in the Mediterranean region where the villagers used extensive storage facilities

---

[6]   In addition to the mass of papyrological data, there were two presses found in the village (Husselman 1979, 54, pl. 92a). For other foodstuffs consumed see Boak 1933. For fishing in Karanis see *P. Oxf.* I 12.
[7]   Husselman 1952 and Gazda 1983, 10–12 note at least seventeen granaries in Karanis of which seven were large. See houses C123 and C65 (Husselman 1979, plans 18 and 19).

to provide security in case of crop failure. For the peasant farmer, the major alternative to storage was to invest surplus in high value durables (coin, etc.) which could be used in times of crisis.[8] The latter strategy is more prudent in an area where crop failure is likely to be due to variations in the micro-climate than in Egypt where the Nile flood was the most important variable.[9] There would seem to be only limited reason for subsistence agriculturalists to become involved in the market. Nevertheless, there is evidence for involvement of the village in a trade network.

Rural traders and craftsmen are frequently attested in the papyrological material. The documentation is far from perfect or easily understood, but it seems likely that specialist craftsmen and traders formed about 6 per cent of the male population of Karanis.[10] Most villages probably had a fairly similar percentage of tradesmen and craftsmen.[11] At Karanis in 172–5, we have attested a flute player, dyers and fullers, weavers, an embalmer, a necropolis worker, wool-sellers, fish-sellers, vegetable-sellers, a butcher, a lamb-butcher, mechanics, wine-sellers, a purple-seller (?), a goldsmith, transporters, shepherds, cowherds, a doctor, a cobbler, hair-cutters and scribes. This is a more extensive range of traders than is attested for many other village sites and suggests that trade within the village was probably not limited to subsistence goods.

I have not been able to identify any shops in the archaeological record from Karanis and it seems likely that there were very few purpose-built retailing outlets in the village. There are no papyrological references to workshops and shops and there is little

[8]   Gallant 1991, 98–101, argues that in ancient Greece 'the market played only a minor, peripheral role in the domestic economy of most Greek peasants' (p. 101).
[9]   Local failures of the irrigation system could produce local dearths that could be met through the market, though the pattern of declarations of unwatered land seems to suggest that general problems were more common. For declarations of uninundated land see Avogadro 1935 with Montevecchi 1988, 187, and *BGU* XV 2489 with additional references.
[10]   Statistics derived from *P. Mich.* IV 223–5.
[11]   This is based on a survey of taxation and other lists from various villages. See R. and R. D. Alston (forthcoming). The relevant texts are *P. Corn.* 21 and 22, *P. Oxy.* XXIV 2412 and *SB* XIV 11715. Tebtunis and Theadelphia may conform to a rather different model (*SB* I 5124; *BGU* IX 1898).

evidence for a market place.[12] If there had been a regular market at Karanis, it would almost certainly have met in the temple *drumos*,[13] but this was precisely the area which seems to have been very heavily damaged by native excavations.[14]

The evidence for markets in other villages is also limited. There was a market at Philadelphia in the early first century AD (*P. Berol. Moeller.* 4; *P. Athens* 14), but I have no later references to it.[15] There was probably also a market at Ptolemais Hormou (*P. Petaus* 86) from where an *agoranomos* was selected in the early second century, and possibly markets at Tebtunis (*P. Lund.* VI 6; *PSI* X 1117), Theadelphia (*BGU* IX 1898; *P. Fay.* 93) and Alexandrou Nesos (*BGU* XIII 2275, 2293, 2336). Other non-urban markets are more difficult to locate. Markets at Elephantine and Karnak are attached to settlements which are difficult to categorise.[16] A sublicence to sell perfume in the Themistes district of the Arsinoite, dating to AD 161 and found at Theadelphia, reserved to the owner of the main licence the right to sell at the *agoron sun paneguresin* (*P. Fay.* 93), suggesting that there were some periodic markets, perhaps associated with religious festivals. Interestingly, the owner of the licence was an Alexandrian and the potential purchaser of the licence was from Ptolemais Euergetis, the *nome* capital.

Ewa Wipszycka (1971) suggests that the small farmers of the villages must have supplemented their incomes by engaging in part-time trading activities. There is, however, little evidence for part-time craftsmen, though one presumes that there was some

[12] Kerkesoucha, a village within the *territorium* of Karanis, is called Kerkesoucha Agora in the late third and early fourth century, but it is unclear whether there was a market in the settlement (*P. Cair. Isid.* 12, 99).
[13] For markets in *drumoi* see Wagner 1972; Rea 1982; Lauffray 1971; Jaritz 1980.
[14] Grenfell *et al.* 1900, 27, note the large open area in front of the temples and describe this as the *agora*. Grenfell and Hunt's archaeological skills and the time spent at the site were limited. The Michigan team described that area as destroyed by Sebakh hunters.
[15] In the Ptolemaic period, village markets appear to have been quite common. For Philadelpia see *BGU* VI 1271; *P. Cairo. Zen.* II 59161, III 59333; *P. Col.* III 13; *P. Freib.* III 26, 34; *P. Lond.* VII 2006, 2191; *P. Ryl.* IV 562; *PSI* IV 354, VII 856; for Tebtunis see *PSI* X 1098; for Magdola see *P. Enteux.* 35, and also *P. Koln.* I 50, 51, V 221.
[16] It is unclear whether these were classed as *metropoleis* or villages.

domestic production of cloth and other goods (Beauchamp 1993; Wipszycka 1965, 36). The Egyptian economy was heavily regulated with nearly all economic activities subject to some form of taxation. Traders were licensed by the government and the licensed, who had to cover the costs of the permit, had a financial interest in preventing unlicensed or part-time competition. In this way, the method of taxation encouraged craft specialisation.

One of the primary means of exercising control over trading activities was through guilds. San Nicolo (1972, 20) pointed out the relationship between trade guilds and religious associations and it seems possible that the guilds of the Roman period evolved from associations of traders attached to temples. Indeed, a religious element remained to the fore in many guild activities. We have little information concerning guild activities at Karanis, but those active at Tebtunis are relatively well attested. From registers of the mid-first century we hear of salt merchants (*P. Mich.* II 123 r. VII 127, r. XXI 40, r. XXII 27), dyers, fullers and oil workers (*P. Mich.* II 123 r. VII 16–19), weavers (*P. Mich.* II 121 v. IV 6, 123 r. III 41, XXI 31, 124 v. II 19), *rabdistoi* (*P. Mich.* II 123 r. XIV 17), carpenters (*P. Mich.* II 123 r. IV 5), and bronze smiths (*P. Mich.* II 123 r. XXII 18). The guilds regulated membership and competition within their area (*P. Mich.* V 245) and probably acted as guarantors of the quality of the product. Their social functions brought the guildsmen to the *metropolis* (*P. Mich.* V 243, 244; *P. Tebt.* II 584), though they met regularly in the village. The monthly guild presidents appear to have had considerable powers: they could impose fines or even arrest guildsmen (Boak 1937). The authorities also used the guilds as a means to organise requisitions and taxation (*BGU* VII 1564 and 1572; Jones 1960). Although the Tebtunis guilds were based in the village, the social and regulatory functions of the guilds brought the traders into contact with the *metropolis*, integrating the village into a wider network. Leasing and sub-leasing of trading concessions probably enhanced this urban–rural interaction. In AD 72, Theon son of Theon, a villager from Karanis, applied to a metropolite for a licence to sell wool in the village (*PSI* V 459). It seems probable that the metropolite held the concession for the area or for the *nome* and that he sub-let to other traders. Even if Theon was the only wool-seller in the village, such an arrangement brought him into contact with a network of wool traders.

The economy of the Fayumic villages appears to have been fairly heavily monetarised. Considerable numbers of coins have been found in Karanis: over 1,600 dating from 31 BC to AD 404, nearly 1,000 of which date to the third century, were found by the Michigan team (Haatvedt and Peterson 1964). The Grenfell and Hunt expedition found a small hoard of ninety-one coins dating probably to the late second century (Grenfell *et al.* 1900, 65). Investigations at Bakchias produced two hoards amounting to 4,483 coins, both of which were probably second-century accumulations (Grenfell *et al.* 1900, 65). Three further second-century hoards were unearthed at Tebtunis, while the casual finds from the site amount to a mere seventy-six Roman and Byzantine coins, mainly dating to the first two centuries AD (Milne 1935). The casual finds from Euhemeria, Philoteras, Theadelphia (Grenfell *et al.* 1900, 65–71), Tebtunis and Soknopaiou Nesos (Boak 1935) show a rather different pattern from the hoards in that the hoards have a preponderance of Neronian types which suggests that they were collections of the better pieces available. It would seem therefore that coinage was not simply fiduciary but that there was an awareness of the bullion value of the coinage.

The papyri attest transactions in both kind and coin and, of course, small transactions tend not to be represented in the papyrological material. A marriage contract from 143 (*P. Mich.* XV 700) lists items given in a dowry. These items were given a monetary value and this seems to have been a fairly standard pattern for dowries (Montevecchi 1936). Rathbone (1991, 318–30) has also argued convincingly that accounts on a large third-century estate were calculated using money as the primary means for calculating value. Analysis of the Appianus estate archives shows the workings of a sophisticated accounting system involving giro transfers, temporary credits and loans. It is difficult to believe that the estate evolved this system in isolation and it seems likely that the workings of the Appianus estate provide at least circumstantial evidence for the sophistication of the banking system in the rest of Egypt. Even though there were a number of exchanges in kind, money appears to have been the dominant medium of exchange within the villages of the Fayum.

There is very little evidence of the involvement of Karanis in long-distance trade, at least for the first two centuries AD, and even for the third century little non-Egyptian pottery is recorded in the site report (Johnson 1981, nos. 213–54). There is, however, evidence for regional trade. The lamps, for instance, appear to have been types which were distributed over quite wide regions. Of the four main types found at Karanis, two were distributed across the north Fayum and the Delta. The third was spread all across Egypt, and the fourth was mainly used in the Delta region near Alexandria (Shier 1978; Alston 1995, 229–30 n. 22).[17]

Karanis was on the road between the Fayum and Memphis and it had a customs post as the last village before the road entered the desert. Various customs taxes were paid but several *ostraka* and papyri attest payment of the Memphis harbour tax (*BGU* III 764, 765; *P. Lond.* II 469 (b), p. 86 *SB* VI 9234; XII 10914; Sijpesteijn 1987). The Memphis harbour tax was probably charged on goods passing between the Delta and Middle Egypt, Memphis harbour being the most obvious place to collect such dues, but payment of the tax at Karanis suggests that some goods would have circumvented Memphis when passing between the Fayum and the Delta and so we must presume that there were other trade routes running north from Karanis. Karanis has not produced any customs house registers which might allow assessment of the volume of goods passing through the customs post. It is likely that donkeys were used for shorter routes, as at Bakchias (see below) and camels for longer distances across the desert. A registration document (*P. Mich.* IX 543) from Karanis dating to 134–6 lists fifty-five camels and ten calves (owned by eight separate people) in the care of a single camel herder. This is a small herd but would have been capable of moving significant volumes of goods, around 350 *artabas* of grain. It is likely though that most bulky materials would have been moved from Karanis by donkey and water. The grain tax was moved mainly to the harbours at Leukagion or at Ptolemais Euergetis by donkey (*P. New York.* 11 (a); *P. Cair. Isid.* 15). One presumes that goods intended for market would follow a similar path.

We have customs house registers for Bakchias (*P. Wisc.* II 80) and Soknopaiou Nesos (*P. Lond.* III 1169; *P. Mich.* inv. 6124 and

---

[17]   T. Wilfong, curator at the Kelsey Museum, pointed out to me that the site of Karanis was so rich that very large numbers of artifacts were left on site (as is obvious from any visit) and that the 'editing' of the finds on site prior to recording biases our record. The rationale behind such choices cannot confidently be assessed but it seems likely that the better pottery would be more likely to be saved.

6131; *P. Amh.* II 77; Sijpesteijn 1987). All bar *P. Amh.* II 77 (AD 139) date to the late second or early third century. These are in the form of day books which appear to attest what was passing through a customs house on a particular day. They may, however, attest only what was registered by a particular tax collector since although all the documents attest the movement of agricultural products, mainly wine, oil, and grain, *P. Amh.* II 77 and *P. Lond.* III 1169 register mainly oil shipments while *P. Mich.* inv. 6124 and 6131 registers mainly grain and there are also discrepancies in the mix of animals used for transport: *P. Mich.* inv. 6124 + 6131 registers 297 camels and eight donkeys, *P. Amh.* II 77 registers thirty-eight camels and three donkeys, while *P. Lond.* III 1169 registers seventy-four camels and forty-five donkeys passing through the customs post at Soknopaiou Nesos. There seems no obvious explanation for such discrepancies unless our account books attest traffic of different types or heading in different directions.

The customs house books allow a certain quantification of what passed through particular accounts (see Table 9.1). This is achieved by calculating the average load, the likely number of loads passing through in the period covered, and the annual load assuming the typicality of the attested period. The annual traffic registered in the busiest individual accounts may have been sufficient to carry approximately 7,600 *artabas* of wheat or equivalent. Given that yield was probably around 10 *artabas/aroura*, 7,600 *artabas* would represent production from 760 *arouras*, about 7 per cent of the territory of Karanis. We cannot reasonably estimate the total volume of goods passing through the customs houses of the region but it would seem likely that the trade was of some economic significance (*contra* Drexhage 1982), especially if we presume that similar volumes passed through Karanis or that our books only attest a fraction of the trade through the particular customs posts.

This trade was clearly not conducted by large capitalistic enterprises. The number of animals per trip was small and we should not envisage great camel and donkey trains snaking across the Western Desert. It is more likely that a number of people invested in transport animals which were being herded within the village by professional herdsmen and then hired out to merchants, or used by the owners themselves to transport goods. The money at stake on any one trip cannot have been great. The major items

Table 9.1 Traffic registered in the customs accounts

Document*	Site	Attested no. of camels	Attested no. of donkeys	Average no. of donkey loads per trip†	Estimated traffic per annum in artabas of wheat
P. Wisc. II 80	Bakchias	—	133	2	7,355
P. Amh. II 77	Soknopaiou Nesos	38 (+ 1 calf)	3	7	6,000
P. Lond. III 1169	Soknopaiou Nesos	74	45	3	1,379
P. Mich. inv. 6124 + 6131	Soknopaiou Nesos	297	8	5.5	7,682

Notes: *Information derived from Sijpesteijn 1987.
†Camels carry twice the load of donkeys (Sijpesteijn 1987, 52–3).

transported were agricultural products. One can estimate that a donkey could carry about 250–500 *drachmae* of oil or 55 *drachmae* of wheat or 35 *drachmae* of wine, though there would have been significant variations according to the quality of the oil and wine and general economic conditions.[18]

The donkeys heading out from Bakchias were presumably on their way to the Nile valley. The camels and donkeys leaving Soknopaiou Nesos may have been heading towards Alexandria, but were more likely intended for the oases of the Western Desert. It is unlikely that this was a major trade route. The oases could be supplied along a route from the south of the Fayum passing through Dionysias where the Romans constructed a fort in the late third or early fourth century, presumably in part to control the route. There was no similar construction in the northern Fayum. Routes from Lykopolis and Oxyrhynchus were probably more important than those from the Fayum.

The arrangements for transport from the northern Fayum may have been similar to those attested in the 'archive of Nikanor' for the transport of goods to the stations and ports of the Eastern Desert and the Red Sea (*O. Petrie* 205–297; *O. Bodl.* 1968–1971; Fuks 1951; Adams 1995). Nikanor and his family seem to have

---

[18]   Prices from Drexhage 1991, 11–24, 43–50, 64–5.

supplied merchants stationed in the Red Sea ports and some soldiers with subsistence goods over a period of approximately seventy years. The merchants were normally agents of a third party who retained an account with Nikanor and his family and the goods delivered would be charged against that account. The amounts delivered suggest that some merchants were supporting small establishments, probably fewer than twenty people, in addition to ensuring their own subsistence needs (*O. Petrie* 228, 231, 257, 269; *O. Bodl.* 1970). Nikanor and his family moved mainly wine, grain, and drugs though they would move a range of materials such as tin (*O. Bodl.* 1968), clothing (*O. Petrie* 254), dye (*O. Petrie* 264) and wood (*O. Petrie* 267). They do not appear to have transported the goods which would have been shipped out to India and it was presumably from these latter goods that the Romans and Alexandrians attested as holding accounts with Nikanor made their money. The India trade probably brought significant profits (Harrauer and Sijpesteijn 1985), but the income of traders like the family of Nikanor is impossible to estimate.

Movement of people provides an indicator of patterns of contact between communities. Karanis is notable for the high number of Roman citizens resident in the village, the vast majority of whom owed their citizenship to military service, suggesting that many left the village at some point, though the relationship of this movement to economic structures is difficult to assess. In 314, inhabitants of the village of Buto in the Memphite *nome* were arrested in Karanis (*P. Cair. Isid.* 128) suggesting some communication or economic link with the Memphite.

Tax rolls from first-century Philadelphia allow some quantification of population movement. *P. Corn.* I 22 lists 114 male resident aliens in the village from a population of around 2,500–2,800 (Rathbone 1990). Depending on whether we presume that their families had come with them, the alien population was 4–13 per cent of the population of the village. Around 20–25 per cent of the aliens were tradesmen or craftsmen. A similar number of male Philadelphians probably resided away from the village. Registers from *c.* AD 49 (*SB* XIV 11481 and *P. Princ.* I 14; Hanson 1974) show that four registered male residents were away near Perseon, two at Boubastis (both Fayum villages) and sixty-four 'around the village'. This latter category probably includes those not at home when the tax man called and need not suggest that they had left the village for an extended period. Sixty-four men were, however, in Alexandria. A similar, though incomplete list (*SB* XVI 12632; Hanson 1980), shows that men were away at the Arsinoite hamlet of Hiera, the *metropolis*, Babylon, Alexandria, Iuliopolis and Parembole, though the document is too badly damaged to allow quantification. It seems that there was a high rate of mobility, especially among the traders and craftsmen of the villages.

We can trace the communication network through the Karanis papyri. I surveyed 850 papyri either from or mentioning Karanis which produced 164 attestations of places other than Karanis, of which eighty-eight dated to the second century. Some results are presented in Table 9.2. Although the military presence in the village skews attestations, links with Alexandria were important even if obviously military texts are excluded. There was some communication with communities beyond Egypt itself, though again this evidence is affected by the soldiers and veterans in the population, and even some of the documents which have no obvious military references may have involved soldiers or veterans. Contacts with non-Arsinoite communities were otherwise few and attestations connecting Karanis with Arsinoite communities, both other villages and the *metropolis*, predominate (61–75 per cent). The villages most commonly attested were those closest to Karanis. There are some surprises; one would have expected closer

Table 9.2 Communities in contact with Karanis (percentage of total attestations)

Place	Second century (all references)	Second century (excluding soldiers' documents)	All centuries
Arsinoite villages	45	55	46
Ptolemais Euergetis	16	20	26
Alexandria	20	10	15
Antinoopolis	5	6	4
Memphis	1	1	1
Herakleopolite	1	1	1
Latopolis	—	—	1
Pselchis	1	1	1
External to Egypt	10	6	7

connections with Antinoopolis[19] and Memphis and the percentage of attestations with Philadelphia (1 per cent) is low (Alston 1995, 61–8). The results do not depend on detailed prosopographic study of documents and where this has been possible, mainly in dealing with soldiers and their families (Alston 1995, 127–9, 137–8), a fuller picture of extra-village communication emerges. Nevertheless, it seems unlikely that the general picture is misleading. Villagers of Karanis communicated mainly with their neighbouring communities, Ptolemais Euergetis and Alexandria. There were few contacts with other communities.

Communications between *metropolis* and village were extensive, as one might expect. Some metropolites had land holdings distributed across the *nome* (Rowlandson 1996; Bagnall 1992; Bowman 1985). There were also links beyond the immediate *metropolis*, especially to Alexandria and from the 130s to Antinoopolis. *P. Fay.* 87 illustrates Alexandrian land holdings in a Fayum village. An estate which had belonged to the philosopher Iulius Asklepiades was managed for the city of Alexandria and seemed to bring in between one and two talents annually for the city. Many Arsinoites were made citizens of Antinoopolis and were expected to reside in the city for certain periods of the year in order to fulfil their civic duties. These families, however, retained their estates in the Fayum which continued to need working and managing (Alston 1995, 61–3; Bell 1940; Braunert 1964, 124–6).

Nomenclature provides some evidence for extreme 'localism' in Egypt. Theophoric names tended to reflect the local deity. The name Petesouchos, for instance, was popular in the Arsinoite where the local god was Souchos, while in the Thebaid *ostraka* the name is hardly attested (Braunert 1964, 20). Soknopaiou Nesos seems to have had a relatively stable population with few outsiders settled in the village (Samuel 1981). As a result, Greek nomenclature had only a limited impact. Soknopaiou Nesos was, however, rather a strange place, with only very limited agricultural land, and it appears to have been dominated by the traditional temple to a greater extent than other villages of the area, but, even here, though residents were mainly 'Egyptian', there seems to

[19]   This may in part be due to over-caution in identifying those active at Antinoopolis and Karanis.

have been contact with other communities and people with Greek or Roman names.

Village economies were essentially agrarian, as one would expect, and show some characteristics of subsistence-type agricultural production as outlined by Gallant (1991). The economy was, however, heavily monetarised and although there were exchanges in kind, many (possibly most) exchanges were expressed or considered in monetary terms. The coinage was not, however, treated as fiduciary as in a fully developed monetary economy. There was limited trade specialisation and although most traders probably catered for subsistence needs, such as clothing, some sold other types of goods. There would, therefore, have been a certain amount of trade conducted within the village, though the absence of trade facilities from some villages suggests that this internal trade may have been limited. The guilds of Tebtunis provide evidence for the local organisation of trade in one area at least and also show that village traders were associated with larger economic and administrative structures, probably based in the *metropoleis*. There was trade in agricultural produce and the trade network extended beyond the village and city to communities outside the *nome*. This trade appears to have been significant, but we should not envisage a high percentage of agricultural products being exported on the basis of the available evidence.[20] The villages of the Fayum were part of a wider trading network, though it does not appear that the network was particularly extensive. Fayum villages do not display autarkic economic organisation.

Cities

There is considerably more evidence for traders in cities than in villages, and traders and craftsmen formed a far higher proportion of the population in these settlements. The available data are problematic and quantification dangerous, but the best available estimate suggests that about 28 per cent of the male population of Oxyrhynchus (*P. Oxy.* XLIV 3300 and *P.Oslo.* III 111) and 27 per cent of the male population of Panopolis (*P. Berol. Bork.*)

---

[20]   Bagnall 1993, 88, argues that commerce in foodstuffs was essentially local. The available material does not contradict that judgement.

were registered tradesmen.[21] These numbers may well under-represent the proportion of the total male workforce employed since manual workers and assistants (Wipszycka 1965, 65) may not have been registered. A high level of craft specialisation is confirmed by a survey of crafts and guilds attested within Oxyrhynchus. Coles (1987, 230–2) lists thirty-three guilds that registered prices with the city authorities in the fourth century.[22] Many guilds and crafts are not represented in these lists.[23] Fikhman (1979) estimates there to be ninety different crafts attested at Oxyrhynchus. Some trades appear to have been mainly or wholly urban: bleachers, *oinemporoi*, dyers, linen weavers, bakers, silver-smiths, and glass makers. The number of craftsmen and the level of specialisation demonstrate the relative importance of trade within the urban economy.[24] To use the services of these traders, and probably those of many others as well, the villagers would have had to visit the city.

In contrast to the relative absence of evidence for retailing facilities from Karanis, there is an abundance of evidence from cities for retail outlets and other trade facilities. The building programmes instituted by the urban elites in the late first and early second centuries seemingly throughout much of Egypt also provided trading facilities. The *stoae* erected along the major thoroughfares were ideal locations for shops and stalls and the city could derive income from renting these spaces. The cities also provided *agorai*. There were at least three in Oxyrhynchus: an *agora* (probably the main market of the city) by the Serapeum (Rea 1982), probably along or beside the processional avenue between the two main temples of the city, a vegetable market in the south-east of the city (*P. Oxy.* I 43 v.), near a gate, and an

---

[21]   The sample for Oxyrhynchus is extremely small (fifty men), but that for Panopolis (410 men) reasonable. The registers list single (main) occupants and if we believe that traders and craftsmen were of a lower economic status than landowners, on average, our figures may seriously under-represent the tradesmen element of the population.

[22]   See also *P. Oxy.* LX 4081.

[23]   For lists of crafts see Fikhman 1965, 24–34, 122–7 (*non vidi*). *PUG* I 24 (provenance unknown) lists thirty-three guilds, not all of which are attested in the Oxyrhynchite lists.

[24]   Van Minnen 1986 may exaggerate the importance of the textile trade, though his calculations as to the relative importance of crafts and trades in Oxyrhynchus (van Minnen 1987) produce a reasonable conclusion.

agora of the shoemakers (*P. Oxy.* VII 1037).[25] The *agora* has not been located in most other cities. In Thebes there were at least two (Palme 1989), a north market (*O. Leid.* 79, 98, 105, 106; *O. Thebes* 49) and a south market (*O. Thebes* 77). One, possibly the north market, was outside the main pylon of the temple at Karnak where a tariff of charges and taxes has been found (see n. 13). At Hermopolis, there appears to have been a covered area which may have been used for retailing (*Stud. Pal. Pap.* V = *CPH* 119). *Macella* appear very rarely. There was a *macellum* in Hermopolis in the late third century (*Stud. Pal. Pap.* V = *CPH* 127v = *Stud. Pal. Pap.* XX 68 = *SB* X 10299) but other references (*P. Tur.* 50; *P. Rain Cent.* 159) refer to probably privately owned structures of the fifth or sixth centuries. The *agora* itself was an important source of income (*Stud. Pal. Pap.* V = *CPH* 102; *P. Herm.* 34).

These markets were rigorously controlled. The *agoranomoi*, who probably had responsibility for the registration of sales, almost certainly supervised the markets as well. Architecture represented the control of the city over trade. The stalls would have been partly obscured by the colonnades, which demonstrated the public nature of the space they occupied. Similarly the *agorai* were obviously public space. The markets near the temples were also dominated by buildings that had represented urban authority in the Pharaonic and Ptolemaic periods (Smith 1976). The market square at Elephantine was enlarged in the Augustan period and in the centre of the market was placed a large tribunal from where the market officials, or, indeed, any other official, could survey the market and the assembled population (Jaritz 1980). Tariffs were presumably posted in the market and the market would be the centre from where civil officials exercised control over trading in the city (Rea 1982; Wagner 1972).

We have no constitutions for guilds of Oxyrhynchus to compare with those of Tebtunis, but the evidence of declarations of prices from Oxyrhynchus (*P. Oxy.* LI 3624–6; LIV 3731–73; *P. Harris* I 73; *PSI* I 85, III 202) demonstrates monitoring of the guilds by the urban authorities. These were fourth-century declarations and represent a level of supervision that is not be attested in earlier periods. Nevertheless, other interventions are attested. The urban authorities in Oxyrhynchus sought to ensure the provision of oil

---

[25]   The sole reference dates to AD 444.

for the city by binding oil sellers by oaths when renting premises that they would supply the city with oil at appropriate prices (*P. Oxy.* XII 1455; cf. *PUG* I 21, 22). From as early as 116, measures were taken to ensure the supply of bread (*P. Oxy.* XII 1454), and the building and equipping of bakeries by officials is attested by 199 (*P. Oxy.* VI 908). By the middle of the third century Oxyrhynchus had a corn dole (*P. Oxy.* XL 2892–2940). Antinoopolis may have had a corn dole from its foundation (*P. Oxy.* XL 2941; 2942). Hermopolis and Alexandria also had doles (*W. Chr.* 425; Eusebius, *HE* 7. 21; Carrié 1975). There were public bakeries in other cities (*P. Hib.* II 220; *P. Sakaon* 23, 25). All this represents massive intervention in the market to secure cheap food for the city and thus improve the security of the urban population. The impact on the economic structure was probably to locate some trade outlets in the city and perhaps, because of increased security of supply of food, encourage trade and craft specialisation.

The archaeological data from cities are less good than those from villages and this has affected the surviving numismatic evidence. Over 1,500 coins were uncovered at Oxyrhynchus, seemingly from stray finds (Milne 1922). The coins date from the Ptolemaic period to the seventh century and show no obviously unusual patterns. The fourth-century coinage comes mainly from Eastern mints. Antioch, Alexandria (35 per cent), Nicomedia, Cyzicus and Constantinople account for 76 per cent of the coinage found. Rome (9 per cent), Aquileia, Arles, Trèves, Tarraco, Siscia and London account for 17 per cent. A certain amount of coinage from outside Egypt reached Oxyrhynchus, though the means by which it arrived cannot be assessed.[26] This pattern can be compared with that of hoards from other parts of Egypt of fourth-century date. These coins are mostly from Fayumic finds (one from Hawara (Milne 1920)) though their provenance cannot normally be more closely established. These four hoards show a range of 41.4–54.7 per cent of coins from Alexandria and 8.8 per cent (all Rome), 7.3 per cent (various mints), 2.8 per cent and 8.62 per cent (7.4 per cent from

---

[26]   Duncan-Jones 1994, 176 suggests that most money moved through the military in the late second century AD. Hendy 1985, 294–6, suggests some demonetarisation in the post-Diocletianic period. The evidence from Egypt seems considerably more optimistic.

Rome) from the West (Lallemand 1966; Milne 1920). The general pattern, therefore, differs slightly from the Oxyrhynchite evidence, with the coins from Oxyrhynchus having more cosmopolitan origins. The evidence is not such, however, to be able to assess whether this difference is due to the urban provenance of the Oxyrhynchus finds or to some other cause.

The papyrological evidence similarly points to the dominance of monetary transactions in the cities of Egypt, though low level economic transactions are rarely attested. Bagnall (1985, 49–55) has argued that there was a shortage of coinage in fourth-century Egypt and that coin continued to circulate as bullion. This seems a likely conclusion, though we should not underestimate the sophistication of exchange systems and the extent to which exchange was monetarised.

The archaeological evidence from cities, as we would expect, suggests a much greater range of trade links than the material from villages. The lamps from Antinoopolis (Donadoni 1974, 95), mainly of the third to fifth centuries, show typological similarities with lamps from across the Eastern Mediterranean, notably from Asia Minor, Greece (though tracing of origins is often problematic), and Africa, though there are a number of purely Egyptian types. This suggests a trade network extending beyond the province. The pottery report from the site is far from complete but, by contrast, the majority of reported finds of both fineware and amphorae were of Egyptian origin (Donadoni 1974, 72–95). The lamps and pottery from Hermopolis (Spencer 1984, 16–24) are not fully published, though a preliminary report on the pottery suggests that there was a small proportion of imported finewares from Tunisia (28 per cent). Local potteries produced 27 per cent of fineware, while Aswan ware (40 per cent) and Delta potteries (4 per cent) provided the rest. The Red Slip Ware shows a slightly different pattern. From the third to the eighth century, imported wares comprise 42 per cent of the attested examples, while local potteries produced 21 per cent and Aswan 29 per cent. A further 7 per cent came from an unknown Egyptian source.[27] The majority of the pottery came from Egyptian potteries, a pottery local to Hermopolis, potteries at Aswan and some wares from the Delta.

---

[27] See also discussion of amphorae and the identification of a Hermopolite type in Spencer and Bailey 1982, 16; Spencer ed. 1983, Appendix 3.

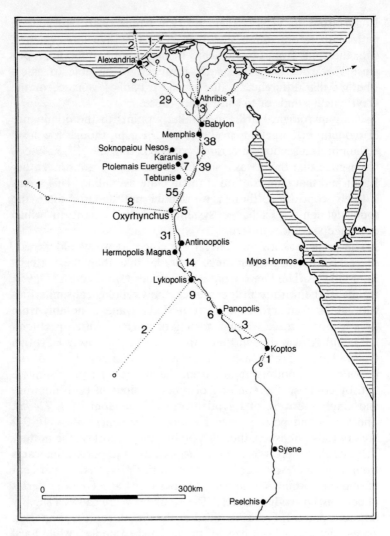

Figure 9.1 Communications from Oxyrhynchus (excluding Oxyrhynchite), first to sixth century AD (in per cent)

The communication network can be assessed from the Oxyrhynchus papyri. The documents are more suitable for such an analysis than the Karanis documents since there are far more documentary texts from Oxyrhynchus, and those published in the *P. Oxy.* series have an established archaeological provenance. Only the *P. Oxy.* volumes (I–LXII) were read for attestations of contacts with communities other than Oxyrhynchus. The majority of the texts come from the second, third and fourth centuries. The network can be plotted on a map and the linear geography of Egypt allows totals to be established for traffic heading to and through the various centres of the province. Of the 201 texts attesting communications with communities outside the Oxyrhynchite, more than half attest links to the north. Twenty-five per cent of the total, fifty texts, attest communication with Alexandria (Figure 9.1). If they are excluded, the north–south divide is remarkably even. We can break down this pattern by century and attempt to incorporate the figures for links with Oxyrhynchite villages. In the second century (n = 93), about 43 per cent of contacts were with localities external to the Oxyrhynchite, of which 12 per cent were to Alexandria. Only 6 per cent of contacts were with communities south of Lykopolis, and, excluding Alexandria, only 4 per cent were with communities north of Memphis (Figure 9.2). The third century (n = 145.5) shows a similar picture. Fifty-eight per cent of contacts were with communities from outside the Oxyrhynchite. Alexandria accounts for 13 per cent of these while 6 per cent of contacts were with communities south of Lykopolis and 6 per cent to Egyptian communities, excluding Alexandria, north of Memphis. Four per cent of contacts were with communities outside Egypt (Figure 9.3). Similar results can be derived for other centuries, though the statistical base is even smaller. Such calculations allow us to posit certain 'zones of intensity of contact'. In the second century, contacts to the north (excluding Alexandria) and south cease to be significant at about 165 km. In the third century, links to the south and north appear to have developed a little further with contact ceasing to be significant at about 200 km. Combining the evidence from the first six centuries AD, we can see that the Oxyrhynchite itself (the district) accounts for 40–50 per cent of all contacts. Zone 2 (the region), which is defined as including those cities that have ten or more contacts with Oxyrhynchus, comprises communities within a radius

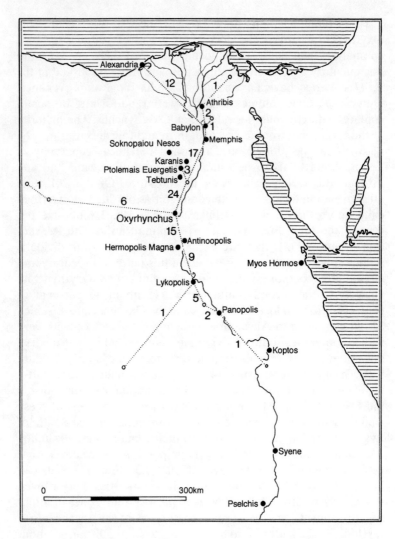

Figure 9.2 Communications from Oxyrhynchus (including Oxyrhynchite), second century AD (in per cent)

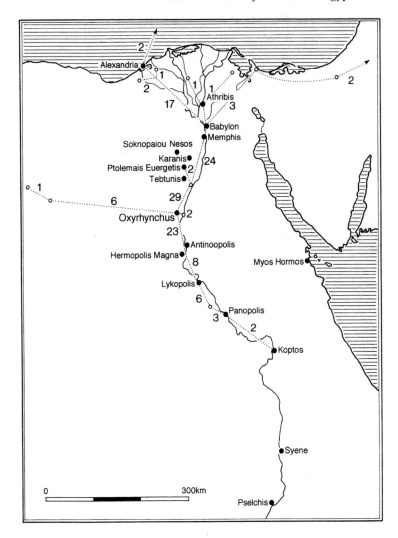

Alexandria
2
1
2
17
1
1
Athribis
3
Babylon
Memphis
Soknopaiou Nesos
Karanis
Ptolemais Euergetis
2
24
Tebtunis
1
6
29
Oxyrhynchus
2
23
Antinoopolis
Hermopolis Magna
8
Myos Hormos
Lykopolis
6
Panopolis
3
2
Koptos
Syene
0
300km
Pselchis

Figure 9.3 Communications from Oxyrhynchus (including Oxyrhynchite), third century AD (in per cent)

of about 90 km of the city and accounts for about 45 per cent of all non-Oxyrhynchite contact. Zone 3 runs for about 230 km north and 260 km south and involves about 17 per cent of all non-Oxyrhynchite contacts (Figure 9.4). Alexandria accounts for 25 per cent of all non-Oxyrhynchite contacts. The rest of Egypt and places external to Egypt account for only about 13 per cent of contacts.[28]

Oxyrhynchus and the other urban centres of Egypt acted as centres for retailing and production. In so doing, each city probably served as the economic centre for its surrounding *nome*, as it served as the religious and administrative centre. The city's trading relations extended beyond the *nome*, to the region, to Egypt beyond and to the rest of the Roman empire. It is, however, notable that although the archaeological, papyrological and numismatic evidence attests trade beyond the frontiers of the province, the majority of contact appears to have been within Middle Egypt and with Alexandria. It seems likely that the majority of non-Egyptian goods, including coinage, passed to these Middle Egyptian communities via the markets of Alexandria. These cities do not appear to have been heavily involved in long-distance trade. Regional trade may, however, have been very important, though the quantification of its absolute economic significance is, of course, impossible.

Conclusions: economic models, Egypt and the Roman empire

The trade network for Middle Egypt appears to conform to our second main model: a regional trade network focused on the urban centre. The cities were the focus of the district trade network but also were part of a regional trade network, communicating with nearby communities within Middle Egypt and presumably

---

[28] It is appropriate to remind the reader here of my initial warnings about the nature of the evidence and the methods used. It seems very likely that the preserved material over-represents the importance of trade outside the Oxyrhynchite since contact with distant places is more likely to produce documentation than contact with those in the nearest village, and the documentation probably over-represents the officially active and the wealthy – groups which may be expected to have more extensive networks of associates.

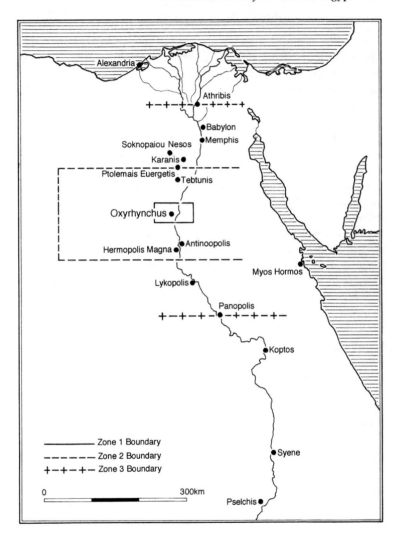

Figure 9.4 Zones of contact

engaging in trade with them, though the customs house registers
suggest that not all regional trade passed through the *metropoleis*.
Although goods from outside Egypt did make their way to the
cities and villages of Middle Egypt, there is little evidence of significant involvement in long-distance trade.

The final section of this study will look at the implications of
the model and its general applicability both to cities in other
regions of Egypt and to the rest of the Mediterranean.

There is substantial evidence of long-distance trade passing
through Egypt in the Roman period, especially trade with India
through the Red Sea ports (Raschke 1978). This trade has left
comparatively little archaeological or other traces in the Nile
valley and it seems likely that most passed straight to Alexandria.
There was almost certainly continual trade with areas further
up the Nile valley and beyond into central Africa. Again, this
trade is difficult to assess though centres like Philae must have
owed some of their importance to the movement of people
between Nubia and Egypt and the placing of a considerable
garrison at Syene may also have been related to trade. The material culture of the Nubian towns does not suggest that they were
benefiting from considerable wealth passing along the Nile.[29]
I have found no evidence to suggest that the Dar el Arbain, the
route into central Africa through the oases of the Western Desert,
was in extensive use in the ancient period (Alston 1995, 193,
237 n. 5).

Goods from the Mediterranean basin other than those intended
for export to the east appear to have passed along the Eastern
trade route. The excavations at Quseir al-Qadim on the Red Sea
coast have produced large amounts of non-Egyptian fineware,
mostly Eastern Sigillata A (*c.* 66 per cent), Eastern Sigillata B
(10 per cent), Cypriot ware (10 per cent) and imitation Arretine,
perhaps from Alexandria (10 per cent) (Whitcomb and Johnson
1982, 64–6). There are parallels between Quseir finds and Indian
kitchen wares, and Nabataean wares also seem to have influenced
the local pottery. The amphorae appear to have been a mixture
of Egyptian, North African and Dressel 2–4 (Whitcomb and
Johnson 1982, 67–9). The lamps are also informative. Of the fifty

[29] Recent excavations at Qasr Ibrim are summarised by Adams 1988.
For Nubian culture in this period see Adams 1977.

lamps analysed, twenty-four were imports (nineteen Italian), and twenty-six were Egyptian, a notably different pattern from that of other sites (Whitcomb and Johnson 1982, 243–4). It is clear that some of the material that supplied the site came from the Nile valley, as is attested by the Nikanor archive, but that there was a far higher proportion of imported goods in Quseir than in the cities and villages of the valley.

Unsurprisingly, a similar pattern emerges from the evidence from Alexandria. All the races of the world met and traded in Alexandria (Dio Chrysostom, *Oratio* 32. 36) and Alexandria not only controlled the trade from India and the East that passed through Egypt, and the trade goods of Egypt itself, but may also have been used as a port of call for ships heading between the west and the Palestine area. One would expect the archaeological remains to show a general East Mediterranean mix. Unfortunately, the state of excavation in Alexandria is deplorable and the study of small finds even less good. The pottery from Kôm el Dikka does, however, provide some guide to trade routes from the third century AD onwards. The pottery groups identified by Rodziewicz (1976) conform largely to the expected pattern. Of the imported wares, Group A is not commonly found in Egypt but was not in fact present in great quantities at Alexandria. Groups C and D were again rare in the rest of Egypt, though common in the East Mediterranean. Only Group B both had a general Mediterranean dispersal and was common throughout Egypt. There were also three common local wares which show different patterns of distribution between Lower and Upper Egypt, the Lower Egyptian forms being more common in Alexandria. Alexandria, as is predictable, was heavily influenced by Mediterranean patterns but seems to have been part of the Egyptian trade network, trading especially with Lower Egypt.

Excavations at Marina el Alamein which have uncovered mainly first- to third-century AD pottery (though there is evidence for the continued occupation of the site until the seventh century) suggest a slightly different pattern and may, given their location, reflect the situation in Alexandria in this period. The pottery shows extensive contacts overseas. There is a considerable amount of western pottery, mostly from Tunisia, but also from Gaul and Spain (though the extremely common Baetican oil amphorae are not attested) (Majcherek 1993).

Pottery excavated at Kellia, a monastic site on the western fringes of the Delta, comes mainly from Egyptian potteries, the two main sources being Abu Mina in the Delta and Aswan. There were some imported amphorae and finewares from Cilicia, Cyprus and Tunisia (Ballet 1988). Kellia was not on a trade route and the pottery seems to be fairly consistent with the pattern attested from the pottery of Hermopolis, though with a higher proportion of imports. The excavations at Tell Atrib in the Central Delta, not fully published, have produced a considerable amount of Roman fineware, suggesting a more cosmopolitan mix than at Hermopolis (Mysliwiec and Herbich 1988).

In the region of Antioch, villagers tended not to come to market in the city but to exchange goods between themselves at rural fairs (De Ligt 1993, 73–4, 126–8; Libanius, *Or.* 11. 230). De Ligt has collected considerable evidence for rural fairs in Syria, Africa and Asia Minor and sufficient attestations of such gatherings from other regions to suggest that they were common in the rest of the ancient world as well. This kind of market was a significant trading phenomenon in the medieval period when fairs would be used to allow exchange across regions. In some cases pre-existing urban centres may have been able to control annual trade fairs.

Most markets, however, probably served fairly homogeneous regions, as is shown by recent work on markets in modern North Africa (Beaujeu-Garnier and Delobez 1979, 113–14). But even these markets were not always based in urban centres in the ancient world. The cases of applications to hold markets on private estates are well known and much discussed (De Ligt 1993, 155–205, 1995). The reluctance of the Roman authorities to grant licences to hold such markets has been related to the security problems that stemmed from markets, but perhaps equally or more significant are the financial implications for any competing urban centre.

Not only could markets be held in places other than cities, but also cities could exist without notable markets. Absence is far more difficult to prove than presence but there does seem to be a notable absence of retailing from many of the cities of second- and third-century Britain (Perring 1991). Although most urban areas had fora, it is not clear that these were used for marketing rather than for exclusively ceremonial and political purposes. The model of the shop-free forum was after all developed in Rome in the Republican period (Wallace-Hadrill 1991). The gentrification of many British urban centres is notable: the small shops disappeared and were replaced by large villas, not a phenomenon one can convincingly parallel from the East. Poulter's work on Danubian cities seems to show a fairly similar picture. The latter stages of urban settlement on the Danube seem to be almost devoid of non-official buildings (Poulter 1992; 1995). The cities are constructed as monuments to Roman governmental power and one presumes that the populations who were to be impressed by these buildings were elsewhere. It seems likely that the only form of exchange carried out in these areas would be connected with taxation.

This cursory survey shows that the place of the city in the trade network varied considerably from region to region and even quite geographically close regions may have cities that had very different trade networks. To seek one economic model to explain the ancient city is to ignore the manifest differences – geographical, historical, cultural and economic – between regions and cities across the Roman world, and to seek to apply a model derived from study of the city in one area to urban systems in a different area is fraught with dangers. The model derived from our evidence for the cities of Middle Egypt cannot therefore be taken as applying to all other Roman cities, though it is possible and even likely that some other areas will have developed similar urban systems. The growing awareness among historians of late antiquity especially of the different histories of particular cities when faced with similar historical and institutional developments should focus our interest again on the phenomenon of ancient urbanism. The high level of architectural and institutional uniformity in the cities of the Roman empire should not blind urban historians to notable diversity in economic structures.

Even within Egypt, there seem to have been notable variations in the role cities played in the trade network. Some communities were on the international trade routes that passed through Alexandria and their material culture and economic status were affected by that trade. The cities of Middle Egypt were something of a backwater by comparison. They display regional networks of trade and craft production which focused on urban centres and into which villages were integrated. We should not think of these districts as isolated territories, with villages and city existing as a distinct economic system, but rather as part of a wide regional network.

The focusing of the trade network on urban communities was in part a result of policy. The authorities controlled markets, often through direct regulation, but also in more subtle ways. We have seen how the guild and licensing system linked village traders into a larger network and also how the direct regulation of trade, especially of the food supply, encouraged traders to provide for urban markets. The urban markets were also dominated by urban architecture and institutions, be they shops situated in the colonnaded avenues of the city, or market stalls loomed over by the temple or supervised from a tribunal.[30] Thus the political institutions helped shape the trade network at a district level, though the forces that created the network and encouraged regional trade cannot be assessed.

Finally, this perspective helps to explain an economic and geographical conundrum. Hadrian founded a large and privileged community in Middle Egypt *c.* AD 130 very close to the pre-existing city of Hermopolis Magna. If the cities acted solely as central places for the surrounding villages, then we would have expected that the proximity of the two cities would have resulted in the failure of one. Both cities, however, appear to have flourished throughout the next centuries. In my model, this can be explained since the cities were not simply solar central places but were part of a complex network of urban and rural communities stretching several hundred kilometres along the Nile. In such a context, the foundation of Antinoopolis probably did not significantly disrupt the regional urban system.

Bibliography

Adams, C. E. P. (1995), 'Supplying the Roman army: *O. Petr.* 245', *ZPE* 109: 119–24.

Adams, W. Y. (1977), *Nubia: Corridor to Africa* (London).

—— (1988) 'Ptolemaic and Roman occupation at Qasr Ibrim', in F. Geus and F. Thill (eds), *Mélanges offerts à Jean Vercoutter* (Paris), 9–17.

Alston, R. (1995), *Soldier and Society in Roman Egypt: A Social History* (London and New York).

---

[30] This desire to control and centralise markets is common to many societies (De Ligt 1995; De Ligt 1993, 155–98, 205–24; Shaw 1981; von Reden 1995, 107–10; Sawyer 1986).

Alston, R. and Alston, R. D. (forthcoming), 'The urban community in Roman Egypt: definitions and differentiation', *JEA* (forthcoming).

Avogadro, S. (1935), 'Le ΑΠΟΓΡΑΦΑΙ di proprietà nell'Egitto greco-romano', *Aeg.* 15: 131–206.

Bagnall, R. S. (1985), *Currency and Inflation in Fourth Century Egypt* (*BASP*. suppl. 5) (Atlanta).

—— (1992), 'Landholding in late Roman Egypt: the distribution of wealth', *JRS* 82: 128–49.

—— (1993), *Egypt in Late Antiquity* (Princeton).

Ballet, P. (1988), 'La céramique des Kellia: Nouvelles orientations de recherches', in E. C. M. van den Brink (ed.), *The Archaeology of the Nile Delta, Egypt: Problems and Priorities* (Amsterdam), 297–312.

Beauchamp, J. (1993), 'Organisation domestiques et rôles sexuels: les papyrus byzantins', *Dumbarton Oaks Papers* 47: 185–94.

Beaujeu-Garnier, J. and Delobez, A. (1979), *Geography of Marketing* (trans. S. H. Beaver) (London and New York).

Bell, H. I. (1940), 'Antinoopolis: a Hadrianic foundation in Egypt', *JRS* 30: 133–9.

Boak, A. E. R. (1933), *Karanis: The Temples, Coin Hoards, Botanical and Zoological Reports: Seasons 1924–31* (Ann Arbor).

—— (1935), *Soknopaiou Nesos: The University of Michigan Excavations at Dime 1931–1932* (Ann Arbor).

—— (1937), 'The organisation of gilds in Greco-Roman Egypt', *TAPA* 68: 212–20.

Boak, A. E. R. and Peterson, E. E. (1931), *Karanis: Topographical and Architectural Report of the Excavations during the Seasons 1924–28* (Ann Arbor).

Bohannan, P. and Dalton, G. (1962), 'Introduction', in P. Bohannan and G. Dalton (eds), *Markets in Africa* (Evanston, Ill.), 1–26.

Bowman, A. K. (1985), 'Landholding in the Hermopolite nome in the fourth century AD', *JRS* 75: 137–63.

Braunert, H. (1964), *Die Binnenwanderung: Studien zur Sozialgeschichte Ägyptens in der Ptolemäer- und Kaiserzeit* (Bonner historische Forschungen, 26; Bonn).

Carrié, J. M. (1975), 'Les distributions alimentaires dans les cités de l'empire romaine tardive', *Mélanges de l'École Française de Rome* 87: 995–1101.

Coles, R. (1987), 'Appendix II: the guilds of Oxyrhynchus', in *P.Oxy.* LIV: 230–2.

De Ligt, L. (1993), *Fairs and Markets in the Roman Empire: Economic and Social Aspects of Periodic Trade in a Pre-industrial Society* (Amsterdam).

—— (1995), 'The *nundinae* of L. Bellicius Sollers', *De Agricultura: Essays in Honour of P. W. de Neeve* (Amsterdam), 238–62.

Donadoni, S. (1974), *Antinoe (1965–1968): Missione Archeologica in Egitto dell' Università di Roma* (Rome).

Drexhage, H. J. (1982), 'Beitrag zum Binnenhandel im römischen Ägypten aufgrund der Torzullquittungen und Zollhausabrechnungen', *MBAH* 1: 61–84.
—— (1991), *Preise, Mieten/Pachten, Kosten und Löhne im römischen Ägypten bis zum Regierungsantritt Diokletians* (Vorarbeiten zu einer Wirtschaftsgeschichte des römishen Ägypten, I; St Katharinen).
Duncan-Jones, R. P. (1994), *Money and Government in the Roman Empire* (Cambridge).
Fikhman, I. F. (1965), *Egipet na rubezhe dvukh epokh* (Moscow).
—— (1979), 'Die spätantike ägyptische Stadt Oxyrhynchos', *Das Altertum* 25: 177–82.
Fuks, A. (1951), 'Notes on the archive of Nicanor', *JJP* 5: 207–16, reprinted in idem (1984), *Social Conflicts in Ancient Greece* (Jerusalem and Leiden), 322–49.
Gallant, T. W. (1991), *Risk and Survival in Ancient Greece: Reconstructing the Rural Domestic Economy* (Cambridge).
Gascou, J. (1985), 'Les grandes domaines, la cité et l'état en Égypte byzantine: recherches d'histoire agraire, fiscale et administrative', *Travaux et Memoires*, 9: 1–90.
Gazda, E. K. (1983), *Karanis: An Egyptian Town in Roman Times* (Ann Arbor).
Grenfell, B. P., Hunt, A. S. and Hogarth, D. G. (1900), *Fayum Towns and their Papyri* (London).
Haatvedt, R. E. and Peterson, E. E. (1964), *Coins from Karanis* (Ann Arbor).
Hanson, A. E. (1974), 'Lists of taxpayers from Philadelphia', *ZPE* 15: 229–48.
—— (1980), 'P. Princeton I 11 and P. Cornell 21 v.', *ZPE* 37: 241–8.
Harden, D. B. (1936), *Roman Glass from Karanis found by the University of Michigan Expedition to Egypt 1924–1929* (Ann Arbor).
Harrauer, H. and Sijpesteijn, P. J. (1985), 'Ein neues Dokument zu Roms Indienhandel. P. Vindob.G.40822', *Anz. der phil.-hist. Klasse der österr. Akad. der Wissenschaft.* 122: 124–55.
Hendy, M. F. (1985), *Studies in the Byzantine Monetary Economy* (Cambridge).
Hopkins, K. (1980), 'Taxes and trade in the Roman empire, 200 BC–AD 400', *JRS* 70: 101–25.
Husselman, E. M. (1952), 'The granaries of Karanis', *TAPA* 83: 56–73.
—— (1979), *Karanis: Excavations of the University of Michigan in Egypt 1928–1935: Topography and Architecture* (Ann Arbor).
Husson, G. (1983), *Oikia: Le vocabulaire de la maison privée d'après les papyrus grecs* (Paris).
Jaritz, H. (1980), *Elephantine III: Die Terrassen vor den Tempeln des Chmnum und der Satet* (Mainz).
Johnson, B. (1981), *Pottery from Karanis: Excavations of the University of Michigan* (Ann Arbor).
Jones, A. H. M. (1960), 'The cloth industry under the Roman empire', *Economic History Review,* second series 13: 183–92, reprinted in idem (1974), *The Roman Economy* (Oxford), 350–64.

Kehoe, D. P. (1988), *The Economics of Agriculture on Roman Imperial Estates in North Africa* (Hypomnemata 89; Göttingen).

Lallemand, J. (1966), 'Trésor de monnaies romaines en bronze découverte en Égypte: Constant à Constance Galle', *CE* 41: 380–94.

Lauffray, J. (1971), 'Abords occidentaux du premier pylone de Karnak: le dromos, la tribune et les aménagements portuaires', *Kêmi* 21: 77–144.

Majcherek, J. (1993), 'Roman amphorae from Marina el-Alamein', *Mitteilungen der Deutschen Archäologischen Instituts, Abteilung Kairo* 49: 215–20.

Milne, J. G. (1920), 'Two Roman hoards of coins from Egypt', *JRS* 10: 169–84.

—— (1922), 'The coins from Oxyrhynchus', *JEA* 8: 158–63.

—— (1935), 'Report on coins found at Tebtunis in 1900', *JEA* 21: 210–16.

Montevecchi, O. (1936), 'Ricerche sociologia negli documenti dell'Egitto gréco-romano II: I contratti di matrimonio e gli atti di divorzio', *Aeg.* 16: 3–83.

—— (1988), *La Papirologia* (Milan).

Mysliwiec, K. and Herbich, T. (1988), 'Polish archaeological activities at Tell Atrib in 1985', in E. C. M. van den Brink (ed.), *The Archaeology of the Nile Delta, Egypt: Problems and Priorities* (Amsterdam), 177–203.

el-Nassery, S. A. A., Wagner, G. and Castel, G. (1976), 'Un grand Bain gréco-romaine à Karanis', *BIFAO* 76: 231–75.

Nowicka, M. (1972), 'À propos des tours – πύργοι dans les papyrus grecs', *Archeologia* 21: 53–62.

Palme, B. (1989), 'Zu den Unterabteilungen des Quartières 'Αγορά in Theben', *Tyche* 4: 125–9.

Perring, D. (1991), 'Spatial organisation and social change in Roman towns', in J. Rich and A. Wallace-Hadrill (eds), *City and Country in the Ancient World* (London and New York), 273–93.

Poulter, A. (1992), 'The use and abuse of urbanism in the Danubian provinces during the later Roman empire', in J. Rich (ed.), *The City in Late Antiquity* (London and New York), 99–135.

—— (1995), *Nicopolis ad Istrum: A Roman, Late Roman and Early Byzantine City: Excavations 1985–1992* (*JRS* Monograph 8) (London).

Preisigke, F. (1919), 'Die Begriffe ΠΥΡΓΟΣ und ΣΤΕΓΗ bei der Hausenlage', *Hermes* 54: 423–32.

Raschke, M. G. (1978), 'New studies in Roman commerce with the East', *ANRW* II 9.2: 605–1363.

Rathbone, D. W. (1990), 'Villages, land and population in Graeco-Roman Egypt', *PCPS* 36: 103–42.

—— (1991), *Economic Rationalism and Rural Society in Third-Century AD Egypt: the Heroninos Archive and the Appianus Estate* (Cambridge).

Rea, J. (1982), 'P. Lond. inv. 1562 verso: market taxes in Oxyrhynchus', *ZPE* 46: 191–209.

Rodziewicz, M. (1976), *La céramique romaine tardive d'Alexandrie (Alexandrie I)* (Centre d'Archéologie Méditerranéenne de l'Académie

Polonaise des Sciences et Centre Polonaise d'Archéologie méditer-
ranéenne dans la République Arabe d'Égypte au Caïre) (Warsaw).
Rowlandson, J. (1996), *Landowners and Tenants in Roman Egypt:
The Social Relations of Agriculture in the Oxyrhynchite Nome* (Oxford
Classical Monographs; Oxford)
Samuel, D. H. (1981), 'Greeks and Romans at Socnopaiou Nesos',
Proceedings of the XVIth International Congress of Papyrology (Chico),
389–403.
San Nicolo, M. (1972), *Ägyptisches Vereinswesen zur Zeit der Ptolemäer
und Römer.* I: *Die Vereinsarten* (Münchener Beiträge zur Papyrus-
forschung und antiken Rechtsgeschichte II, 1; Munich).
Sawyer, P. (1986), 'Early fairs and markets in England and Scandinavia',
in B. L. Anderson and A. J. H. Latham (eds), *Markets in History:
Papers Presented at a Symposium at St George's House Windsor Castle
held 9–13 September 1984* (London), 59–77.
Shier, L. A. (1978), *Karanis: Terracotta Lamps from Karanis, Egypt: Excavations of the University of Michigan* (Ann Arbor).
Shaw, B. D. (1981), 'Rural markets in North Africa and the political
economy of the Roman empire', *Ant. Afr.* 17: 37–83, reprinted in
idem (1995), *Rulers, Nomads and Christians in Roman North Africa*:
I (Aldershot).
Sijpesteijn, P. J. (1987), *Customs Duties in Graeco-Roman Egypt* (Studia
Amsterdamensia ad Epigraphicam Ius Antiquum et Papyrologicam
pertinentia, 17; Zutphen).
Smith, H. S. (1976), 'Society and settlement in Ancient Egypt', in G. W.
Dimbleby, R. Tringham and P. J. Ucko (eds), *Man, Settlement and
Urbanism* (London), 705–9.
Spencer, A. J. (ed. 1983), *British Museum Expedition to Middle Egypt:
Ashmunein 1982* (London).
—— (1984), *British Museum Expedition to Middle Egypt: Ashmunein
1983* (London).
Spencer, A. J. and Bailey, D. M. (1982), *British Museum Expedition to
Middle Egypt: Ashmunein 1981* (London).
Van Minnen, P. (1986), 'The volume of the Oxyrhynchite textile trade',
MBAH 5: 88–95.
—— (1987), 'Urban craftsmen in Roman Egypt', *MBAH* 6: 31–88.
von Reden, S. (1995), *Exchange in Ancient Greece* (London).
Wagner, G. (1972), 'Inscriptions grecques du dromos de Karnak II',
BIFAO 71: 161–79.
Wallace-Hadrill, A. (1991), 'Elites and trade in the Roman town', in J.
Rich and A. Wallace-Hadrill (eds), *City and Country in the Ancient
World* (London and New York), 241–72.
Whitcomb, D. S. and Johnson, J. H. (1982), *Quseir al-Qadim: Prelimi-
nary Report* (ARCE 7) (Malibu).
Wipszycka, E. (1965), *L'industrie textile dans l'Égypte romaine* (Warsaw).
—— (1971), 'Les impôts professionels et la structure de l'industrie dans
l'Égypte romaine: À propos de la ΚΟΠΗ ΤΡΙΧΟΣ', *JJP* 16–17: 117–30.

10

Trading gods in northern Italy

Mark Humphries

Introduction

This chapter will examine the role of trade networks in the diffusion of private religious cults in the Roman empire, focusing on
Christian origins in northern Italy.[1] Historians of early Christianity
have sometimes supposed that merchants were instrumental in
the spread of the church (e.g. Frend 1964). A foreign element
in the early churches of the west is undeniable: until the late second
century, the literary output of these communities was exclusively
in Greek (Mohrmann 1965, 72–4). Yet the precise nature of the
contribution of traders has been hard to define because they are
difficult to identify in early Christian communities (Lane Fox 1986,
272–3). This chapter aims to move the debate forward by concentrating on *trade networks* rather than individual traders. To this
end, it begins by describing the sort of circumstances conducive
to the spread of religious information, showing how trade networks
fit the criteria demanded. Then it demonstrates the correlation
between north Italian trade networks and the distribution there
of private pagan cults, especially that of Isis. Finally, it will be

---

[1] This chapter is substantially revised from the version presented at
the St Andrews conference. It has been improved enormously by
the comments of Jill Harries, Helen Parkins, John Serrati, Christopher
Smith, Michael Whitby and the participants at the conference. All dates
are CE.

shown how Christianity fits into this pattern, and, by focusing on the well-attested congregation at Aquileia, it will argue for a connection between the origins of Christian communities in certain centres and the location of those centres in the north Italian trade network.

Definitions: trade networks and religious diffusion

Trade networks and social dynamics

It is necessary to begin by defining what I mean by the term 'trade network'. Although some overlap is inevitable, at the outset I want to distinguish the idea of trade networks both from communications networks and from the activities of individual traders. Being an important node on a communications route was not enough to guarantee a settlement significance in trading terms. To take an example from southern Italy: Aecae commanded the two ancient roads from Beneventum to Luceria but never became an important market centre. In commercial terms it was overshadowed by Luceria itself, where the markets could offer goods drawn from a wide catchment area. That this was so highlights the importance not just of good communications but of locally available resources and commodities in the location of markets (Frayn 1993, 41–2, 79–84).

Rather, the term 'trade network' means not simply the exchange of goods at market centres but the whole matrix of social relations associated with that trade. This includes the new social relations accruing to a town or city because of its commercial importance. These relations could exist at an official level, such as the dispersal of state personnel to administer the collection of customs duties (cf. De Laet 1949). At another level, they can be perceived in the altered social dynamics of a trading centre, in terms of the composition of its population, which could often come from a wide range of social, racial and cultural backgrounds. Precisely such a profile was presented by the Piraeus in the late classical and hellenistic periods. Here was a society teeming with foreigners and their gods (Parker 1996, 158–98; von Reden 1995, 30–3). As with early Christianity, however, the precise role of individual foreigners in religious diffusion at the Piraeus is hard to determine (Parker 1996, 160–1, 197–8, 333–42). Even so, trade networks had profound implications for the social horizons of anyone involved in commerce, such as the unnamed merchant Demosthenes defended against Apatourios:

> Because I have visited many places and because I spend my time in your market (*emporion*), I know most of the seafarers, and I am on intimate terms with these fellows from Byzantion because I have spent much time there.
>
> (Dem. *Or.* 33. 5).

For the purposes of this chapter, therefore, the *significance* of a trade network is not the existence of commerce but its impact on the society in which it took place.

Networks and religious diffusion

How is this relevant to the dissemination of religions? At this stage it needs to be stated what is meant by a *private religious cult*. The religious groups discussed herein must be distinguished from *public* cults which were spread primarily by public, state-sponsored initiatives: even supposedly conservative Roman religion was subject to radical change by the interference of the state (North 1976). *Private religious cults* were spread by the private initiative of particular individuals or groups. Of course, a blanket term like this covers a multitude of differences. Cults such as Mithraism or Isis worship appealed to very different constituencies, whereas others, such as Judaism and Christianity, could find themselves subject to censure, indeed persecution, at the hands of the authorities.[2] Moreover, adherence to an exclusive monotheistic cult such as Judaism or Christianity required a very different set of responses in terms of identity than did adoption of cults belonging to an inclusive polytheistic system (Gallagher 1993; Goodman 1994, 20–37). Similarly, the strategies by which such private cults increased their membership could vary widely, even between two such closely related cults as Judaism and Christianity in the first century (Goodman 1994).

[2] For differences between the memberships of Mithraism and the Isiac cult: Martin 1987, 72, 118. For Judaism: Goodman 1989, 40–4. For Christianity: Lane Fox 1986, 419–92.

Yet for all that, there seem to be strong similarities in the kind of environments which stimulated the geographical expansion of such private religions. Because they were not fostered by the agency of the state, these private cults relied on private initiatives for such projects as the erection of altars or the construction of cult buildings (White 1990). Likewise, their dissemination to new centres also depended on the movement of adherents from one centre to another. In the case of Christianity, this was soon accompanied by a proselytising mission to seek out new converts (Goodman 1994, 91–108).

The expansion of a cult, like the dissemination of any body of ideas, depends, therefore, on close personal interface with potential converts (Stark 1996, 13–21; cf. Kraabel 1994; Matthews 1989). This process could happen in a variety of ways, but recently the geographer Chris Park has categorised two major mechanisms by which it might occur. First, there is *expansion diffusion*, whereby 'the innovation grows by direct contact, usually *in situ*' when 'an idea is communicated by a person who knows about it to one who does not'. Then there is *relocation diffusion* which 'involves the initial group of carriers themselves moving, so they are diffused through time and space to a new set of locations' (Park 1994, 99–101). Although he acknowledges the role played by different mechanisms, Park sees early Christian diffusion occurring primarily by relocation diffusion (Park 1994, 105–7). This derives from his reliance on narratives which personalise the process by emphasising the role of individual missionaries in Christian expansion.[3] Yet for the empire as a whole, and the western provinces in particular, it is impossible to know who spread the Christian message (Lane Fox 1986, 276). Any effort at understanding early Christian expansion must acknowledge that it is largely an anonymous process. Far from being able to know *who* was responsible for its growth, it is better to ascertain what circumstances encouraged this remarkable expansion.

A key to unlocking this problem has been provided in recent decades by work on early Christianity (primarily the New

---

[3]   For example, the Acts of the Apostles; cf. Park 1994, 106: 'Christian missionaries like Paul travelled from town to town spreading the good news (of the gospel) [*sic!*]'. Likewise, the efforts of Gallagher 1993 depend on three ancient romances: cf. Goodman 1994, 22 for the problems of such an approach.

Testament) informed by approaches derived from the social sciences. Between Jesus and Paul there occurred a significant change in the social environment of the early Christian movement, as it moved from the rural milieu of the Gospels to the urban framework of Acts and the Pauline epistles (Sanders 1993, 98–103; Hengel 1992): 'Paul was', as Wayne Meeks so aptly called him, 'a city person' (1983, 9). This was crucial, for in the cities of the Mediterranean basin the early Christian movement found precisely that environment of interpersonal contact crucial to the spread of its ideas. Even better were those cities which lay along trade networks and had constantly shifting and diverse populations: here a heady mixture of *in situ* expansion diffusion and mobile relocation diffusion could work together to produce new Christian communities.

Already by Paul's time this factor was influencing the pattern of Christian expansion. Much of his missionary effort took in the trading cities of the Aegean, such as Ephesos, Thessalonika and Athens (Meeks 1983, 40–50; cf. Destro and Pesce 1995: 43–63). When he preached to the Gentiles at Athens, he chose the market place (*agora*) as his venue (Acts 17: 17), not because he sought to make converts of the traders, but because the *agora* was the trade network in microcosm: the area in the city where the largest congregations of people were to be found. In the west, when Paul arrived in Italy at Puteoli, he found that a small Christian community was already established there (Acts 28: 13). Puteoli was the most important port and market on the Bay of Naples and in Paul's day it still functioned as the major port of Rome (Frayn 1993, 89–91). The city boasted a diverse population and a rich range of religious life, from local cults to Judaism and eastern mysteries (Frederiksen 1984, 330; Grant 1986, 29–32), and it is unsurprising that it should have acquired a Christian presence so early. Indeed, Paul's arrival there gives some hint as to how this might have occurred. He did not go to Puteoli on a planned mission but as a prisoner *en route* to Rome (Acts 27: 1–4); even so he was able to mix freely with people in the city (Acts 28: 14). He arrived, furthermore, on a ship sailing from Alexandria through the straits of Messina to Puteoli (Acts 28: 11–13), precisely the route used by grain ships supplying the imperial capital with food (Rickman 1980, 128–9). Paul's arrival at Puteoli provides a vignette of how trade networks could be important in the unplanned diffusion of religions.

Trade networks and private cults in northern Italy

Turning now to northern Italy, there is the same correlation between trade networks and patterns of private cult diffusion. Of the various soteriological cults which spread into the region, there is a particularly rich and coherent body of evidence for devotion to Isis (Figure 10.1). Diffusion of this cult in northern Italy and the surrounding areas occurred in the mid- to late second century. The scatter of Isiac material is revealing: there are concentrations in and around the major port cities of the region at Ariminum, Ravenna, Tergeste and, especially, Aquileia (Malaise 1972a, 4–13, 23–32); moving inland, the cult spreads along the major trade routes stretching into the Po valley (Malaise 1972b, 335–51).

A particularly revealing picture can be drawn of the diffusion of the cult on the Alpine fringes of northern Italy and into north-western Illyricum. At Sublavio, near the Brenner pass between Verona and Augusta Vindelicorum (Augsburg) in Noricum, dedications to Isis were set up by slaves of one Ti. Iulius Saturninus (*CIL* v. 5079–80). Similar dedications were made at Poetovio (Ptuj in Slovenia), on the road from Aquileia to the Danube, by slaves of a certain Q. Sabinus Veranus (*ILS* 4243–4), while an altar to Isis Victrix and Serapis was set up by the equestrian C. Ulpius Aurelius Gaianus (Selem 1980, 13, no. 17). All these devotees of Isis were employed by the *publicum portorii Illyrici*, the customs network covering the Balkans (De Laet 1949, 175–92; Selem 1980, 69–74), and their activities are but a minute sample of the many employees of this organisation who made dedications – not just to Isis but to other soteriological deities throughout the region.[4]

In northern Italy itself, the pattern is repeated, with the highest proportions of foreign cults found at important commercial centres such as Aquileia and Verona (Chevallier 1983, 455–70). The inscriptions recording these dedications show that the propagators of such cults in northern Italy and the Balkans were often foreigners or Romans involved in trade or with the *portorium*

---

[4] Another slave of Iulius Saturninus made a dedication to Mithras at Senia on the Dalmatian coast (*AE* 1940, 101), as did a slave of C. Antonius Rufus, who was also employed by the bureau (*ILS* 4225). Indeed, Antonius Rufus' stewards were also active in the Mithraic community at Poetovio: Selem 1980, 99–100.

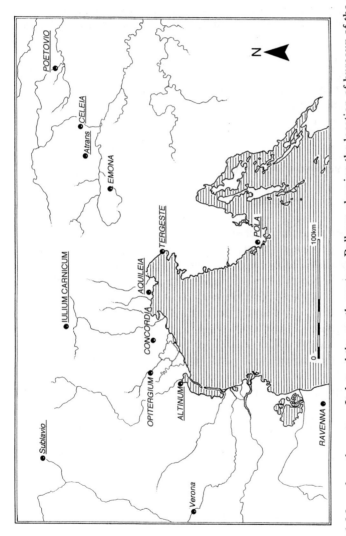

Figure 10.1 Map of north-eastern Italy and the north-western Balkans, showing the location of bureaux of the *publicum portorii Illyrici* (underlined), centres of commercial activity by the Barbii family of Aquileia (in capitals), and centres of Isiac and Mithraic worship (in italics). Based on Budischovsky 1976; De Laet 1949; Malaise 1972a, 1972b; and Sasel 1966.

(Chevallier 1983, 458–70; Malaise 1972b, 321–32). Of course, their dedications were made to satisfy their own needs, not out of any missionary zeal (Goodman 1994, 28). A more striking example of such expansion without a mission comes from the Jews, who by the fourth century were established in several of northern Italy's most important commercial cities (Ruggini 1959). Unlike the Christians, however, the Jews of northern Italy seem not to have indulged in a proselytising mission (cf. Goodman 1994), leading to the conclusion that the Jewish presence, which was strongest in commercial centres, must be attributable to the trade networks of northern Italy.

Trade networks and Christian origins in northern Italy

Sources and problems

Early north Italian Christianity is very poorly attested, with no reliable documentary testimony of its existence prior to the fourth century. Then, at Rome in 313 and Arles in 314, four north Italian bishops – Merocles of Milan, Constantius of Faventia, Stennius of Ariminum and Theodore of Aquileia – appear at councils convened by Constantine to resolve the Donatist schism in the Carthaginian church. Over the next century, the number of north Italian bishoprics increased so that, by the death of bishop Ambrose of Milan in 397, Christian communities certainly existed also at Vercellae, Novaria, Dertona, Eporedia, Comum, Cremona, Placentia, Parma, Bononia, Ravenna, Brixia, Vicetia, Verona, Tridentum, Patavium, Concordia, Altinum, Tergeste (Lanzoni 1923, 421–577; see Figure 10.2).

To know of the existence of bishoprics, is not, however, to know their origins. What is more important is that some Christian communities evidently existed without bishops,[5] a reminder that

[5] The clearest evidence comes from Eusebius of Vercellae's letter to Christian congregations at Dertona and Eporedia, indicating that these congregations were under the jurisdiction of Vercellae. Yet, by the time of the Council of Aquileia (381) Dertona had its own bishop (Lanzoni 1923, 476–7). This probably reflects a deliberate effort by Ambrose of Milan to erode the influence of the Vercellese church (McLynn 1995, 285–6).

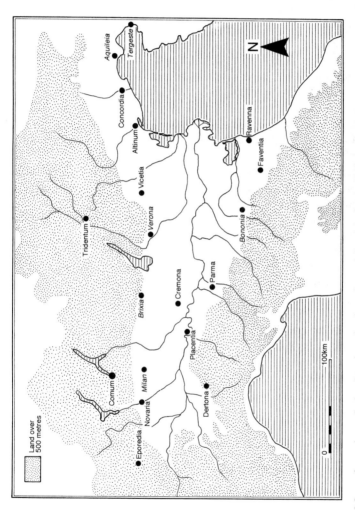

Figure 10.2 Map of northern Italy showing the location of Jewish (in italics) and Christian communities by the early fourth century. Based on data in Lanzoni 1923 and Ruggini 1959.

the appearance of a bishopric represents the culmination, not the beginning, of a process of Christian growth (Lanzani 1984, 356). By the end of the fourth century, however, the dynamics of Christian expansion in northern Italy had changed, as bishops of centres such as Milan, Tridentum and Aquileia actively sought to propagate the faith in new centres (Lizzi 1989, 59–70, 151–9). The issue is also clouded by the existence of a number of medieval texts which purport to narrate Christian origins in northern Italy. While such texts have been the basis for most studies of Christian origins in Italy until very recently, it is clear that they were often fabricated with an eye to ecclesiastical power politics (Otranto 1991, 3–21; Picard 1988).

So where should a study of Christian origins in northern Italy begin? Plainly the medieval texts need to be ignored or treated with extreme caution. Since they present Christian origins in terms of apostolic missions modelled on the activities of Paul in the New Testament, they characterise the process as relocation diffusion. In what follows, however, I will present a more anonymous picture of expansion diffusion operating through the trade networks of northern Italy. As for determining a group of Christian communities to use as a basis for this study, I propose to use the list of congregations known by the time of the Council of Ariminum (359) as the starting point, in order to avoid the complexities presented by an internal mission directed by certain bishops. This consists of the bishoprics of Aquileia, Ariminum, Brixia, Faventia, Milan, Parma, Patavium, Ravenna, Vercellae and Verona, as well as the non-episcopal congregations at Dertona, Eporedia and Novaria (see Figure 10.2).

Christian centres and market centres

Many of these cities were also important commercial centres. Aquileia will be dealt with in greater detail below, but for now it is worth noting that it was the most prosperous port in the region. Strabo records that Ariminum was also a significant port (5. 1. 11). It was also positioned at the hub of an important road network: from here the Via Aemilia turned north-west into the Po valley (Livy 39. 2), as well as leading south to Fanum Fortunae and the easiest crossing of the Appennines towards Arretium (cf. Strabo 5. 2. 9). Ravenna was situated at the mouth of the river Po, which was used for the transport of imports into northern Italy (Pliny, *HN* 3. 123). It is worth noting that the earliest evidence for Christianity at Ravenna comes not from the centre of the city, but from its extramural harbour settlement at Classis (Deichmann 1976, 233–4). Indeed, until the development of Ravenna as a capital after 402 by Roman emperors, Ostrogothic kings and Byzantine exarchs, it seems that the Christian presence was stronger at Classis than in the city itself (Deichmann 1989, 49–53).

Moving inland, the Christian centres of the Po valley cluster in important commercial cities, many of them associated with the cloth trade. Patavium and Faventia were important centres in the textile industry, while the latter was also the starting point of a trans-Appennine road, the Via Faventina (Frayn 1984, 25; Chevallier 1983, 7). Brixia was an important centre of the wool trade, where the raw material was also manufactured into goods (Tozzi 1971). Milan, too, was an important textile market, as well as being a trading city with links through the Alps to Gaul and southwards to Apulia (*CIL* v. 5911, 5925; Garnsey 1976, 19–22). Similar conditions prevailed at Verona, which was a wool-market in addition to the starting point for trade routes into the central Alps (De Laet 1949, 157–8, 182–3; Frayn 1984, 25; Sartori 1960, 222–3). Parma, too, was an important centre of wool production (Martial 2. 43, 4. 37, 5. 13, 14. 155). As for Vercellae, there is only one inscription which records a trader there (*CIL* v. 8939), but the large number of amphorae found there, many of them stamped at *fabricae* elsewhere in Italy, confirm that it was one of the region's most flourishing cities (Chevallier 1983, 271). Indeed, Tacitus brackets Vercellae with Novaria and Eporedia as important cities in this part of the Po valley (*Hist.* 1. 70).

Clearly there is considerable overlap between the distribution of early Christian centres in northern Italy and the region's pre-existing trade network. The new religion seems to have appeared earliest in cities which acted as markets, centres of industrial production or both. This economic prominence gave these centres social networks covering a broad area, even connecting them with each other: the Gavii of Verona, for example, had freedmen at Aquileia (Chilver 1942, 90–1). This trade network was deeply embedded, therefore, in the social matrix of the region as a whole. This is worth remembering, for it would be a simplistic analysis indeed which asserted that trade networks were the only factors contributing to Christian expansion. At Vercellae, for example, bishop Eusebius' contacts with the Christian congregation at Dertona fit into an existing pattern of administrative social relations: one C. Marius Aelianus of Dertona, for example, held civic office at Vercellae (*CIL* v. 7373).

This noticeable overlap suggests that the social consequences of trade networks, which would have created circumstances conducive to the spread of private cults, were important for the diffusion of Christianity in northern Italy. While the evidence, it must be admitted, is circumstantial, in one centre at least there are more compelling reasons for supposing that these trade networks were indeed crucial to the evangelisation of the region. In the next section, I argue that this was the case at Aquileia.

Trade networks and early Christianity at Aquileia

Trade, society and religion at Roman Aquileia

Of the Roman cities of northern Italy, few have yielded more of their ancient secrets than Aquileia. Now a mere village, with extensive tracts of its ancient area lying in open fields, the site has been the subject of archaeological investigation since the eighteenth century. The large corpus of inscriptions and numerous pottery assemblages from Aquileia give a detailed picture of the city's position in the ancient trade networks of northern Italy, the Balkans, the Adriatic and the wider Mediterranean world. This is a picture also known from ancient authors. Strabo called the city 'the emporium of those Illyrians who live near the Danube' (5. 1. 8; cf. 4. 6. 10). The most interesting description of the city is provided by Herodian in the early third century, which encapsulates nicely the social implications of trade:

> Aquileia has always been an important city with a large local population. Sited as it is on the coast commanding the hinterland of the Illyrian territories, it has acted as a trading post (*emporion*) for [northern] Italy by providing sea traders with a market for goods from inland by land or river. Similarly, essential goods which cannot be produced in the Illyrian countryside because of the winters, come by sea and are sent from Aquileia up country to the people of the inte-

rior. They farm land which is particularly fertile for the vine, and export a great quantity of wine to people who do not grow grapes. As a result of this, the city is teeming with local citizens, aliens and traders.

(Herodian 8. 2. 3)

All the key elements are here: good communications and local resources combining to create a market centre which attracted a diverse population. Some of the city's trading connections counted for more than others, and their particular importance must have changed over time. Diocletian's Price Edict records what must have been a flourishing trade with Alexandria (§37. 5, see Lauffer 1971, 201), but it is uncertain if this survived unscathed after Constantine diverted the riches of Egypt to his new capital on the Bosphoros after 330 (cf. Rickman 1980, 198). Likewise, trade with Africa seems to have increased in the late third and fourth centuries, as Aquileia became an important distribution centre for goods supplying the military garrisons in the north-eastern Alps (Whittaker 1983, 165–7; Cipriano 1986, 140–3). One area of trade was of continuous, if fluctuating, importance throughout the period, and that was with the north-western Balkans (see Figure 10.1). It was here that some of Aquileia's greatest trading families, such as the Barbii, made their fortunes (Cipriano 1986; cf. Sasel 1966).

Herodian's description of the ethnic diversity of Aquileia's population cannot be doubted: inscriptions from altars and tombstones excavated in the city show that it was inhabited by immigrants from all over the empire (Calderini 1930, 338–57; Cuscito 1974), many of whom chose to leave their mark in their native Greek tongue (*IG* xiv. 2337–78). In addition, trade brought the scrutiny of officialdom, as Aquileia was a centre for a bureau of the *publicum portorii Illyrici*; this too would have brought immigrants to the city (De Laet 1949: 179–80). This ethnic diversity was reflected in the city's religious profile. Private soteriological cults are unusually well represented, with dedications to deities such as Magna Mater, Mithras and Isis (Calderini 1930, 123–37), and a thriving Jewish community, many of them immigrants, also lived here (Ruggini 1959, 192–213).

Although some allowance must be made for the extraordinary detail available about Aquileia as compared with the other cities of northern Italy, it seems that the cosmopolitan nature of its population and pantheon far exceeded that of any other city in the region. That this was so cannot be divorced from the importance of the city as a crucial node on several interlocking trade networks. It has long been noticed that Aquileia is the pivot about which the personnel of a number of private cults revolve. The Mithras and Isis worshipping stewards of several *praefecti vehiculorum* working for the Illyrican *portorium* can be traced along trade routes emanating from the city towards the Brenner, into north-western Balkans and along the Danubian coast (Budischovsky 1976; Selem 1980). Turning to Christianity, it appears that Aquileia's importance in those trade networks was to influence its religious life once more.

Trade networks and Christianity

As has been noted, it is not until the reign of Constantine that Aquileia's Christian community enters the documentary record, but, as entrances go, it is a dramatic one. Theodore, the bishop of Aquileia who attended the Council of Arles in 314, was discovered in the early years of this century to have constructed an enormous complex of cult buildings in the city which were decorated with over a thousand square metres of sumptuous, polychrome mosaic (Menis 1965). The building itself was a renovation and enlargement of an earlier structure on this site, either bought by the church or donated by a member of the congregation (White 1990, 129–31, 146–7). This spectacular discovery reveals that Aquileia's Christian community was already extremely wealthy in the opening decades of the fourth century. In a city which had made its fortune on trade, such an ostentatious display by the Christians of Aquileia arouses suspicions that some of them were associated with the commercial life in the city in some way, perhaps as traders themselves. As always, direct evidence is lacking, but there is enough circumstantial evidence to suggest a link between the Christian community and Aquileia's importance as a centre of trade.

First, there is a close correlation between the geographical sphere of influence of the Aquileian church and the trade networks in which the city occupied a central role. It has been shown that Africa had strong mercantile links with the city, and this is mirrored in the life of the Christian community. Fortunatianus, bishop of Aquileia in the 340s and 350s, came from Africa (Jerome, *de vir. ill.* 97). The link may be discernible also in Theodore's church complex. Strong similarities have been noted between the style of its mosaics, particularly the large seascape with its depiction of the story of Jonah, and those being executed by North African workshops at this time (Dorigo 1971, 169). Indeed, it seems that North African mosaicists were active elsewhere in northern Italy in the fourth century, laying the magnificent pavements of the villa at Desenzano on the shores of Lake Garda (Dunbabin 1978, 214–16).[6]

Aquileia's strong connections with the north-western Balkans had an impact on Christianity too. The bishops of Aquileia held considerable prestige among the Christian communities of the lands beyond the Julian Alps, a relationship which would crystallise into Aquileia's medieval patriarchate (Menis 1978). The Christian community of Jerome's home town of Stridon, for example, was within Aquileia's sphere of influence by the mid-fourth century (Jerome, *Epp.* 6, 7). After the death of the homoian[7] emperor Constantius II in 361, Bishop Valerian of Aquileia was seen as a leader of the effort to eradicate homoian bishops – by now deemed heretical – from Illyricum (Basil, *Ep.* 91). These connections already existed by the time of Constantine's conversion. When Theodore of Aquileia attended the Council of Arles in 314, he was recorded as coming from Dalmatia, unlike Merocles of Milan, who is clearly recorded as coming from Italy (Gaudemet 1977, 58–9). This designation implies that the Christian communities Theodore represented at the council in addition to Aquileia were those of the north-western Balkans.

The cosmopolitan character of Aquileia's population extended to the city's Christians. Bishop Fortunatianus was, as we have seen, an African. The Christian congregation included a large section drawn from the Greek east (*IG* xiv. 2353–60), particularly Syria, some of whom built their own church to the north of the city in the late fourth century (Chevallier 1990, 105). This poly-

[6] Duval (1974, 196–7) paints a charming – though self-confessedly fanciful – picture of Bishop Caecilian of Carthage, *en route* to see Constantine at Milan, suggesting the use of African mosaicists to Theodore.
[7] Subscribers to this doctrine held that Christ was 'like' (*homoios*) God the Father.

glot nature was evident already in Theodore's day. The inscription which records his dedication of his church complex acknowledges the help he received 'from Almighty God and the flock given [him] by heaven' (*ILCV* 1863: *adiuuante Deo omnipotente et poemnio caelitus tibi traditum*). The word used in this inscription to describe Theodore's flock is a curiosity: rather than use the customary Latin word *grex*, the inscription uses *poemnium*, a Latin transliteration of *poimnion*, the Greek for 'flock'. Use of the term *poemnium* points to the same Greek element in the Christian population of Aquileia observable in the epigraphic record.

It is worth considering also the place of Theodore's church in the topography of Aquileia (see Figure 10.3). It was built within the walls, in an area enclosed as part of the late third-century development of the city as a supply base for the army in the northeastern Alps (Jäggi 1990, 163–7). Immediately to the south of the Christian complex there was an enormous *horreum*, the plan and location of which recalls the military warehouse built at Augusta Treverorum (Trier) in the tetrarchic period.[8] Theodore's complex rose, then, in an area of Aquileia given over to trade. It is possible that the donor of the site was somehow engaged in commerce, especially if Raymond Chevallier is right in identifying the building underlying the complex as a *horreum* (1990, 106).

The evidence at Aquileia, therefore, points to a strong connection between its Christian and trading communities. Not only was its most important church building in an area of the city associated with commercial activity, but the Aquileian faithful were a cosmopolitan lot, drawn from the parts of the empire with which the city had trading networks. Extending out of the city, there were Christian networks of influence which followed precisely the trade routes used most frequently by merchants operating out of the city. These links were well established, moreover, by the time that the Aquileian church emerges into the light of history under Constantine. If these connections stretch back to the very beginnings of Christianity in the city – and I see no reason to doubt

---

[8]   Bertacchi 1982, 340–8 and fig. 2; cf. Rickman 1971, 264–5, on the example at Augusta Treverorum. The building was so vast that a topographical painter of the seventeenth century took its imposing remains for a ruined patriarchal palace: Jäggi 1990, plate 1C.

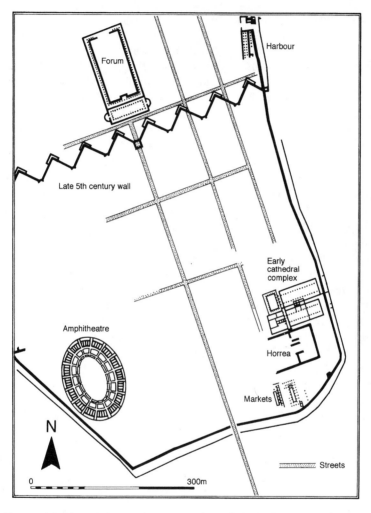

Figure 10.3 Plan of the southern part of Aquileia, indicating the location of Theodore's church complex, the imperial *horreum* and the extent of the tetrarchic expansion of the city. Based on Bertacchi 1982 and Jäggi 1990.

that they do – then it seems that at Aquileia Christian origins were profoundly influenced by the city's importance in ancient trade networks.

Implications and conclusions

The evidence from northern Italy has demonstrated a correlation
between trade networks and patterns of religious diffusion for the
pagan soteriological cults and for Judaism and Christianity. In
some cases a direct link can be drawn between the spread of a
cult and individuals involved in trade, such as the personnel of
the *publicum portorii Illyrici* who set up altars to Isis at Sublavio
and Poetovio. At Aquileia, a major market centre, it has been
suggested that by 314 the Christian community reflected the
wealth, geographical horizons and ethnic mix of the city's trading
population. Although circumstantial, this evidence is enough to
suggest that the social repercussions of trade had contributed to
the development of Christianity at Aquileia, and probably also at
other centres in northern Italy.

A number of implications can be drawn from this case-study
for the history of religious diffusion in the Roman west as a whole.
Whereas we can often identify traders or customs officials as
disseminators of private pagan cults, the paucity of material on
early Christianity allows no such vivid picture. We can make little
more than the general observation that the social dynamics
fostered by trade networks provided an environment of close
personal interface and geographical mobility which were crucial
for any kind of religious diffusion from centre to centre, and which
were probably central to the success of Christianity.

The model constructed in this chapter for northern Italy is
applicable to other parts of the western Mediterranean. One area
where the debate over the role of traders in Christian origins has
raged most strongly is the Rhône valley in southern Gaul. The
early congregations at Lugdunum (Lyon) and Vienna (Vienne)
were clearly composed of immigrants from the Greek east. As
at Rome, their earliest literature – Irenaeus' *Adversus Haereses*
(*c.* 185) – was written in Greek; while Eusebius of Caesarea's
account of the martyrdoms of Christians from both cities in 177
was gleaned from a report sent by 'Christ's servants at Vienna
and Lugdunum to the brethren in Asia and Phrygia' (Eus. *HE* 5.
1. 3). Such evidence has prompted the conclusion that Christianity
came to the Rhône valley by 'the main trade routes linking
Gaul with the eastern Mediterranean' (Frend 1964, 126–7). Other
analyses suggest, on the contrary, that early Christianity at

Lugdunum and Vienna originated in the predominantly Greek Christian community at Rome (Pietri 1978). In the model proposed in this chapter, however, it does not matter from where southern Gaul first received its Christianity. Instead, we can understand why Christianity should develop at Lugdunum and Vienna by the mid-second century, because trade networks had created in those cities an environment conducive to the diffusion of private cults (Audin 1975; Rivet 1988, 305–14).

A word of caution before concluding. As noted before, it would be absurd to suggest that trade networks were the only factors encouraging the growth of Christianity. The example of southern Gaul is instructive in this regard because Christianity developed earlier and faster at Lugdunum than it did in Massilia (Marseille), the region's greatest port (Gilliard 1975, 31). This was so because Lugdunum was important not just in terms of trade networks: it was the effective capital of the Three Gauls, at the hub of a vast communications network, and the centre of political, cultural, administrative and religious activity (Audin 1975, 31–54; Fishwick 1987, 97–137). Thus there were several reasons why it should have had a diverse and changing population creating an environment congenial for the diffusion of new cults. Yet this does not undermine the argument of this chapter. Instead, it emphasises the point made earlier that the significance of trade networks was that they helped create a social environment in which diffusion could occur. At Lugdunum the trade networks supplemented other networks, and this would have been true, to a greater or lesser degree, of every centre discussed in this chapter.

To conclude, this analysis of northern Italy – together with its brief foray into southern Gaul – has shown the significant, but not exclusive, importance of trade networks in explaining the processes of religious diffusion. The importance of trade for any society cannot be reduced to economic formulae or the mere exchange of goods. Trade is deeply embedded in the society within which it occurs, bringing people from distant areas into contact and fostering environments of cultural plurality. I have written in the knowledge that some have dismissed the search for Christian origins as a 'fruitless and insoluble' undertaking (Mitchell 1993, 43). To an extent I agree: the true origins of north Italian Christianity will never be known. Yet it seems worth while to me to attempt an answer, by viewing the spread of Christianity in the context of the

complex social, economic, political and cultural networks which
made up the ancient Mediterranean world. The endeavour does
not seem pointless when one considers their importance in other
better-attested processes of religious diffusion, such as the spread
of Manichaeism along the Silk Road to Turkestan and China (Lieu
1985, 69–72), or the movement of first Hinduism and then Islam
through the trading centres of Malaya and the Sumatra archipel-
ago (Park 1994, 102, 109–11). Trade networks helped provide the
conditions of cultural plurality which would assist the spread of a
private cult such as Christianity. Teeming with a multiplicity of cul-
tures, religions, races and languages, the plural societies of places
like Aquileia, Puteoli or Lugdunum demonstrate that there were
additional non-economic aspects to the relationship between trade,
traders and the ancient city.

Bibliography

Audin, A. (1975), 'Lugdunum: colonie romaine et capitale des Gaules',
    in A. Latreille (ed.), *Histoire de Lyon et du Lyonnais* (Toulouse), 23–59.
Bertacchi, L. (1982), 'Edilizia civile nel IV secolo ad Aquileia', *Antichità
    Altoadriatiche* 22: 337–57.
Budischovsky, M.-C. (1976), 'La diffusion des cultes égyptiens d'Aquilée
    à travers les pays alpins', *Antichità Altoadriatiche* 9: 207–27.
Calderini, A. (1930), *Aquileia romana: Ricerche di storia e di epigrafia*
    (Milan).
Chevallier, R. (1983), *La romanisation de la Celtique du Pô* (Rome).
—— (1990), *Aquilée et la romanisation de l'Europe* (Tours).
Chilver, G. E. F. (1942), *Cisalpine Gaul* (Oxford).
Cipriano, M. T. (1986), 'Aquileia (Veneto): Le anfore del Museo', in A.
    Giardina (ed.), *Società romana e Impero tardoantico* 3 (Rome and Bari),
    139–43.
Cuscito, G. (1974), 'Africani in Aquileia e nell'Italia settentrionale', *Anti-
    chità Altoadriatiche* 5: 143–63.
Deichmann, F. W. (1976), *Ravenna: Hauptstadt des spätantiken Abend-
    landes. II Kommentar 2* (Wiesbaden).
—— (1989), *Ravenna: Hauptstadt des spätantiken Abendlandes. II
    Kommentar 3* (Wiesbaden).
De Laet, S. J. (1949), *Portorium: Étude sur l'organisation douanière chez
    les Romains surtout a l'époque du Haut-Empire* (Brugge).
Destro, A. and Pesce, M. (1995), *Antropologia delle origini cristiane*
    (Rome and Bari).
Dorigo, W. (1971), *Late Roman Painting* (London).
Dunbabin, K. M. (1978), *The Mosaics of Roman North Africa* (Oxford).

Duval, Y.-M. (1974), 'L'influence des écrivains africains du IIIe siècle sur les écrivains chrétiens de l'Italie du Nord dans le seconde moitié du IVe siècle', *Antichità Altoadriatiche* 5: 191–225.

Fishwick, D. (1987), *The Imperial Cult in the Latin West* (Leiden).

Frayn, J. M. (1984), *Sheep-Rearing and the Wool Trade in Italy during the Roman Period* (Liverpool).

—— (1993), *Markets and Fairs in Roman Italy* (Oxford).

Frederiksen, M. (1984), *Campania* (London).

Frend, W. H. C. (1964), 'A note on the influence of Greek immigrants on the spread of Christianity to the west', in *Mullus: Festschrift Th. Klauser* (Munster), 125–9.

Gallagher, E. V. (1993), 'Conversion and community in late antiquity', *Journal of Religion* 73: 1–15.

Garnsey, P. D. A. (1976), 'Economy and society at Mediolanum under the principate', *PBSR* 44: 13–27.

Gaudemet, J. (1977), *Conciles gaulois du IVe siècle* (Paris).

Gilliard, F. D. (1975), 'The apostolicity of the Gallic churches', *Harvard Theological Review* 68: 17–33.

Goodman, M. (1989), 'Nerva, the fiscus Judaicus and Jewish identity', *JRS* 79: 40–4.

—— (1994), *Mission and Conversion: Proselytizing in the Religious History of the Roman Empire* (Oxford).

Grant, R. M. (1986), *Gods and the One God* (London).

Hengel, M. (1992), 'The pre-Christian Paul', in J. Lieu, J. North and T. Rajak (eds), *The Jews among Pagans and Christians in the Roman Empire* (London), 29–52.

Jäggi, C. (1990), 'Aspekte der städtebaulichen Entwicklung Aquileias in frühchristlicher Zeit', *Jahrbuch für Antike und Christentum* 33: 158–96.

Kraabel, A. T. (1994), 'Immigrants, exiles, expatriates, and missionaries', in L. Bormann, K. Del Tredici and A. Standhartinger (eds), *Religious Propaganda and Missionary Effort in the New Testament World* (Leiden), 71–88.

Lane Fox, R. (1986), *Pagans and Christians* (Harmondsworth).

Lanzani, V. (1984), 'Ticinum: le origini della città cristiana', in *Storia di Pavia 1. L'età antica* (Pavia and Milan), 349–68.

Lanzoni, F. (1923), *Le origini delle diocesi antiche d'Italia* (Rome).

Lauffer, S. (1971), *Diokletians Preisedikt* (Berlin).

Lieu, S. N. C. (1985), *Manichaeism in the Later Roman Empire and Medieval China* (Manchester).

Lizzi, R. (1989), *Vescovi e strutture ecclesiastiche nella città tardoantica (l'Italia Annonaria nel IV–V secolo d. C.)* (Como).

McLynn, N. B. (1995), *Ambrose of Milan: Church and Court in a Christian Capital* (Berkeley).

Malaise, M. (1972a), *Inventaire préliminaire des documents égyptiens decouverts en Italie* (Leiden).

—— (1972b), *Les conditions de pénétration des cultes isiaques en Italie* (Leiden).

Martin, L. H. (1987), *Hellenistic Religions* (New York).

Matthews, J. F. (1989), 'Hostages, philosophers, pilgrims, and the diffusion of ideas in the late Roman Mediterranean and Near East', in F. M. Clover and R. S. Humphreys (eds), *Tradition and Innovation in Late Antiquity* (Madison), 29–49.

Meeks, W. A. (1993), *The First Urban Christians* (New Haven).

Menis, G. C. (1965), *I mosaici cristiani di Aquileia* (Udine).

—— (1978), 'Rapporti ecclesiastici tra Aquileia e la Slovenia in età paleocristiana', *Arheolski Vestnik* 29: 368–76.

Mitchell, S. (1993), *Anatolia: Land, Men and Gods in Asia Minor. 2: The Rise of the Church* (Oxford).

Mohrmann, C. (1965), 'Les origines de la latinité chrétienne à Rome', in eadem, *Études sur le latin des Chrétiens* 3 (Rome), 67–126.

North, J. (1976), 'Conservatism and change in Roman religion', *PBSR* 44: 1–12.

Otranto, G. (1991), *Italia meridionale e Puglia paleocristiane: Saggi storici* (Bari).

Park, C. C. (1994), *Sacred Worlds: An Introduction to Geography and Religion* (London).

Parker, R. (1996), *Athenian Religion: A History* (Oxford).

Picard, J.-Ch. (1988), *Le souvenir des évêques: Sépultures, listes épiscopales et culte des évêques en Italie du Nord des origines au Xe siècle* (Rome).

Pietri, Ch. (1978), 'Les origines de la mission lyonnaise: remarques critiques', in *Les Martyres de Lyon* (177) (Paris), 220–31.

Rickman, G. E. (1971), *Roman Granaries and Storage Buildings* (Cambridge).

—— (1980), *The Corn Supply of Ancient Rome* (Oxford).

Rivet, A. L. F. (1988), *Gallia Narbonensis: Southern Gaul in Roman Times* (London).

Ruggini, L. (1959), 'Ebrei e orientali nell'Italia settentrionale tra il IV e il VI secolo d. C.', *Studia et Documenta Historiae et Iuris* 25: 186–308.

Sanders, E. P. (1993), *The Historical Figure of Jesus* (Harmondsworth).

Sartori, F. (1960), 'Verona romana', in *Verona e il suo territorio* I (Verona), 161–259.

Sasel, J. (1966), 'Barbii', *Eirene* 5: 117–37.

Selem, P. (1980), *Les religions orientales dans la Pannonie romaine: Partie en Yougoslavie* (Leiden).

Stark, R. (1996), *The Rise of Christianity: A Sociologist Reconsiders History* (Princeton).

Tozzi, P. L. (1971), 'Iscrizioni latine sull'arte laneria bresciana e Virgilio *Georgiche* IV. 277–8', *Athenaeum* n.s. 49: 152–7.

von Reden, S. (1995), 'The Piraeus – a world apart', *G&R* 42: 24–37.

White, L. M. (1990), *Building God's House in the Roman World. Architectural Adaptation among Pagans, Jews and Christians* (Baltimore).

Whittaker, C. R. (1983), 'Late Roman trade and traders', in P. Garnsey, K. Hopkins and C. R. Whittaker (eds), *Trade in the Ancient Economy* (Cambridge), 163–80.

11

Ancient economies: models and muddles

John K. Davies

I

In a gentlemanly and mostly implicit way, the papers given at the St Andrews Conference touched on some of the most intractable questions of ancient economic history. My brief off-the-cuff summing up in the final session attempted to sketch the components of a possible framework of wider reference, within which the chapters published in this volume could be related to each other and could find a comfortable home. The chapter which follows here, transformed and much enlarged from those initial remarks,[1] is that sketch. It is undoubtedly inadequate, and is quite probably incompetent. All I claim for it is that by recognising how wide the spectrum of approaches to the subject currently is, by acknowledging their various legitimacies, and by sketching (however crudely) their components and their inter-relationships, it attempts to map the field of ideas in such a way as to help the

[1] An intermediate version, entitled 'Greek economies: where has the conversation got to?', was given to a Research Seminar at Liverpool in February 1997. I am most grateful to colleagues there present for helpful comments, especially to Zosia Archibald, Chris Mee, Graham Oliver, and Christopher Tuplin. The usual disclaimers of responsibility apply. Once more, I am glad to acknowledge the support of the Leverhulme Trust for this, as for other fruits of the productive *schole* which its award to me has provided.

tiro to orient herself. If A. N. Other can replace this crude model
by a more precise or a more wide-ranging one, so much the better.

A first task is to make explicit what remained implicit. First and
foremost is the challenge of locating any discussion of trade,
traders, and the city within the broader task of writing the
economic history of antiquity. Especially if, as symbolised by
the very proper inclusion of Kuhrt's chapter on the Assyrian
colonies, we understand by 'antiquity' not just that portion of it
which is accessible via texts in Greek and Latin but the whole
sweep of economic and social development from first literacy until
the transformation of most of the Roman empire into something
else, the range of relevant environments in time and space is so
huge as to render the task self-defeating – not to mention the
overwhelming case for seeing even such boundaries (of 'antiquity'
as thus defined) as highly problematical constructs. Inevitably,
therefore, contributors zoomed in onto specific areas where the
mutual influences of traceable exchange patterns, the perceptible or assumed influence of a city or group of cities (whether
as markets, or as power-wielding manipulators of the terms of
exchange, or as both at once), and the observable behaviour
of individuals became a matter of analysis or debate. Yet, equally
inevitably, contributors were therefore addressing different questions and casting 'cities' in different roles.

A first helpful step may be to locate them at various points
along a spectrum. At one, minimalist, extreme, for Lawall the city
(here Chios) merely lurks in the background, whether as the
authority possibly responsible for codifying the markings on
amphorae or as the political community conscious enough of its
role and reputation as producer and exporter (presumably of wine)
to place an amphora and bunch of grapes on its coinage from the
early fifth century onwards.[2] So too for Paterson, who focuses on
orbis Romanus rather than *urbs Roma* in order to bring out, *contra*
the post-Finley near-orthodoxy, the exceptional scale, nature, and
complexity of Roman trade during the principate and in order to
emphasise the importance of the individuals who exploited the

---

[2] For basic references see Kraay 1976, 242 n. 2. A more extended
comparison with Pouilloux's model of the linkage at Thasos between
economy and polity (Pouilloux 1954, with the critiques of Finley 1965,
28–32 and Garlan 1983, 2ff.) would be a helpful next step.

new conditions. Likewise, for Laurence cities as such – as distinct from the spatial integration of the 'wider economy' – barely appear, the villa appearing instead as the main motor alike of production and of consumption. Smith in contrast finds it possible to move outwards from the basic tasks of classifying and dating artifacts towards the social role of the artisan in late archaic central Italy in buttressing the identities and ideologies which were needed for the new types of urban form and urban social cohesion. Tsetskhladze too moves outwards, but in a wholly different way, from the colonising cities of the Aegean to the Black Sea, from the artifacts found (and not found) in the latter region, and from the commodities putatively 'traded', in order to sketch relationships which were based on tribute-exaction and gift-giving rather than market-based exchange. In further contrast, to a greater or lesser degree the remaining contributors place cities at the centre of the exchange activities which they describe. For Humphries, Aquileia was indeed a city, through the institutions of which the spread of ideas could be plausibly postulated, but without itself having any collective or directed role in that spread. Alston portrays the central role of urban centres, small and large, in the economy of Roman Egypt and their participation in regional if not international trade networks, while reminding us that 'not only could markets be held in places other than cities, but also cities could exist without notable markets' (p. 196 above). Finally, at the maximalist end of the spectrum, Whitby portrays a city (Athens) actively attempting both to manage trade in one essential commodity and to manage the traders involved, while Kuhrt portrays a city (Ashur) which was not merely attempting to manage trade in one essential commodity but actually consisted of the men (and, it seems, women) who were the traders involved.

Though particular interpretations in these chapters may be debatable, the general impression of an immensely wide spectrum of patterns of exchange activity is as unassailable overall as it is awkward for the generalising or pattern-making instinct. Further case-studies would fill out the spectrum[3] and might even extend

---

[3] Hellenistic Rhodes is an obvious candidate, as also would be a non-Greek city-state such as Tyre in the light of Ezekiel xxvii–xxviii (with Bondi in Krings ed. 1995, 268–89), while an update of Meiggs on Ostia might usefully revisit the relationship between occupational guilds and decurions.

it,[4] but will make it no easier to bring all such activity within a single formula. That is hardly surprising, for various reasons. First and foremost, each component of the triad of this book's title has a bibliography and a body of theory (or rather, of competing theories) of its own. This is not the occasion to describe them, even in outline (though some components will be cited below), but simply to state the palpable fact that, e.g. theories of the city (Weberian or other) and theories of exchange currently have different focuses, different vocabularies, and different ideological presuppositions. Nor, second, is there any agreement among the practitioners of the craft of economic historian of antiquity on the best unit of description and analysis. It is notable that all contributors to this volume have focused on a specific city, or region, or exchange pattern, and that nearly all have elected to use a synchronic mode of description rather than analyse a process of change through time. Good reasons of practicality will have driven such choices, but thereby leave open – or, again, implicit – their theoretical rationale. To take only one issue thereby submerged: those economic geographers who look to J. H. von Thünen as their founding father tend to write in terms of the 'region' as the unit of discourse, however loosely that concept may be defined,[5] whereas economic geographers of literate antiquity are perhaps more tempted to write in terms of the political unit, be it Roman province or Greek city-state. Given the intimate links between economy and public economy (see below), that choice may be just, but it still needs to be justified.

A third reason, the difficulty of harmonising conclusions drawn from differing genres of evidence, can be illustrated from the chapters in this very volume. Tsetskhladze, using almost exclusively the tangible evidence of pottery, coinage, and metal objects, together with the increasing palynological evidence of what was grown, where, and when, casts such severe doubt on 'trade'

---

[4] Study of the balance between fiscally driven and independent 'trade' in pre-Persian Babylon or Ptolemaic Alexandria would illuminate the complex situation where a city economy is also a royal economy.

[5] For a valuable introduction see Smith 1976b. Samuelson's commemorative paper (Samuelson 1983) is no less stimulating, as a sample of the possibilities, for being highly mathematical and for focusing on the single-centre model of exchange.

as the main motor of Greek involvement with, and settlement in, the Black Sea region as to challenge much of what still passes for current orthodoxy and to reduce to nil the need to ascribe explicit policies to any of the Greek states concerned with the region. Whitby, in contrast, uses literary and epigraphic evidence in order to restate, *contra* Garnsey, the older view that population pressure on indigenous food resources forced fifth- and fourth-century Athens to look abroad for supplementary supplies on a large and continuous scale and to stimulate and control the grain trade via public policy and intervention. Paradoxically, both contributors are probably right, for the distance between them can be greatly reduced by adopting the hypothesis that the Milesian settlements in Pontos and Propontis were prompted not by 'trade' but by the search for the kind of *lebensraum* which was unobtainable in the Milesian hinterland once Lydian pressure on the Greek seaboard cities became intense; that a century later knowledge of an initially spasmodic but gradually growing effective demand in Athens for certain foodstuff staples spread among the *emporoi* and *naukleroi* of the Aegean, stimulating the growth of exchange patterns which initially piggy-backed onto the existing links with Miletos; and that those patterns eventually created a collective interest among the inhabitants of Attika which was strong enough to prompt military and political action by the Athenian polity once Miletos ceased to be a major regional power after 494. None the less, even if such a reconciliation has its attractions, the methodological challenge remains: issues of exchange patterns (direct or indirect),[6] of the scale of exchange, of the degree of intervention by a polity (*polis* or other), and of the interests which drove such intervention, all come into play.

[6]   Neither author cites the *syngraphe* of Dem. 35. 10–13, with its clear evidence for a triangular exchange pattern: from Athens in ballast, but with 3,000 drachmas in silver, to be used to buy wine at Mende or Skione in Chalkidike, which would then be taken into Bosporos and the Black Sea and exchanged for goods (presumably grain, though the contract does not say so) which were to be brought back to Athens (translation and discussion in Davies 1993, 223–4). By their nature such triangular patterns are hard to detect, but their existence would help to bridge the gap between the near-total absence of Athenian coins from Black Sea hoards, rightly noted by Tsetskhladze (this volume, p. 58f.), and the literary evidence.

These and other considerations[7] are all part of a general problem which runs though the entire discourse of ancient economic history: the lack of a clear and generally accepted answer to the question 'What do we regard as a satisfactory framework for the description, analysis, and interpretation of economic activity in antiquity?' As things are, regrettably, much of what we write comprises 'a discourse in search of a method':[8] much of what we say to each other ends in impasse.[9] Rather than join the debate, it may therefore be now more helpful to deconstruct it, by identifying its components and its presuppositions: which in turn involves delving into the history of the debate reflected in the title of the present volume. The main body of this chapter will therefore try to describe the main intellectual currents, to criticise them in various ways, and to set out an alternative route forward. What follows here may therefore seem at once elementary, disjointed, and remote from the themes of the foregoing chapters. I can but beg the reader to have patience for a few pages.

II

First in importance among the intellectual currents to be considered must be the discipline of economics itself. This is not the moment for a survey, historical or other, even if I were competent to provide one,[10] but merely to note the general directions and tendencies of the discipline: towards abstraction and analytic concepts, towards quantification (for economists, an economy is a thing which you *measure*, by GNP, demand curves, annual growth, inflation, price/earnings ratios, unemployment, etc.), and over-

---

[7] One other is so bleak that I put it in a footnote: most of us (I include myself) would be seen as little more than amateurs, alike in handling theories and in handling such quantitative evidence as we have, if suddenly transferred into a serious university department of economic history. (For an honourable exception to the latter, Duncan-Jones 1974 and 1990.)

[8] The phrase is borrowed from the title of Penn 1990.

[9] I understand this was the verdict reached by a panel meeting on the topic at the APA meeting at New York in December 1996 (G. J. Oliver, pers. comm.). Cf. also Kuhrt's view (this volume, p. 28) that the debate about the ancient economy 'seems to me to have run its course and it has not got a lot more to offer'.

[10] Cf. rather Roll 1961, among many others.

whelmingly towards analysis in terms of *markets* and of *economic man*. Almost at random, I pick an illustrative quotation:

> The central working assumptions of the new classical school are three:
> Economic agents *maximize*. Households and firms make *optimal* decisions. This means that they use all available information in reaching decisions and that those decisions are the best possible in the circumstances in which they find themselves.
> Decisions are *rational* and are made using all the relevant information. Expectations are rational when they are statistically the best predictions of the future that can be made using the available information. Indeed, the new classical school is sometimes described as the *rational expectations school*, even though rational expectations is [*sic*] only one part of the theoretical approach of the new classical economists. The rational expectations implication is that people eventually will come to understand whatever government policy is being used, and thus that it is not possible to fool most of the people all the time or even most of the time.
> *Markets clear*. There is no reason why firms or workers would not adjust wages or prices if that would make them better off. Accordingly, prices and wages adjust in order to equate supply and demand: in other words, markets clear. Market clearing is a powerful assumption, as we shall see presently.
>
> (Dornbusch and Fischer 1990, 7)

Admittedly, this is an extreme example, representing the tenets of the Neo-classical school rather than those of the new Keynesians, whose faith in the operations of markets is not as fundamentalist as that of the Friedmanites or of the neo-Hayekians, but for our purposes what the two schools have in common is more important: a concentration on Now, on capitalist economies, on the fiscal policy of polities (i.e. nation-states), etc., with virtually no reference to the past or to older schools or gurus such as the Marginalists' concept of social value or Veblen's notion of conspicuous consumption, let alone Marx. The trouble is, ancient historians cannot isolate themselves from these traditions, assumptions, and tendencies. They do influence our discourse, all the more importantly because they may do so indirectly, even subconsciously or surreptitiously, as well as because there are historians writing on the economic history of antiquity who reflect such approaches (for example, Thompson 1978, 1982; Figueira 1984; Burke 1992; Silver 1995). Whether such approaches *should* influence us is a question which has therefore to be brought into the open. The underlying

problem is whether the concepts and theories which the discipline
of economics uses are social universals or not. Some, such as marginal utility or the law of substitution, probably are, but others
pretty certainly are not: at the extreme, Heichelheim's attempt
to detect Kondratieff-style trade cycles in the economy of the
Hellenistic eastern Mediterranean can hardly be said to have been
a success.[11] It is therefore meaningful to ask whether the statement
'The ideal economy must be neo-classical in structure' is like
saying 'The ideal house must be neo-classical in structure' (which
is a matter of aesthetic judgement), or is like saying 'The ideal
house must conform to the laws of the country wherein it is built'
(which is true but contingent), or is like saying 'The ideal house
must conform to the laws of physics and mechanics' (which is true,
unavoidable, obvious, and unhelpful). Neo-classical economists,
I suspect, would prefer the third formulation. Development
economists would demur. A wise economist colleague of mine once
defined economics as concerned with what lies in between
technology and psychology,[12] rightly thereby emphasising the
human and context-contingent parameters of the activity. To
be fair, even an extreme neo-classical such as Morris Silver
acknowledges that 'Marx's capitalist and the modern economic
theorist's profit-maximizing entrepreneur are after all caricatures
or models, not realistic representations of businesspersons' (Silver
1995, 175), or that

> the location of ancient economies along a 'disembeddedness'–'embed-
> dedness' scale with respect to the socio-political sphere is variable not
> constant. Moreover, ancient economies, Near Eastern and Graeco-
> Roman, experienced 'Dark Ages', periods of crisis, in which household
> economy increased greatly in importance relative to both markets and
> hierarchies. The proper task of the historical economist is to probe
> the sources of this observed variation.
>
> (Silver 1995, 196)

That 'mission statement' may be debatable, or too limited, but it
helps to remind us that present-day economic theory as a set of
potentially applicable ideas cannot be ignored.

---

[11] Heichelheim 1930, with the critique of Reger 1994, 157f.
[12] Derek Morris (pers. comm. *c.* 1975).

A second component, linked to the first but best kept separate from it, is the polarisation between 'primitivists' and 'modernisers', or alternatively between 'substantivists' and 'formalists'. A description by Paul Cartledge neatly encapsulates the differences:

> For the formalists, the ancient economy was a functionally segregated and independently instituted sphere of activity with its own profit-maximizing, want-satisfying logic and rationality, less 'developed' no doubt than any modern economy but nevertheless recognizably similar in kind. Substantivists, on the other hand, hold that the ancient economy was not merely less developed but socially embedded and politically overdetermined and so – by Neoclassical standards – conspicuously conventional, irrational, and status-ridden. It is crucial that this much more interesting and important 'substantivist'–'formalist' debate should not be confused, as it often is, with the 'primitivist'–'modernizer' debate. Not even the most ardent primitivist would deny that actually quite a lot of extra-household economy went on in Greece. Not even the most ardent modernizer would deny that some quite basic aspects of ancient Greek economy were really quite primitive. The most serious misunderstandings can arise when the debate about the level and quantity of Greek economic life becomes confused with the argument over its politico-social location.[13]

(Cartledge forthcoming)

Helpful though this is, the background needs to be sketched more fully. Basic is the collision between two models of social and economic development in antiquity. The first, developed from an idea of Rodbertus by the 'Nationalökonom' Karl Bücher in the lectures which became his 'unpretentious little book' *Die Entstehung der Volkswirtschaft*[14] saw human history as a linear progression through three types of 'economy': first *Hauswirtschaft* (Rodbertus's 'Oikenwirtschaft'), in which the entire circuit of the economy from production to consumption was carried out within

---

[13] I am most grateful to P. A. Cartledge for permission to cite this paragraph in advance of publication.

[14] The phrase 'Anspruchsloses Büchlein' is Bücher's own (Bücher 1922, 2 in Finley 1979). Not in fact that the book was as 'unpretentious' as all that, for it went through at least fifteen editions by 1920 and was translated into French, English, Russian, and Bohemian. (For the English edition, see Wickett 1901.)

the closed circle of the household (family, or descent-group); second, *Stadtwirtschaft* as typified by the city-states of medieval Germany, in which direct exchange among the members of a civic community through a regulated market maximised the self-sufficiency of that community and minimised the need for capital; and third, *Volkswirtschaft* as exemplified especially by the Colbertian system of seventeenth-century France, wherein the government of a post-Renaissance national state took pains to maximise gainful economic activity in order to maximise its tax revenue.

Though Bücher acknowledged at one point that traces of *Stadtwirtschaft* were visible in antiquity, and at another that his three modes were not a mutually exclusive sequence (but only that at any one moment one mode predominates), he insisted that 'neither among the peoples of Antiquity nor in the early Middle Ages did the circumstances of daily demand support a regular exchange'.[15] He thus laid himself open to an onslaught from Eduard Meyer, Julius Beloch, and others, on the explicit ground that he had seriously underestimated the *amount* of market-based economic activity in antiquity. In terms of specific texts and data, they had the better of the argument, but underlying their use of them was both a sound implicit objection (that the development of economic systems was not as linear as he had assumed) and an explicit but probably *un*sound alternative model. This latter is the more interesting, for it has coloured the argument ever since. Its core was a perceived analogy between the growth of the archaic and classical Greek city-states on the one hand and that of the medieval city-states on the other, with their wealth based on long-distance trade and concentrated in corporations of entrepreneurial merchant-dynasts. For Meyer in particular, thinking in cultural as well as in economic terms, the post-Mycenaean period was 'Das griechische Mittelalter', the seventh, sixth and fifth centuries BC corresponding to the fourteenth, fifteenth and sixteenth centuries AD:[16] for Beloch in particular, the motifs were industry, factories, production, (mass)-consumption, competition, markets,

---

[15]   Respectively Bücher 1922, 116, 148 and 111.
[16]   For the title, Meyer 1937, 231–491, with 267–9 for an explicit engagement with the analogy; for the century-by-century correspondences, Meyer 1895/1924, 118–19.

and money.[17] Their authority, the accessibility of the terminology, and the degree of palpable confirmation available from texts and artifacts, have given this interpretative tradition, with or without the medieval colouring, a long run for its money. The extreme position in this direction was probably that of Ure, with his portrait of the archaic Greek tyrants as merchant princes owing their power to commercial or industrial activity and to the 'financial revolution' of coinage, but the underlying approach is still contributing substantially to the debate.[18]

So of course is its antithesis, represented *imprimis* by Hasebroek's two books of 1928 and 1931. By arguing, with reference especially to archaic and classical Greece, that most known traders were not actually Greek, and that they remained poor, politically inert, and socially disreputable, his contribution was immensely influential in challenging the mercantilist model. Though his first point has to some degree been controverted by more recent work (cf. Bravo 1977; Reed 1981), the remainder of his argument was strong enough to transform the debate, partly by providing some of the theoretical input for Finley's new synthesis of 1973, partly by forcing historians to re-identify the interests which *polities* (as distinct from persons) can be reliably seen to have had in stimulating and protecting markets, trade, and traders. The latter activity has helped attention to turn instead to fiscal interests and to the degree to which polities took steps, not to maximise exports, but to maximise reliable access to, and reliable supplies of, essential primary materials: i.e. towards the ascription of an *import*

---

[17] Cf. Beloch 1899, 1902, and especially the chapter 'Die Umwälzung im Wirtschaftsleben' in Beloch 1924, 264–308. Its running heads are eloquent: Erwachsen der Industrie, Natürliche Hilfsquellen, Mittelpunkte der Gewerbtätigkeit, Industrielle Emanzipierung vom Oriente, Handwerkerstand, Sklaverei, Größere Betriebe, Seehandel, Nautik, Kanalbauten, Verkehr zu Lande, Handelsplätze, Entwickelung der Städte, Landfrieden, Proxenie, Kampf gegen den Seeraub, Maß und Gewicht, Griechische Systeme, Münzprägung, Ionische Elektronprägung, Kroesos' Münzsystem, Euboeische und aeginaeische Währung, Pangaeische Währung, Fortdauer der Naturalwirtschaft, Bergbau auf Edelmetalle, Thesaurierung, Preise, Der Zins, Ackerbau, Viehzucht, Verteilung des Grundeigentums, Ländliche Arbeiter, Verschuldung des Bauernstandes.
[18] Ure (1922, 2 and 286) explicitly compares the Medici with the early Greek tyrants. Cf. also the works cited in note 2 above, and French 1964. Even Jeffery 1976 lurches into mercantilist language from time to time.

interest or an *imperialist* interest, not of an *export* interest. It is hardly surprising, therefore (as we saw above), that the debate about the Athenian corn trade should be a hardy perennial, all the more since Lysias' Speech XXII 'Against the corn-dealers' allows us, via the careful analysis of Seager (1966), to see the conflicting interests involved and takes us back to the triad of our present title.

A third component of the conversation is that provided by the comparatively new discipline of economic anthropology.[19] Two of its contributions deserve particular notice. The first is the work of Karl Polanyi. His basic idea, carried through in the 1940s and 1950s in a heroically cross-cultural series of studies, was that much of what passes as 'trade' in antiquity was not conducted in free markets via a price-demand mechanism but comprised a set of exchange transactions which were embedded in social relationships, specifically reflecting relationships of reciprocity between the transacting parties.[20] Both terms, 'embeddedness' and 'reciprocity', have become terms of art in the literature, taken up by Finley and many others. They do indeed have their attractions. They seem, for example, to capture the flavour of exchange transactions in Homer or Hesiod, which clearly are not 'market' exchanges but rather social acts which reflect a complex link between the 'social value' of gift and counter-gift (as determined by the relative statuses of the parties) and their exchange value. They seem also to capture the flavour of the many 'non-economic' transactions attested in classical Athens, i.e. those contracted for non-productive purposes, for the maintenance of prestige, to help friends, etc. They seem too to accord with Greek attitudes as reflected in the disapproving tone of Aristotle's remarks on money-making (*chrematistike*) as an activity, on profit as a motive, or on coinage as a medium of value. (Arist. *Pol.* i 8–11, 1256 a 1–1259 a 36) They help to explain the apparent absence of 'capitalist' institutions from the societies of antiquity. Such an approach

---

[19]   For which see *imprimis* the annual *Research in Economic Anthropology*, since 1978.

[20]   Basic orientation from Polanyi *et al.* 1957 and Polanyi and Dalton eds 1968. Evaluations and celebrations of Polanyi are legion. I know of Humphreys 1969; Garlan 1973; Valensi 1974; Dalton 1975; Lowry 1979, 77ff., Figueira 1984; Block and Somers 1984; Elwert 1987; and Silver 1995, 95ff.; others are cited by Lowry and by Block and Somers.

therefore has appealed to historians, both because it had evidence in its favour and because it offered a middle way between Marxist analysis of the past on the one hand, and neo-classical economics, oriented towards the detection of 'free markets', on the other. There has of course been a reaction against the approach, to the point where 'embeddedness' has perhaps had its day,[21] but the notion of 'reciprocity' is alive and well.[22]

The second contribution of economic anthropology, reinforced by the preoccupations and findings of archaeological survey work, has been to divert attention away from towns and traders towards landscapes and their unurbanised inhabitants. Reasonably so, for persons whom common sense would call 'peasants' litter the pages of Greek literature from Hesiod through Aristophanes to the novelists. Notoriously, however, 'peasant' has proved to be a very debatable term. Does it denote a genuine social type *sui generis*, or a rural population reduced to economic dependence upon a town (hence *contado*, *contadini*), or one reduced to dependence upon a landlord? – at which point the term begins to merge with the equally complex and debatable category of 'serf'. It may be most helpful (and in no sense original) to see 'peasants' as the sum of five characteristics:

1   a livelihood gained predominantly by agrarian or pastoral work on a landholding;
2   dependence on a landlord, via obligations to provide cash rent, or share-cropping, or corvée services;
3   a pattern of settlement which is either fully dispersed (i.e. non-nucleated) or nucleated in villages but not in city-size settlements;
4   a lack of significant economic differentiation, by task or size of holding, among the population of a district; and
5   what is fundamental, a lifestyle where the unit of production is the household and where the bulk of production stays within the household for its own use, with exceptions only for (a) whatever may be siphoned off by a landlord, (b) direct or indirect taxes, and (c) rare exchanges for major durables (salt, ironware, etc.) not produceable within the household.

[21]   Though I note it has now reached Egyptology (Kemp 1989, 231ff.).
[22]   Cf. Gallant 1991, 145ff.; Millett, 1991 *passim*, and Seaford 1994, 191ff.

In this way, though with shifting emphases,[23] there has emerged from recent scholarship, whether focused on prehistory (Halstead 1987, 1989), the classical period (Walcot 1970), or present-day observation (Forbes 1982), a set of models for 'peasants' as a social type which shows a strong family resemblance, while the basic idea of a 'peasant economy' is generally traced back to the Russian economist Chayanov and to the detailed high-quality economic and statistical work from the 1880s onwards on Russian peasant economic problems to which he was heir.[24] Such models may eventually prove to be inadequate, or conceptually flawed, but the basic perception underlying them is unlikely to be discarded.[25] If so, two important consequences follow. First, they force us to be cognisant of the need to construct descriptive frameworks for economic systems which make at most a marginal use of market mechanisms, which are dominated by the so-called 'domestic mode of production', and which have the household, perhaps even a one-person household, as their primary economic unit. Second, they force us to construct descriptive frameworks for economic activity wherein the objectives are *not* those of neo-classical *homo economicus*, *nor* those of the classic pages of Adam Smith on the economies in manufacturing pins to be gained by the extreme division of labour, *nor* those of Morris Silver's entrepreneur trying to reduce 'transaction costs', but (1) to be self-sufficient and therefore not beholden to others, (2) to 'have a little of everything',[26] (3) to survive by having enough in store to tide a household over for a bad year or two, and fundamentally (4) to minimise risk, e.g. by planting a variety of crops (which therefore are less likely all to fail in the same year) or by having land not in one place but in a number of different places with different micro-environments (so that frost or flood does not damage the

---

[23] Various approaches and formulations in Forbes 1982, 17–19; Shanin 1982; and Gallant 1991, 4–5.

[24] Basic source Chayanov 1966/1986, with Schmitt 1992 for a useful assessment of the theoretical validity of his approach. (Schmitt appears not to be aware of the use which historians of antiquity are making of the Chayanov model.) Sketches of Zemstro-based scholarship by Shanin in Chayanov 1986, 14f., and by Thorner in Chayanov 1966/1986, xii.

[25] Though one notes the brisk counter-statement of Paterson in this volume ('The concept of the self-sufficient peasant is a myth', p. 158).

[26] Cf. the title of Forbes 1976.

crop of an entire holding). The case for supposing that much 'peasant' behaviour in antiquity was governed by such considerations, most recently and most forcibly put by Gallant with much cross-cultural comparison (Gallant 1991, *passim*), has now to be a principal starting-point. It carries the subversive but pointed implication that all three components of the triad of our title are secondary phenomena, generated either by such very limited effective demand as 'peasants' could exert or by the more effective but differently focused demand for goods of status, luxury, and power which a landlord or chiefly class may have been able to wield.

A fourth component, caustically but justly termed 'a fetish of scholars and stockbrokers' in a recent book (von Reden 1995, 171), is money, or rather the specific form of it which we call coinage as developed in the Aegean in the seventh century BC. The topic needs to be broached, above all in a book with such a title as the present one, if only to call attention to a strange phenomenon. Notoriously the topic has been a battlefield for decades. The strong view saw (and still sees) coinage as having been developed early in the seventh century as an aid to trade in the areas with the strongest trading activity, as both helping and being helped forward by the procedures of profit-making, as a part of the mercantilist activity of the Greek states, and as an innovation which made Greece a monetary economy, perhaps the first in the world.[27] The weak view argues that coinage was a late seventh-century development, not adopted by most Greek states till *c.* 550 or later; that it had no perceptible commercial purpose initially, being first used to facilitate payments to or by the individual Greek states (e.g. payment of taxes, or to mercenaries); that coins remained bullion first, second, and last; that circulations largely remained regional or local, the boundaries being reinforced by the different and incompatible weight standards: that the use of coins in a retail market context is not to be inferred until low denomination silver and bronze issues appear; and that its use in long-distance trade is a secondary development of the late sixth century, when significant gatherings of coin first appear in hoards.[28] The most recent, very weak view resiles even from the second formulation to profess agnosticism (Howgego 1995, 3). The net

[27] Beloch 1924, 287ff., remains classic, with Figueira 1984.
[28] See the studies cited by Burke 1992, 213 n. 52.

result is a strangely deserted battlefield,[29] which is being occupied not so much by economic historians (or even by numismatists) as by cultural historians who use the reflections of Aristotle and others on coinage as a peg on which to hang the study of Greek conceptions of value (cf. von Reden 1995, 171ff.). Such study is far from irrelevant, but needs to be identified as a separate type of enquiry before any meaningful synthesis can be attempted.

The fifth component of the conversation has to be the set of confusions uncovered, and to some degree perpetuated, by the debate between Polanyi (in Polanyi *et al.* 1957, 64–97) and Finley (1970) over the claim 'Aristotle discovers the economy'. It takes us to the other extreme of the spectrum of discourse, wherein historians of economic thought attempt to detect, in Aristotle and other classical writers, more or less developed formulations, or pre-echoes, of modern economists' ideas and theories. To re-open that enquiry is futile, for there are at least six different quests involved:

1   to understand the mechanisms, routes, and institutions within which economic transactions took place;
2   to understand the ways in which those mechanisms recognisably approached the classifications currently or recently in use among economists;
3   to understand the descriptive or analytical concepts (if any) which were applied by the historical culture itself to such activities;
4   to understand the values or mentalities with which the historical culture itself, or individual authors from within it,[30] engaged in, or viewed, such activities;

[29]   As evidenced by the absence of any coin-based chapter from the present book.

[30]   That distinction too is important. At one extreme we may accept at face value the famously Keynesian tone of Xenophon's ideas for regenerating Athens and Athenian public revenues after 355 in his *Poroi* without calling such writing 'economic analysis' in Schumpeter's sense (Schumpeter 1954, 40 and 57); at the other extreme we might want to accept that one hyperintelligent scholar in the 330s was doing real 'economic analysis' in respect of the concepts of 'exchange' and 'value' without thereby asserting that the society he lived in ever followed him. For the record, and to stimulate exploration, I note the straightforwardly descriptive tone in *HOPE* of the accounts of the economic thought of al-Ghazali (Ghazanfar and Islahi 1990), the Eastern Church Fathers (Karayiannis 1994), and Ibn Khaldun (Soofi 1995).

5 to understand the extent to which the concepts detectable within the historical culture itself were appropriate to the economic activities of that culture; and

6 to understand the extent to which such concepts were the recognisable forerunners of those used in modern disciplines.

Even more simply, and excluding as anachronistic irrelevance such notions as that of tracing an 'archaeology of economic ideas',[31] one may separate out three independent variables:

(a) quantities and ranges (of items exchanged and services provided);
(b) structures, institutions, and systems (within which exchange took place);
(c) mentalities (of those participating in such exchanges).

However, lest anyone should be tempted to try to use those variables as the three dimensions of a matrix within which the economic activity of historical societies might be located, I note, first, that I see no means of reducing to linear form the terminology or the phenomena to be included under (c), and second and fundamentally, that whatever classificatory or analytical system we use has to accommodate, in a way that the *monocolore* and essentially synchronic constructs of Bücher or Finley cannot, a possible extreme diversity of types of activity within the same society. Some goods, such as, say, sculpture or mercenary service in archaic Greece, may be 'traded' while others remain within a Domestic Mode of Production: some men write 'Salve lucrum!' on their mosaic floors while others are concerned first and foremost to minimise risk; some estates, as Paterson argues in this volume, can be seen by their owners simultaneously as instruments of self-sufficiency and as generators of market-derived profits. Nothing will serve more decisively to dissolve the current polarisation of discourse than an acceptance that an 'economy' (whether defined as that of a geographical region or as that of a polity – see next paragraph) does not have to be *monocolore*, does not have to be labelled according to its 'predominant pattern', and does not have to be more than a loosely articulated *mélange* of separate systems each with its own rules, purposes, and ideology.

---

[31] Thus Lowry 1987a, with Lowry 1987b.

My sixth and last component is the old-fashioned distinction[32] between 'economy' and 'public economy', which ought to be in the conversation but isn't. The notion of a 'public economy' is perfectly clear, denoting those movements of goods, labour, or money from individuals or from groups into the control of the polity which (a) are not in any direct sense exchanges of one good/service for another, (b) are therefore one-way movements, (c) are exacted compulsorily, (d) happen only within the area controlled by that polity, and (e) may be sometimes or partially compensated for by redistribution among those taxed, but may equally well be retained in order to be sent out of the area controlled by the polity, or used to employ persons other than the primary taxees. To define a public economy thus is not necessarily to portray it in Friedmanite terms as an incubus upon a scene of economic activity which would do better without it, for (a) economic activity requires security (which carries costs), (b) some economic activity requires investment in infrastructure, and (c) the redistribution of the resource thus exacted can contribute substantially to social cohesion (cf. Athenian *misthos*). To define it thus is however to try to signal, and to try to reduce, a major current confusion, for an area or region controlled by one fiscal or public economy is not necessarily the same as – indeed is almost certainly not the same as – an area of such significantly bounded economic interaction in 'real' (i.e. non-fiscal) terms as to count as an identifiable economic region. At one extreme, it would be at best unhelpful to group together as one 'economy' all the regional interactions taking place within the fifth-century Achaemenid or Athenian empires as single fiscal units; at the other, it would be equally unhelpful to categorise separately the 'economies' of Naxos and of Paros, separate fiscal units though they usually were.

III

At this point, faced on the one hand with a broad spectrum of patterns of exchange activity (section I above) and on the other with a bewildering array of irreconcilably diverse analytical approaches (section II above), the reader might be forgiven for

[32]   Cf. the title of Böckh 1817. It would be of value to trace, as Lewis 1971 does not, the influences which led Böckh to formulate his title thus.

concluding that any attempt to create a unified field theory even for the specific activities encompassed within our triad 'Trade, Traders and the City', let alone for the whole range of the economic activities of 'antiquity', is a fool's errand. This final section will attempt to subvert that conclusion. It starts from five perceptions. The first is that the notion of creating a 'unified field theory' is not identical with that of hypostatising a 'large unified economic space' in the way justly criticised by Finley (1986, 77), but denotes a way of creating a long-range (indeed infinitely extensible) map on which flows can be traced. The second is that the essential movements, the sum of which comprises an 'economy', are not necessarily *exchanges* (even if we include deferred returns) so much as *flows*, whether of goods, services, or money. Some of them are indeed two-way, or directly reciprocal, but others, as we have seen, may be three-way (cf. n. 6 above) or (as with fiscal redistribution) diffused through a system in far more complex, indirect, or capillary ways. The third is that, viewed spatially, all flows and exchanges of resource occur within or between cellular structures.[33] Such structures may be minimally small (at the extreme, the single individual living a Robinson Crusoe-like existence and circulating[34] resource only within his one-man *oikos*), while others will occur both within the wider zones formed by the circumferences of each of the components of a nested series (village, canton, *polis*, regional landscape, Roman province, etc.) and across cellular boundaries. It is of course with the latter type of flow that many of the chapters in this book have been concerned (especially those of Alston, Kuhrt, Paterson and Whitby). It is not an objection to this perception that 'cell' may be a very procrustean concept, for we positively need concepts which are topologically fluid enough to reflect the complexities of human behaviour, and a good case can be made for thinking that in Graeco-Roman terms the 'city' is and has to be seen

---

[33] The use of such terminology derives from Duncan-Jones's fundamental observation about the Roman empire that 'The underlying reality could be a cellular economy in which monetary anomalies were relieved only to a limited extent by fiscal or market mechanisms' (Duncan-Jones 1990, 44). Foraboschi's approach, as cited by Paterson in this volume (p. 164f.), is closely similar.

[34] Not in fact a misuse of the word, for storage of goods is a form of circulation, or of flow from Person-Now to Person-Future, within the dimension of time rather than space.

as a component within a cellular structure. The fourth perception is
that any models which we construct for 'ancient economies' must
be qualitative and descriptive, not quantitative. That requirement
derives not just, or even primarily, from the all-too-well-known fact
that, for all the labours of Duncan-Jones and others, we have no
quantitative data for the economic activities of antiquity which
even begin to bear comparison with those available for post-1500
Europe, nor even from the need to be independent of the presence
or absence of coinage, or of recognisable 'money'. It stems rather
from the need to construct models which have some diachronic
validity, in order that the effect of an increased flow in one area
(say, of an increased bullion flow from Laureion, or an increased
movement of wine from central Italy to Gaul) can be seen to diffuse
through a system. A fifth perception, arising from the fourth, is that,
in direct conflict with modern economists' commodity-oriented
systems, no models for antiquity (or, I dare say, for contemporary
societies either) can be satisfactory which do not admit, as flows
which are in some sense commensurable with monetary, commodity, or other resource flows, both 'non-monetary' returns (such as
'negative reciprocity' or *charis*) and exchange-patterns which are
managed or are in a Polanyian sense 'embedded'. Sixth and last
is the perception, to which I hope to animadvert in more detail
elsewhere, that the importance of the economic roles of cults and
temples needs to be recognised in the same way as that of public
revenues and expenditures.

Using these perceptions, and agreeing for good heuristic reasons
that any model which is proposed for antiquity must contain cells
of at least two orders of magnitude – the 'household' (*oikos*) level
and the 'regional' (*polis vel sim.*) level – I suggest the following
schema. For convenience it is presented in three stages, but with
no pretence that they represent a real chronological development.
All three stages use the concepts of 'flow' and of 'resource' as
sketched above. Stage 1 is presented in Figure 11.1. It starts with
households as the minimal unit, encompassing thereby not merely
the 'family farm' of much economic anthropology[35] but also the

[35]   Cf. Burford Cooper 1977–8, and also Isaac 1989, 2–4 and the literature he there refers to. At some stage the welter of information about
intra-familial economics, as sketched e.g. by Bergstrom 1996, will need
to be integrated with the discussion.

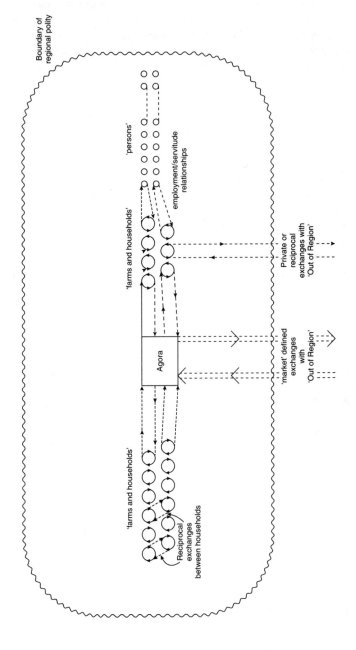

Figure 11.1 A flow diagram of resource movement, stage 1: modified household autarky

thes or landless labourer. However, it also postulates a place of exchange which for convenience is called *Agora* without any accompanying presumption that exchange is governed by market behaviour or that the proportion of a region's resource which flows through it is much if at all greater than zero. We can then map the following transactions:

1   within the individual household, via the Domestic Mode of Production, storage, and autarky;
2   between households on an exchange basis or a lend-and-return basis;
3   between households via the forced or bought use of labour from outside the household (hired hands, slaves, shepherds, etc.);
4   between households and a market, or periodic fair, or festival, whether at a sanctuary or at a border or on a seashore or in a 'real' marketplace or a souk or wherever;
5   between household and 'out of region', whether by direct exchange, via piracy or *syle*, or via mercenary service, or however;
6   between Agora and 'out of region'.

It must be understood that what is being thus mapped is a network of channels for the flow of resource within topological space, so that the number of basic units can be small or large, and the flows can be small, or large, or changing, without affecting the network of relationships. It can therefore map with equal ease a market-dominated landscape, where flows through Agora predominate, or a Millettian landscape, wherein flows through type 2 transactions predominate. What it cannot do in this elementary form is to represent the sorts of flows and transactions which are described in the case-studies of this volume. A second stage of complexity is required, which is set out in Figure 11.2. We can now incorporate entities other than the autarkic farm, or manor, or peasant household, such as landowners with a rent element in their portfolio of holdings, or private employment entities such as quarries or mines or workshops or ships, cult entities such as temples and sanctuaries, or partnerships. A wider range of transactions can thereby be mapped, namely:

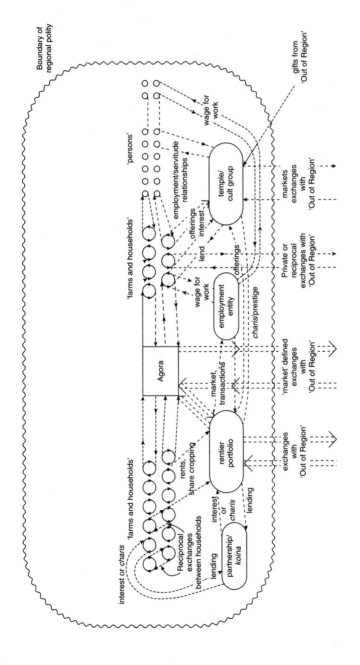

Figure 11.2 A flow diagram of resource movement, stage 2: complex flows

7   rents in money or kind accruing from 'farms' owned;
8   income from other investments in the 'employment entity'
    group;
9   wage nexus between outfits in that group and households/
    persons (whether spasmodic, or seasonal, or long term);
10 gifts and sacrifices to 'temples' (sometimes reciprocal, as when
    a sacrificed animal is eaten by the members of a cult group),
    the return for which in the form of psychological security is
    unreal in economists' terms but is real enough in terms of
    cultural history or economic anthropology and has to be built
    into the model;
11 gifts and sacrifices to 'temples' etc., for which the return is
    not just psychological security but also social prestige (*charis*),
    accruing especially to the owners of *rentier* portfolios;
12 concentrations of resource into partnerships (*collegia*, *koina*,
    etc.). Some will be *charis*-bearing instruments of social
    reciprocity, some are interest- or yield-bearing[36] (e.g. bottomry
    loans), but functionally do not differ all that much;
13 exchanges with 'out of region', more likely to be on a signif-
    icant scale when transacted by *rentier* entities or by temples.[37]

However, even that more complex structure is inadequate to map
a developed Greek or Italic city, or an imperial *civitas* area such
as Humphries's Aquileia, or the flows within Roman Egypt as
analysed by Alston. One missing component is the 'state' itself,
conceptually separable from the flows and entities sketched above
even in respect of polities which minimised the gulf between
polites and *koinon*, let alone for polities wherein governments are
remote and tax-collectors a separate species. If we therefore move
to Stage 3, represented in Figure 11.3, the separateness of the
koinon as a set of channels for the flow of resource via its various

---

[36] With Cohen's rendering of *tokos* (Cohen 1992, 44ff.).
[37] The resources involved in temple-building, as well as the 'trading'
activities involved, have yet to be properly evaluated, especially in an
archaic or classical Greek context where various public and cultic expe-
dients were required in contrast to the Hellenistic or Roman norm, where
resource tended to come from booty or from noble or royal munificence.
Cf. however Snodgrass 1980, 58–62 and 140ff., and the proceedings of
the various Uppsala symposia published as *Boreas* 15 (1987), 21 (1992),
and 24 (1996).

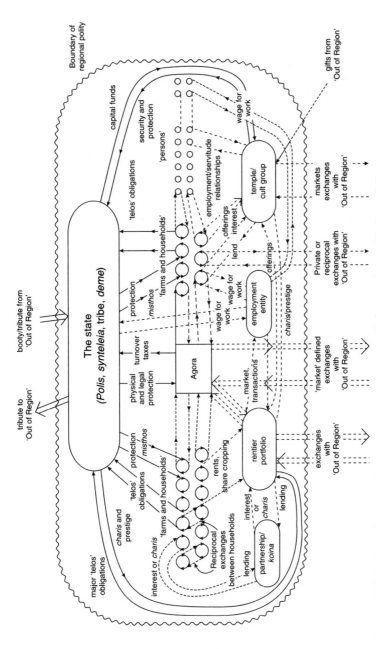

Figure 11.3 A flow diagram of resource movement, stage 3: interactions with the public economy

(and themselves separable) economic functions can be recognised. We can then map further transactions such as:

14   *telos*-type obligations (military service, corvée work, participation in the management of the polity, jury service), balanced by protection of person, property, and family, access to law, etc., and perhaps also by

15   *misthos* (in certain regions and polities);[38]

16   extended *telos*-type obligations on the part of the socially prominent, conveying non-quantifiable but none the less real return in the form of social prestige (*charis* or *gratia*);

17   turnover taxes from Agora, again reciprocated by the provision of facilities, security, legal protection, etc.;

18   direct wages in return for work for the state (received as contractor or employee, not as recipient of *misthos*);

19   transfer of resource from polity to temples and sanctuaries, again with a non-quantifiable but real return;

20   links with 'out of region', which may or may not be genuinely reciprocal.

The complex map which Stages 1–3 have generated is admittedly a model for a *Kleinstaat* such as Athens or Samos or Corinth or the Etruscan, Italic, or Campanian city-states of republican Italy. However, the network would not be significantly different if plotted for a monarchy such as Thrace or Macedon, and will even work for Sparta if we regard *syssitia* as segmental components of the state or as cells to be inserted at an intermediate level between household and state. It will adequately represent the sorts of flows recognised by Alston for a Roman province, at least for one so comparatively uniform and integrated as Egypt, and can comfortably accommodate the effects on transport, and therefore on the economists' 'transaction costs', described by Laurence for the developed road network of central Italy. What it will not do

---

[38]   I am aware that the types of transaction described in 14–15 could be argued not to be productive and not to be 'economic', but since they involve the use of time and resource and are inter-personal, they cannot be excluded from any portrait of the channels through which resource flows in a particular society. I hope to pursue this fundamental point of definition elsewhere.

on its own is to map adequately large-scale polities such as contemporary Britain, with separable regional economies likely to respond differently to a single shift in the fiscal regime,[39] or as the Achaemenid empire, which has to be seen economically as a partially interlocking set of separate local–regional economies, overladen by the two mildly unifying factors of a tax system and of estate holdings in provincial/satrapal areas on the part of Persian grandees. Nor will it on its own map the sorts of relationships between two regions which are described by Lawall (Chios–Phrygia), Kuhrt (Ashur–central Anatolia), or Whitby (Athens–Black Sea). What will do so, however, is to envisage a more complex map consisting of at least two 'cells' each of the internal complexity portrayed in Figure 11.3. Even a two-cell universe would be adequate to represent the inter-regional relationships just mentioned, while the number of cells can of course be increased without limit[40] and provides thereby a means of portraying a more complex set of flows with many centres, such as that envisaged by Tsetskhladze for the Black Sea, or a far larger geographical entity, such as pre-Roman Italy or Spain, or a much larger polity such as the Achaemenid empire or even the Roman empire.

There is no doubt in my mind that a framework of description such as has been sketched above provides a means of tracing on a single surface all the economic flows that can be detected for the societies of antiquity. Its limitation is that it describes structures and networks, not human needs or the motivations of those who, as traders or travellers, traversed the pathways of those networks. None the less, if, as argued above, the present need is to separate the mapping and the measurements of such flows from the assessment of whatever incompatible *mélange* of ideologies may have stimulated or inhibited such flows, such a deconstruction may actually be helpful.

[39] Cf. H. Davies 1997 on the likely differential effects of an interest rate change.

[40] I am aware of attempts which are being made to use the mathematics of fractals in order to model the systems generated by the repetition of simple or complex patterns, but this is not the place, nor have I the skills, to explore the idea in detail. I am grateful to Zosia Archibald and David Gibbins for preliminary steers in this direction.

Bibliography

Andreades, A. M. (1933), *A History of Greek Public Finance*, I (Cambridge).

Andreau, J. and Etienne, R. (1984), 'Vingt ans de recherches sur l'archaïsme et la modernité des sociétés antiques', *REA* 86: 55–83.

Austin, M. M., and Vidal-Naquet, P. (1972), *Économies et sociétés en Grèce ancienne* (Paris), translated as *Economic and Social History of Ancient Greece: An Introduction* (London, 1977).

Beloch, K. J. (1899), 'Die Grossindustrie im Altertum', *Z. für Socialwissenschaft*, 2: 18–26; repr. in Finley 1979, third item.

—— (1902), 'Zur griechischen Wirtschaftgeschichte', *Z. für Socialwissenschaft* 5: 95–103 and 169–79; repr. in Finley 1979, fourth item.

—— (1924), *Griechische Geschichte* I², 1 (Berlin and Leipzig).

Bergstrom, T. C. (1996), 'Economics in a family way', *JEL* 34: 1903–34.

Block, F. and Somers, M. R. (1984), 'Beyond the economistic fallacy: the holistic social science of Karl Polanyi', in T. Skocpol (ed.), *Vision and Method in Historical Sociology* (Cambridge), pp. 47–84.

Böckh, A. (1817), *Die Staatshaushaltung der Athener* (Berlin).

Bravo, B. (1977), 'Remarques sur les assises sociales, les formes d'organisation et la terminologie du commerce maritime grec à l'époque archaïque', *Dialogues d'histoire ancienne* 3: 1–59.

Bücher, K. (1906), *Die Entstehung der Volkswirtschaft* (Tübingen). (The first edn is of 1893, but the reproduction in Finley 1979 (as the first item) is of pp. 85–150 of the 1906 edn.)

—— (1922), 'Zur griechischen Wirtschaftgeschichte', in idem, *Beiträge zur Wirtschaftsgeschichte* (Tübingen), 1–97, repr. in Finley 1979, fifth item.

Burford Cooper, A. M. (1977/8), 'The family farm in ancient Greece', *Classical Journal* 73: 162–75.

Burke, E. M. (1992), 'The economy of Athens in the classical era: some adjustments to the Primitivist model', *TAPA* 122: 199–226.

Cartledge, P. A. (forthcoming), 'The economy (economies) of ancient Greece', in *Dialogos* 5 (1998).

Chayanov, A. V. (1966), *A. V. Chayanov on the Theory of Peasant Economy*, eds D. Thorner, B. Kerblay and R. E. F. Smith (Homewood, Ill., 1966; repr. with foreword by T. Shanin, Manchester and Madison, 1986).

Cohen, E. E. (1992), *Athenian Economy and Society: A Banking Perspective* (Princeton).

Dalton, G. (ed. 1967), *Tribal and Peasant Economies: Readings in Economic Anthropology* (Garden City, N.Y.).

—— (1971), *Economic Anthropology and Development: Essays on Tribal and Peasant Economies* (New York and London).

—— (1975), 'Karl Polanyi's analysis of long-distance trade and his wider paradigm', in J. A. Sabloff and C. C. Lamberg-Karlowsky (eds), *Ancient Civilization and Trade* (Albuquerque) [*nondum vidi*].

Davies, H. (1997), 'Britain's regional economies: how different are they; and how should those differences affect monetary policy?', *RSA Journal* 145, no. 5476 (Jan./Feb.): 40–8.

Davies, J. K. (1975), Review article of Austin and Vidal-Naquet (1972) in *Phoenix* 29: 93–102.

—— (1993), *Democracy and Classical Greece* (2nd edn, London).

De Sainte Croix, G. E. M. (1972), *The Origins of the Peloponnesian War* (London).

Dornbusch, R. and Fischer, S. (1990), *Macroeconomics* (5th edn, New York).

Duncan-Jones, R. (1974), *The Economy of the Roman Empire: Quantitative Studies* (2nd edn 1982, Cambridge).

—— (1990), *Structure and Scale in the Roman Economy* (Cambridge).

Elwert, G. (1987), 'Ausdehnung der Käuflichkeit und Einbettung der Wirtschaft: Markt und Moralökonomie', in K. Heinemann (ed.), *Soziologie wirtschaftlichen Handelns* (Opladen), 300–21.

Figueira, T. J. (1984), 'Karl Polanyi and ancient Greek trade: the port of trade', in *Early Trade and Traders in the Mediterranean: The Ancient World* 10 (1–2): 15–30.

—— (1988), *Aegina: Society and Politics* (Salem, N.H.).

Finley, M. I. [1952], *Studies in Land and Credit in Ancient Athens, 500–200 BC* (New Brunswick, N.J., n.d.: cited variously as Finley 1951 and Finley 1952).

—— (1965), 'Classical Greece', in *Deuxième Conférence internationale d'histoire économique, Aix-en-Provence, 1962, I: Trade and Politics in the Ancient World* (Paris and La Haye), 11–35.

—— (1970), 'Aristotle and economic analysis', *Past and Present* 47: 3–25, repr. in Finley (1974), pp. 26–52.

—— (1973), *The Ancient Economy* (London).

—— (1974), *Studies in Ancient Society* (London).

—— (ed. 1979), *The Bücher–Meyer Controversy* (repr. of five contributions by Karl Julius Beloch [1899 and 1902], Karl Bücher [1906 and 1922], and Eduard Meyer [1924] on the ancient (esp. the Greek) economy) (New York).

—— (1986), *The Ancient Economy* (2nd edn, Berkeley and Los Angeles).

Foraboschi, D. (1994), 'Economie plurali ed interdipendenze', in *L'Italie d'Auguste à Dioclétien* (Rome), 215–18.

Forbes, H. A. (1976), ' "We have a little of everything": the ecological basis of some agricultural practices in Methana, Trizenia', in M. Dimen and E. Friedl (eds), *Regional Variation in Modern Greece and Cyprus: Toward a Perspective of the Ethnography of Greece* (New York), 236–50.

—— (1982), *Strategies and Soils: Technology, Production, and Environment in the peninsula of Methana, Greece* (Ph.D. thesis, University of Pennsylvania; Ann Arbor, Mich.).

French, A. (1964), *The Growth of the Athenian Economy* (London and New York).

Gallant, T. W. (1991), *Risk and Survival in Ancient Greece* (Stanford).

Garlan, Y. (1973), 'L'oeuvre de Polanyi: la place de l'économie dans les sociétés', *La Pensée* 171: 118–27.

—— (1983), 'Greek amphorae and trade', in P. Garnsey, K. Hopkins, and C. R. Whittaker (eds), 27–35.

Garnsey, P. (1985), 'Grain for Athens', in P. Cartledge and F. D. Harvey (eds), *Crux: Essays Presented to G. E. M. de Ste Croix on his 75th Birthday* (Exeter), 62–75.

—— (1988), *Famine and Food Supply in the Graeco-Roman World: Responses to Risk and Crisis* (Cambridge).

Garnsey, P., Hopkins, K. and Whittaker, C. R. (eds 1983), *Trade in the Ancient Economy* (London).

Garnsey, P. and Whittaker, C. R. (eds 1983), *Trade and Famine in Classical Antiquity* (Cambridge).

Ghazanfar, S. M. and Islahi, A. A. (1990), 'Economic thought of an Arab scholastic: Abu Hamid al-Ghazali (A.H. 450–505/AD 1058–1111)', *HOPE* 22: 381–403.

Halstead, P. (1987), 'Traditional and ancient rural economy in Mediterranean Europe: plus ça change?', *JHS* 107: 77–87.

—— (1989), 'The economy has a normal surplus: economic stability and social change among early farming communities of Thessaly, Greece', in P. Halstead and J. O'Shea (eds), *Bad Year Economics: Cultural Responses to Risk and Uncertainty* (Cambridge), 68–80.

Hasebroek, J. (1928/1933), *Staat und Handel im alten Griechenland* (Tübingen, 1928), tr. L. M. Fraser and D. C. MacGregor as *Trade and Politics in Ancient Greece* (London, 1933; repr. New York, 1965).

—— (1931), *Griechische Wirtschafts- und Gesellschaftsgeschichte bis zur Perserzeit* (Tübingen).

Heichelheim, F. M. (1930), *Wirtschaftliche Schwankungen der Zeit von Alexander bis Augustus*, Heft 3 of Arthur Spiethoff (ed.), *Beiträge zur Erforschung der wirtschaftlichen Wechsellagen: Aufschwung, Krise, Stockung* (Jena; repr. New York, 1979).

Hopkins, K. (1980), 'Taxes and trade in the Roman empire, 200 BC–AD 400', *JRS* 70: 101–25.

Howgego, C. J. (1995), *Ancient History from Coins* (London and New York).

Humphreys, S. C. (1969), 'History, economics and anthropology: the work of Karl Polanyi', *History and Theory* 8: 165–212; repr. in Humphreys (1978), 31–75.

—— (1970), 'Economy and society in classical Athens', *ASNP*[2] 39: 1–26; repr. in Humphreys (1978), 136–58.

—— (1978), *Anthropology and the Greeks* (London).

Isaac, B. L. (1989), 'Introduction', *REconAnth* 11: 1–11.

Jeffery, L. H. (1976), *Archaic Greece: The City-States c. 700–500 BC* (London and Tonbridge).

Karayiannis, A. D. (1994), 'The Eastern Christian Fathers (AD 350–400) on the redistribution of wealth', *HOPE* 26: 39–67.

Kemp, B. J. (1989), *Ancient Egypt: Anatomy of a Civilization* (London and New York).

Kraay, C. M. (1976), *Archaic and Classical Greek Coins* (London).
Krings, V. (ed. 1995), *La civilisation phénicienne et punique: manuel de recherche* (Leiden, New York and Köln).
Lewis, D. M. (1971), 'Boeckh, Staatshaushaltung der Athener, 1817–1967', in *Acta of the Fifth International Congress of Greek and Latin Epigraphy, Cambridge 1967* (Oxford), 35–9.
Lowry, S. T. (1979), 'Recent literature on ancient Greek economic thought', *JEL* 17: 65–86.
—— (1987a), *The Archaeology of Economic Ideas: The Classical Greek Tradition* (Durham, N.C.).
—— (ed. 1987b), *Pre-Classical Economic Thought: From the Greeks to the Scottish Enlightenment* (Boston, Mass.).
—— (1987c), 'The Greek heritage in economic thought', in Lowry (1987b) [*non vidi*].
Meyer, E. (1895/1924), 'Die wirtschaftliche Entwicklung des Altertums', *Jahrb. f. Nationalök. und Statistik* 64/9 (1895), 1–70; repr. in idem *Kleine Schriften* I² (Halle, 1924), 81–168, thence in Finley 1979, second item.
—— (1937), *Geschichte des Altertums*, III² (Stuttgart).
Michell, H. (1940/1957), *The Economics of Ancient Greece* (Cambridge).
Millett, P. (1991), *Lending and Borrowing in Ancient Athens* (Cambridge).
Morgan, C. (1990), *Athletes and Oracles: The Transformation of Olympia and Delphi in the Eighth Century BC* (Cambridge).
Morris, I. (1993), 'Poetics of power: the interpretation of ritual action in archaic Greece', in C. Dougherty and L. Kurke (eds), *Cultural Poetics in Archaic Greece: Cult, Performance, Politics* (Cambridge), 15–45.
Penn, R. (1990), 'History and sociology in the new economic sociology: a discourse in search of a method', in S. Kendrick, P. Straw and D. McCrone (eds), *Interpreting the Past, Understanding the Present* (Basingstoke), 165–76.
Polanyi, K. and Dalton, G. (eds 1968), *Primitive, Archaic and Modern Economies* (New York).
Polanyi, K., Arensberg, C. M. and Pearson, H. W. (eds 1957), *Trade and Market in the Early Empires* (Glencoe, Ill.).
Pouilloux, J. (1954), *Recherches sur l'histoire et les cultes de Thasos, I: De la fondation de la cité à 196 avant J.-C.* (Paris).
Reed, C. M. (1981), 'Maritime traders in the Greek world of the archaic and classical periods' (D.Phil. thesis, University of Oxford).
Reger, G. (1994), *Regionalism and Change in the Economy of Independent Delos* (Berkeley, Los Angeles and Oxford).
Roll, (Sir) E. (1961), *A History of Economic Thought* (London).
Sallares, R. (1991), *The Ecology of the Ancient Greek World* (London).
Samuelson, P. A. (1983), 'Thünen at two hundred', *JEL* 21: 1468–88.
Schmitt, G. (1992), 'The rediscovery of Alexander Chayanov', *HOPE* 24: 925–65.
Schumpeter, J. A. (1954), *A History of Economic Analysis* (ed. by E. Boody Schumpeter) (New York).
Seaford, R. (1994), *Reciprocity and Ritual: Homer and Tragedy in the Developing City-State* (Oxford).

Seager, R. J. (1966), 'Lysias against the corndealers', *Historia* 15: 172–84.
Silver, M. (1995), *Economic Structures of Antiquity* (Westport, Conn., and London).
Shanin, T. (1982), 'Defining peasants: conceptualisations and de-conceptualisations', *Sociological Review* 30: 407–32.
Smith, C. A. (ed. 1976a), *Regional Analysis, I: Economic Systems*, and *II: Social Systems* (New York, San Francisco and London).
—— (1976b), 'Regional economic systems: linking geographical models and socioeconomic problems', in Smith ed. 1976a: I, 3–63.
Snodgrass, A. M. (1980), *Archaic Greece: The Age of Experiment* (London, Melbourne and Toronto).
Soofi, A. (1995), 'Economics of Ibn Khaldun revisited', *HOPE* 27: 387–404.
Starr, C. G. (1977), *The Economic and Social Growth of Early Greece 800–500 BC* (New York).
Thompson, W. E. (1978), 'The Athenian investor', *Rivista di Studi Classici* 26: 403–23.
—— (1982), 'The Athenian entrepreneur', *Antiquité Classique* 51: 532–85.
Ure, P. N. (1922), *The Origin of Tyranny* (Cambridge; repr. New York, 1962).
Valensi, L. (1974), 'Anthropologie économique et histoire: l'oeuvre de Karl Polanyi', *Annales: Economies, Sociétés, Civilisations* 29: 1311–19.
Von Reden, S. (1995), *Exchange in Ancient Greece* (London).
Walcot, P. (1970), *Greek Peasants, Ancient and Modern: A Comparison of Social and Moral Values* (Manchester).
Wickett, S. M. (1901), Translation of Bücher 1893 as *Industrial Evolution* (New York and London).
Will, E. (1954), 'Trois quarts de siècle de recherches sur l'économie grecque antique', *Annales: Economies, Sociétés, Civilisations* 9: 7–22.

Indexes

The terms *bis* and *ter* indicate, respectively, two and three occurrences of a topic on one page.

The following abbreviation is used: 'R' = Roman.

1 GENERAL INDEX

Passing mentions of topics, and contributors to this volume, are not listed. A few general references to ancient authors are included, but specific citations are in index 2. Modern authors are indexed if their views are the focus of a discussion.

For headings, 'word-by-word' alphabetisation is used (e.g. 'market towns' before 'marketplaces'). Subheadings are arranged alphabetically, including any prepositions.

Italic page numbers indicate illustrations (e.g. *52* = figure on page 52). Figures are not specifically indexed if they fall within a discussion of the same topic.

Agora (term of analysis in Davies's model), *245*, 246
agorai, in cities of R Egypt, 184–5
agoranomoi, in cities of R Egypt, 185
agriculture, and trade, not opposed, 158
Alexandria, and Egyptian trade, 195
amphoras:
(1) general: and economic history, 95–6; and olive oil trade, 162–3; in Black Sea, 60; study of, 76–7; uses, 76;

(2) Chian: distribution, 86–8; economic significance, 3, 6, 90–1, 93–6; forms, 78–81, 93; markings, 81–5; numbers traded, 88–90
Anatolia (*see also* Old Assyrian trading system): Ashur's trade with, 24–5; political structure, 25
animals, for transport, 26
annona, 157
anthropology, and ancient economy, 236–9
Antinoopolis, in Egyptian trade, 198

Aquileia: economy, 214–15; population, 215–16, 217–18; role in spread of ideas, 227; site, 214; topography, 218, *219*; trade and Christianity at, 214–19, trade links, 216–17
architectural decoration, in central Italy, 43–6
aristocracy, Chian, role in trade, 93–5
Aristotle, whether formulated economic theory, 240
Arrius, S. (trader), 160
artisans (*see also* craftsmen), in Italy: 2–3, 11; and architectural decoration, 43; and patrons, 40, 42–3, 45; and political messages, 41, 42, 43; and urbanisation, 48; in source traditions, 36–8; organisation, 38–41; role in economy, 32; social role, 46–7, 48, 227
Ashur (Iraq), 9–10; and Anatolia, 24–5, 26; as trading community, 227; civic structure, 22–3; location and site, 18–19; Mesopotamian traders at, 21–2; textile production at, 27
assemblies (civic), at Ashur, 22–3
Assyria, *see* Old Assyrian trading system
Athens (*see also* grain supply; grain trade): Chian amphoras at, 87–8, 89; effect on Attica, 105–6; population, 109–14
Attica: cultivable area, 104–7; effect of Athens on, 105–6; fallow regime, 104–5; grain production, 103–8; productivity, 107–8

barley, consumption of, 114–17
Beloch, K. J., on ancient economy, 234–5 & n. 17
bishoprics, N. Italian, 210, 212
Black Sea, 5, 227; amphoras in, 60; Attic pottery in, 55, 59–62; coins from, 58–9; colonisation,

52–4; grain trade, 53, 54–63, 123–5; metal trade, 63–7; Pericles' expedition, 56–7; slave trade, 67–8
Bonghi Jovino, M., on Italian workshops, 39–40
Bosporan kingdom: grain production, 62–3; grain trade with Athens, 57–9, 123
boule, Athenian, and size of population, 110
Bücher, K., on ancient economy, 233–4

Campania, regional identity of, 34
caravans, Assyrian, organisation of, 26–7
Cato: on benefits of roads, 139, 140; on cost of land transport, 131–3
cellular structures, in ancient economy, 243–4, 251
census, by Demetrius of Phaleron, 109
Central Italy, *see* Italy
ceramics, *see* pottery
cereals, *see* grain
Chios (*see also* amphoras): economic history, 3, 6, 92–5, 226; political history, 91–2, 94–5
Christianity: and cities, 206–7, 212–13; and trade, 11, 220–1, 222; diffusion, 210–12, 221
Cicero, on building roads to estates, 141
cities (*see also* city-states; towns): and ancient economy, 4; and Christianity, 206–7, 212–13; and economic activity, 226–7, 228–9; and trade networks, 197–8; as cellular units, 243–4; economic intervention by, 226, 229; in R Egypt, 183–92 *passim*, *193*; without markets, 196–7
city-states (*see also* cities): in S. Iraq, 17–18; in Anatolia, 25

coins: and ancient economy, 239–40; colonisation of, 52–4; Cyzicene, 58–9; in Black Sea trade, 58–9; in cities of R Egypt, 186–7; in villages of R Egypt, 176, 183

Colchis: Attic pottery in, 61; Greeks trade metalwork with, 67

collegia, 248

colonisation, of Black Sea, 52–4

Columella, on benefits of roads, 139, 140

commerce (*see also* trade), in R empire, 150–2

commercial law (Roman): development of, 153–4; on wine trade, 154–5

communication networks: of Karanis, 181–2; of Oxyrhynchus, 189

communication patterns, in R Egypt, 170

'consumer city' model, 4, 144

copper, traded in Anatolia, 27

crafts (*see also* craftsmen), 169; interaction between, 46

craftsmen (*see also* artisans; crafts), at Karanis, 173

cults (*see also* private cults), economic role of, 244

customs dues, in R Egypt, 177–8

Cyzicene coins, in Attic trade, 58–9

Davies, J. K., new model of ancient economy, 12–13

Demaratus of Corinth, 37, 38 *bis*, 45, 46

Demetrius of Phaleron, census of, 109

democracy, Chian, and trade, 94

development, in economy of R empire, 163–4

diaitetai, Athenian, 111

diffusion, of ideas, defined, 206

Diocletian's Price Edict, and cost of land transport, 133–5

dipinti, on Chian amphoras, 82–3, 84

distances, reduced by roads, 145

docks, organisation of, 161

Domestic Mode of Production, 238, 241, 246

donkeys, in Old Assyrian trade, 26

economic anthropology, 236–9

economic policies, ancient, 226, 229, 235

economic theory: relevance to ancient history, 230–2; whether existed in antiquity, 240–1

economy, ancient (*see also* economic policies; economic theory): alternative models, 1–2, 4–5, 11–13, 233–42; growth in R period, 163–4; micro-economies in, 164; not *monocolore*, 241; sterility of debate, 28–9

'economy of substitution', 165

Egypt, Roman (*see also under* trade networks): city economies, 183–92 *passim*, *193*, 194–5, 198; coinage, 176, 183, 186–7; communication patterns, 170; customs dues, 177–8; economy, 227; international trade, 3, 171, 187–92 *passim*; inter-regional trade, 3, 5, 171, 181–2; long-distance trade routes, 194–5; trade, 3, 5, 9, 178–80, 183, 194–5, 198; trade networks, 9, 171, 187, 189–92, *193*; village economies, 172–81, 183

Ekphantos of Corinth, 37 *bis*

Eleusis, first-fruits inscription from, 107–8

elites (*see also* aristocracy): and Black Sea trade, 67; Italian, as patrons of artisans, 40, 42–3, 45, 47, 48; Roman, and estates, 158–9

Elizavetovskoe, Attic pottery at, 60
'embeddedness', in ancient economy, 236, 244
empire, Roman, *see* Roman empire
employment, in Davies's model, 246–8
estates, Roman: and elites, 158–9; and roads, 141
ethnic identity, and pottery styles, 35–6
Etruria, regional identity of, 33
exchange: and Athenian grain supply, 229; or flows? 243; varieties of, 226–8
'expansion diffusion': and Christianity, 212; defined, 206
export policies, not operated by ancient polities, 235

fairs (*see also* markets), 196
fallow regime, of Attica, 104–5
Felix, Cn. Sentius (trader), 161
field theory (unified), concept of, 243
Finley, M. I., 4, 157; ghost of, *passim*
first-fruits, Eleusinian, 107–8
fiscal policies, ancient, 235
flows, in Davies's model, 243, 250–1
formalist view of ancient economy, 233
freedmen, in R trade, 161–2

gift-giving, 67, 236
gold supply, in Greece, 64–5
Gordion, Chian amphoras at, 88–9
graffiti, on Chian amphoras, 82–5 *passim*
grain consumption, in Greece, 114–17
grain production: in Attica, 103–8; in Bosporan kingdom, 62–3

grain supply, Athenian (*see also* grain production; grain trade), 7, 102–3, 125–7; citizens' attitude, 117–20; importance, 125, 229; management, 120–5, 227
grain trade (*see also* grain supply), Athenian: alternative views, 102–3; management of, 120–3, 126–7; re-export in, 125–6; with Black Sea, 53, 54–63
grave-goods, in Latin culture, 41
Greeks: and Italian art, 37–8, 45–6; and Scythia, 66; and Thrace, 66–7; colonise Black Sea, 52–4; trade metalwork with Colchis, 67
growth, in economy of R empire, 163–4
guilds, in R Egypt: in cities, 184, 185; in villages, 175

harbours, organisation of, 161
Hasebroek, J., on ancient traders, 235
Hauswirtschaft, 233
Hellespont, and Athens' grain supply, 125
Hermopolis Magna, in Egyptian trade network, 198
Hopkins, K., on ancient economy, 2, 8
households: in ancient economy, 238; in Davies's model, 244–6

Ilushuma (Assyrian king), attracts traders to Ashur, 21–2
import policies, ancient, 235–6
incentives, in managing grain supply, 122–3
institores, 161–2
integration, economic: 5–10 *passim*; of Italy, promoted by roads, 144–5
interdependence, 5–10 *passim*
international trade, in R Egypt, 3, 5, 171, 181–2

inter-regional trade, 5; in R
  Egypt, 3, 171, 187–92 *passim*
intervention, by cities: 226, 229; in
  R Egypt, 186
Ionians, colonise Black Sea, 52–3
Isis, diffusion of, in N. Italy, 208,
  209
Italy, Central (*see also* artisans):
  economy, 33; trade patterns, 35

Jews, in N. Italy, 210, *211*
Jones, A. H. M., 4
Jupiter, temple at Rome, 36, 46

Kanesh (Anatolia), 9, 10;
  chronology, 20–1; in Old
  Assyrian trading system, 26;
  site, 19–20
Karanis (Egypt), 172–4; economy,
  176–7
karum (trading quarter), 23, 26
Kellia, in Egyptian trade, 195
king (of Ashur), as vice-gerent of
  god, 22
koina (partnerships), 248
koinon (community), 248
Kôm el Dikka (Alexandria), in
  Egyptian trade, 195
Kültepe, excavations, 19–20

land transport (*see also* caravans):
  complemented by waterborne,
  143; cost, 8, 9, 130–6, 137;
  in 18C England, 135–7
ˈLatium, regional identity of, 34
law, commercial (Roman): about
  wine trade, 154–5; development
  of, 153–4
limmum (official at Ashur), 23
luxuries, imported, in central
  Italy, 33

macella, in cities of R Egypt, 184
Mamurius Veturius (craftsman),
  47
mancipes, 152
Marina el Alamein, in Egyptian
  trade, 195

Marius Phoebus, L. (oil trader),
  163
market towns, and Christianity,
  213–14
marketplaces, in R Egypt: in
  cities, 184–5; rare in villages,
  174
market (the): complexity of, in
  R economy, 156–7; and
  peasants, 158
markets (*see also* market towns;
  marketplaces): alien to R estate
  economy, 159; cities with none,
  196–7; do not imply modern
  economy, 165; in R empire,
  164–5; rural, 196; supervision
  of, in cities of R Egypt, 185
mercantilist model of ancient
  economy, 234–5
mercatores, 152, 154, 157, 160 *ter*,
  163
merchants, *see* traders
metal trade, between Black Sea
  and Greece, 63–7
metalwork: at Miletus, 65;
  produced in Black Sea, 66, 67;
  traded there, 66–7
metics (Athenian), numbers of,
  111–12
Meyer, E., on ancient economy,
  234
micro-economies, in R empire,
  164
Miletus, metalwork at, 65
modernising view of ancient
  economy, 4, 233
monetarisation (*see also* money),
  170; in cities of R Egypt,
  186–7; in villages of R Egypt,
  176, 183; reflected in R law,
  153–4
money (*see also* monetarisation;
  non-monetary flows), in ancient
  economy, 239

navicularii, 157, 163
negotiatores, 152, 157, 159, 160
  bis, 164, 165

neo-classical economics, 231–2
Nikanor (Egyptian trader), 179–80
non-monetary flows, in ancient
  economy, 244

Old Assyrian trading system, in
  Anatolia: 3–4, 9, 23–4, 25–7;
  and textile trade, 28
oligarchy, Chian, and trade, 93–4,
  95
olive oil trade: organisation,
  162–3; peak of development,
  165
Osborne, R., on pottery and
  trade, 5–6
Osteria dell'Osa (Latium), pottery
  finds at, 41–2
Oxyrhynchus: economy, 183–7
  passim, 189–92; trade links, 189,
  192, *193*

partnerships, in Davies's model,
  246–8
patronage, of artisans, in Italy, 40,
  42–3, 45, 47, 48
Paul (Saint), missionary activity
  of, 207
peasants: and markets, 158; as
  term of analysis, 237–9
Pericles, Black Sea expedition of,
  56–7
Phoebus, L. Marius (oil trader),
  163
Pichvnari, Attic pottery at, 60
Pliny the Elder, on artisans in
  Italy, 36–7
Polanyi, K., on ancient economy,
  236
policies, economic, 226, 229,
  235–6
Pontecagnano (Campania),
  pottery finds at, 42
Pontus, grain imported from,
  123–4
population: of Aquileia, 215–16,
  217–18; of Athens, 109–14
population movements, between
  villages of R Egypt, 180–1

ports, organisation of, 161
positivism, in study of trade, 96
pottery (*see also* amphoras): and
  ethnic identity, 35–6; and
  Greek trade, 5–6; at Osteria
  dell'Osa, 41–2; at
  Pontecagnano, 42; Attic, in
  Black Sea, 55, 59–62;
  commercial value, 6 n., 35, 60,
  61, 75; Greek, in Scythia, 53–4;
  in cities of R Egypt, 187; social
  significance of styles, in Italy,
  41–3
prices, of grain: Athenian
  awareness of, 119, 120;
  favourable to citizens, 125,
  126
primitivist model, 4, 5, 12, 165–6,
  233
private cults: defined, 205; in
  N. Italy, 208–10
public cults, defined, 205
public economy, defined, 242

qualitative description (of ancient
  economy), recommended, 244
quantification (of ancient
  economy), problems of, 7, 168,
  244
quantitative data, difficulty of
  handling, 230 n.
Quseir al-Qadim, in Egyptian
  trade, 194–5

Ravenna, Christianity at, 213
re-export trade (in grain), 125–6
reciprocity, in ancient economy,
  236
redistribution, in economy of
  R empire, 157–8
regions: as unit of discourse, 228;
  economic, not same as areas of
  economic control, 242
regulation (*see also* intervention):
  of Athenian grain supply,
  121–2; of craft production, 169;
  of markets, 185
religion, *see* cults

'relocation diffusion': defined, 206; rejected as explanation, 212

rents, in Davies's model, 246–8

roads: and Settefinestre, 142, 143; and villas, 140–1, 142, 143; economic importance, 9, 136–8; effects on Italy, 138–40, 144–5

Roman empire: economic growth, 163–4; markets, 164–5; micro-economies, 164; redistributive model, 157–8; trade in, 150–2, 155–6, 226

Rostovtzeff, M., 4

Scarico Granozio (Pontecagnano), 42

sculpture, *see* statues

Scythia: and Greeks, 66; Greek pottery in, 53–4

self-sufficiency, in R economy, 158, 165

Sentius Felix, Cn. (trader), 161

Settefinestre, location of, 142–3

ships, Greek, cargo capacities of, 124

shipwrecks, as evidence for R economy, 152

shops: in cities of R Egypt, 184–5; not attested at Karanis, 173–4

slave trade, in Black Sea, 67–8

slaves, Athenian, numbers of, 113–14

Spain, as source of olive oil, 162–3

Stadtwirtschaft, 234

stamps, on Chian amphoras, 82, 84, 85

state, in Davies's model, 248–50

statues, seated, 44–5, 46

storage, in villages of R Egypt, 172–3

styles (ceramic), social significance of, 41–3

substantivist view of ancient economy, 233

'substitution', 165

Syria, influences Italian sculpture? 44, 45

temples: economic role, 244, 246; of Jupiter, at Rome, 36, 46

terracotta architectural decoration, 43–6

textiles, in Assyrian trade, 26, 27, 28

Theodore (bishop of Aquileia), building projects of, 216, 218

theory, *see* economic theory; unified field theory

Thrace: and Greeks, 66–7; Attic imports, 60–1

tin: imported to Assyria, 28; traded through Ashur, 26–7

towns (*see also* cities; market towns), interdependent with villas, 146

trade (*see also* coins; export policies; import policies; re-export trade; law; *and next three entries; see also under specific commodities, personnel, or places, and under* cities; Christianity; Egypt; Roman empire): and colonisation, 52–4; and urbanisation, 48; in central Italy, 35; in early economy, 29; in R Egypt, 3, 5, 177, 178–80, 183; in R empire, 150–2, 155–6, 226; not opposed to agriculture, 158; personnel, 152, 160; positivism and, 96; specialisation, 169

trade networks: and Christianity, 207, 213–14; and cities, 197–8; and private cults, 208, 210; defined, 204–5; in R Egypt, 9, 171, 187, 189–92, *193*

trademarks, on amphoras, 81–5

traders (*see also* trade, *and technical categories*): and expansion of R empire, 150–2; and spread of Christianity, 220–1; and wine production, 159–60; at Ashur, 21–2, 23, 26; at Karanis, 173; Hasebroek on, 235; in ancient economy, 10–11,

165; in Black Sea, 61; in cities
of R Egypt, 183–4; in R
redistributive economy, 157–8;
in villages of R Egypt, 174–5
transport, *see* donkeys; land
transport *and next item*
transport systems,
complementary, 143
tribute, as form of trade, in Black
Sea, 66, 67

unified field theory, concept of,
243
urbanisation, and trade, in Italy,
47–8

Vani, Attic pottery at, 60
Varro, on roads and villas,
139–40
Veturius, Mamurius (craftsman),
47

vice-gerent (Assyrian title), 22
villa economy, importance of
roads in, 139–41, 142–3
villages, of R Egypt, economies
of, 172–80, 183
villas: both produce and consume,
145–6; economic role, 227;
interdependent with towns, 146;
locations, 142, 146
Volkswirtschaft, 234
Vulca (artisan), of Veii, 36, 46

wabartum (caravanserai?), 24, 26
wheat, consumption of, 114–17
passim
wine trade, Roman: and law,
154–5; growth, 152–3;
organisation, 159–60; peak of
development, 165
workshops (of artisans), in Italy,
39–41

2 INDEX OF ANCIENT AUTHORS

References to books, chapters, sections, and lines are in parentheses; page numbers of this volume are outside the parentheses; but **bold** numerals (outside the parentheses) replace book or poem numbers when they would otherwise be frequently repeated.

Abbreviations follow *The Oxford Classical Dictionary* (3rd edn, ed. S. Hornblower and A. Spawforth; Oxford: Oxford University Press, 1996). An asterisk (*) indicates a quotation, usually an extended extract.

Acts (17: 17), 207; (27: 1–4; 28: 11–13, 13, 14), 207
Aesch. *Pers.* (883), 91
Aeschin. (3. 171–2), 57 n.
Amm. Marc. (31. 5. 15), 68
Arist. *Pol.* (1. 8–11. 1256 a 1–1259 a 36), 236; (8. 1338 b), 68; *Rhet.* (1. 4. 11), 119
'Arist.' *Ath. pol.* (51. 3), 120; (51. 4), 121; (52. 2), 122
Ar. *Ach.* (719–835), 105
Basil, *Ep.* (91), 217
Caes. *B Gall.* (2. 15; 4. 2; 4. 20), 150
Cato, *RR* (*De agricultura*) (22. 3), 130, 131; (52), 142
Cic. *Planc.* (64), 151*; *Prov. cons.* (31), 150*; *Q Fr.* (3. 1), 141*; *Verr.* (2. 2. 6), 151*; (2. 5. 154), 151*
Columella, *RR* (*Rust.*) (1 pr. 2), 165*; (1. 1. 3), 159; (1. 3. 4), 140; (1. 5. 6–7), 142; (3. 3), 159
Dem. **4** (21), 110; (32), 108; **18** (241), 125; **20** (*Lept.*) (29–31), 123 n.; (31), 118; (31–3), 123; (32), 58; (32–3), 57, 123; (33), 125; **33** (5), 205*; **34**, 58; (10–13), 122 n.; (37), 121; (39), 125 n.; **35** (10–13), 229; (50–1), 121; **47** (53), 106; **50** (4–6), 123; **56** (5–8), 125 n.; (8–10), 122; **58** (8–9), 121; (12), 121

Dig. (8. 3. 6), 158*; (11. 1. 1), 133; (18. 1. 1), 153*; (18. 1. 71), 154; (18. 6. 1), 160; (18. 6. 2 pr.), 154; (18. 6. 2), 160; (18. 6. 16), 155; (33. 7. 27. 3; 33. 9. 4. 2), 160; (40), 161; (40. 9. 10), 161–2*; (41. 1. 7), 159; (50. 6. 6. 3 ff.), 157
Dio Chrys. (32. 36), 195; (36. 5), 61*
Diod. (13. 20), 116 n.; (18. 18. 5), 109; (20. 25), 67
Euseb. *Hist. eccl.* (5. 1. 3), 220*; (7. 21), 186
Ezek. (27–8), 227
Gai. *Inst.* (2. 79), 159*
Hdn. (8. 2. 3), 214–15*
Hdt. **1** (18, 142), 91 n.; (161, 165), 91; **3** (90), 91; **4** (137), 91; **5** (33; 98), 91; (101), 64; **6** (5), 56; (8–16), 91; (26), 56; (30), 91; (43), 93; **8** (132), 91; **9** (107), 92
Hyperides (fr. 29), 113
Irenaeus, *Adv. haereses*, 220
Jer. *De vir. ill.* (97), 217; *Ep.* (6, 7), 217
Lib. *Or.* 11 (230), 196
Livy (39. 2), 212; (40. 51. 2), 143; (41. 27. 10–11), 144
Lycurg. *Leoc.* (27), 121
Lys. 22 (*Against the Grain-dealers*), 58, 236; (5), 120; (8), 120 *bis*; (16), 120

Mart. (2. 43; 4. 37; 5. 13; 14. 155), 213
Ov. *Pont.* (4. 5. 8), 132
Philoch. (*FGH* 328) (F 162), 124
Plin. *Ep.* (2. 17), 133; (8. 2), 159
Plin. *HN* (3. 100), 133; (3. 123), 213; (6. 15. 16), 68; (14. 2), 149; (17. 28), 140; (34. 33; 35. 6–8, 152, 157), 36
Plut. *Nic.* (29. 1), 116 n.; *Num.* (8), 37; (13. 3), 47; *Per.* (20), 56; (50), 68; *Phoc.* (28. 7), 109; *Popl.* (13), 39
Polyb. (2. 8), 150; (4. 38), 67
Rev. (18: 11 ff.), 149*
Strabo (4. 6. 10), 214; (5. 1. 8), 214; (5. 1. 11), 212; (5. 2. 9), 213; (7. 3. 12), 68; (7. 4. 6), 54, 57*; (11. 2. 3), 67 *bis*; (11. 2. 12), 68
Suet. *Claud.* (18), 157
Tac. *Hist.* (1. 70), 213; (3. 47), 68

Theophr. *Hist. pl.* (8. 8. 2), 107*
Theopomp. (*FGH* 115) (F 292), 124
Thuc. **1** (19, 116–17), 92; **2** (13. 6–7, 31. 1–2), 112; (56), 92; (97), 66; **3** (32), 92; **4** (13), 92; (16. 1), 116; (51, 129), 92; **5** (84), 92; **6** (20. 4), 118; (31), 92; **7** (87. 2), 116; **8** (5, 14), 92; (24), 95; (40), 92
Varr. *LL* (*Ling.*) (5. 35), 140; *Rust.* **1** (16. 2–3), 139*; (16. 2–6), 139; (16. 3), 139
Xen. *Anab.* (7. 5. 12), 67; *Hell.* (2. 2. 10), 57 n.; *Mem.* (3. 6. 13), 118; *Oec.* (20. 22–6), 106; *Poroi*, 240; **2** (1–5), 112; **3** (1–2), 122; (3–5), 122; (5), 126; (12–13), 122, 126; **4** (3–7, 11–12), 114; (13–39), 113; (17, 23), 113; (39), 114
Zos. (1. 28), 68

3 INDEX OF INSCRIPTIONS

AE 1940 (101), 208 n.
CIL:
  v (5079–80), 208; (5911, 5925), 213; (7373), 214; (8939), 213
  vi (1935), 163
  xiv (409), 161
  xv (3943–56), 163
Harding, *Translated Documents* (82), 123 n.; (121), 125 n.
IG:
  ii^2 (360), 122, 126 n.; (398, 408), 122; (1672), 107 n.; (1926, 2409), 111 n.

xiv (2337–78), 215; (2353–60), 217
ILCV (1863), 218
ILS (4225), 208 n.; (4243–4), 208; (7489), 163
IOSPE 1^2 (24), 59
ML (31), 92 n.; (45), 94 n.; (65), 57 n.; (67), 92 n.
Selem, *Religions* (13 no. 17), 208
Tod (163, 167), 123 n.; (200), 125 n.

4 INDEX OF PAPYRI AND OSTRACA

BGU:
iii (764, 765), 177
vi (1271), 174 n.
vii (1564, 1572), 175
ix (1898), 173 n., 174
xiii (2275, 2293, 2336), 174
xv (2489), 173 n.
CPH (102, 119, 127v), 185
O. Bodl. (1968–71), 179; (1970), 180
O. Leid. (79, 98, 105, 106), 185
O. Petrie (205–97), 179; (228, 231, 254, 257, 264, 267, 269), 180
O. Thebes (77), 185
P. Amh. ii (77), 178 (4 times), 179
P. Athens (14), 174
P. Berol. Bork., 183
P. Berol. Moeller (4), 174
P. Cair. Isid. (12), 174 n.; (15), 177; (99), 174 n.; (128), 180
P. Cairo Zen.:
ii (59161), 174 n.
iii (59333), 174 n.
P. Col. iii (13), 174 n.
P. Corn. i (21–2), 173 n.; (22), 180
P. Enteux. (35), 174 n.
P. Fay. (87), 182; (93), 174 *bis*
P. Freib. iii (26, 34), 174 n.
P. Harris i (73), 185
P. Herm. (34), 185
P. Hib. ii (220), 186
P. Koln.:
i (50–1), 174 n.
v (221), 174 n.
P. Lond.:
ii (469b), 177
iii (1169), 177, 178 *bis*, 179
vii (2006, 2191), 174 n.
P. Lund vi (6), 174
P. Mich.:
ii (121v), 175; (123r), 175 (9 times); (124v), 175
iv (223–5), 173 n.
v (243, 244, 245), 175
ix (543), 177

xv (700), 176
(inv. 6124), 177, 178 *bis*, 179; (inv. 6131), 178 *ter*, 179
P. New York (11a), 177
P. Oslo. iii (111), 183
P. Oxf. i (12), 172 n.
P. Oxy.:
i–lxii, 189
i (43v), 184
vi (908), 186
vii (1037), 185
xii (1454, 1455), 186
xxiv (2412), 173 n.
xl (2892–940, 2941, 2942), 186
xliv (3300), 183
li (3624–6), 185
liv (3731–73), 185
lx (4081), 184 n.
P. Petaus (86), 174
P. Princ. i (14), 180
P. Rain. Cent. (159), 185
P. Ryl. iv (562), 174 n.
P. Sakaon (23, 25), 186
PSI:
i (85), 185
iii (202), 185
iv (354), 174 n.
v (459), 175
vii (856), 174 n.
x (1098), 174 n.; (1117), 174
P. Tebt. ii (584), 175
P. Tur. (50), 185
PUG i (21, 22), 186; (24), 184 n.
P. Wisc. ii (80), 177, 179
SB:
i (5124), 173 n.
vi (9234), 177
x (10299), 185
xii (10914), 177
xiv (11715), 173 n.; (11481), 180
xvi (12632), 181
Stud. Pal. Pap.:
v, 185 *ter*
xx (68), 185
W. Chr. (425), 186